But What
Do I DO?

**Strategies From A to W for Multi-Tier
Systems of Support**

Catherine Collier

CORWIN
A SAGE Publishing Company

FOR INFORMATION:

Corwin

A SAGE Company

2455 Teller Road

Thousand Oaks, California 91320

(800) 233-9936

www.corwin.com

SAGE Publications Ltd.

1 Oliver's Yard

55 City Road

London, EC1Y 1SP

United Kingdom

SAGE Publications India Pvt. Ltd.

B 1/I 1 Mohan Cooperative Industrial Area

Mathura Road, New Delhi 110 044

India

SAGE Publications Asia-Pacific Pte. Ltd.

3 Church Street

#10-04 Samsung Hub

Singapore 049483

Program Director: Jessica Allan

Senior Associate Editor: Kimberly Greenberg

Editorial Assistant: Katie Crilley

Production Editor: Veronica Stapleton Hooper

Copy Editor: Michelle Ponce

Typesetter: C&M Digitals (P) Ltd.

Proofreader: Dennis W. Webb

Indexer: Nancy Fulton

Cover Designer: Karine Hovsepian

Marketing Manager: Jill Margulies

Printed in the United States of America

ISBN: 978-1-5063-5115-5

This book is printed on acid-free paper.

Certified Chain of Custody
Promoting Sustainable Forestry
www.sfiprogram.org
SFI-01268
SFI label applies to text stock

16 17 18 19 20 10 9 8 7 6 5 4 3 2 1

Contents

Preface

This book contains most of the strategies I have used myself and is designed for use by teachers, counselors, and learning support or intervention teams. All strategies are appropriate and beneficial for all students K–12 unless otherwise noted. Many of these were first published in my book *RTI for Diverse Learners* published by Corwin, but we have added many more and added additional suggestions for implementation and monitoring. The strategies have been used with students in general education classrooms; at-risk programs; special education programs; English language learning classrooms; learning assistance programs; and in clinical, inclusive, and mainstream classrooms.

Mention is made relative to common tiers within Multi-Tiered Systems of Support or Multi-Tiered Support Systems (MTSS), Response to Intervention (RTI), and the Response to Instruction and Intervention (RTII) process used in many school districts. The strategies are frequently included in problem-solving interventions provided to English language learners (ELL) and English as an additional language students.

The strategies are listed in alphabetic order for ease in locating specific strategies after teachers identify the appropriate strategy for the instruction or intervention need of the target student. A selection grid is provided for identifying the appropriate strategy based upon the need identified as having priority for the student. Recommended strategies and interventions are listed with research sources, desired outcomes, and an example of application. Citations to recommended texts are provided where appropriate throughout the document. Some of these strategies are listed in several sections, as they yield distinctive and varied benefits in multiple assistance situations.

Acknowledgments

I wish to acknowledge the contributions of Sheri M. Collier. She went through almost all of these strategies and assisted with updating and trying out their effectiveness with diverse learners.

About the Author

Catherine Collier, PhD, has over 45 years of experience in equity, cross-cultural, bilingual, and special education. Dr. Collier is a nationally recognized expert on diverse learners with learning and behavior needs. She established and directed the Chinle Valley School, *Dine Bitsiis Baa Aha Yaa,* bilingual services for Navajo students with severe and multiple disabilities for the Navajo Nation. She was the director of a teacher-training program, *Ikayurikiit Unatet* for the University of Alaska for seven years, preparing Yup'ik Eskimo paraprofessionals for certification as bilingual preschool, elementary, and special educators. She was an itinerant (diagnostician/special education) for Child Find in remote villages in Alaska. For eight years, Dr. Collier worked with the BUENO Center for Multicultural Education, Research, and Evaluation at the University of Colorado, Boulder, where she created and directed the Bilingual Special Education Curriculum/Training project (BISECT), a nationally recognized effort. She is active in social justice activities for culturally and linguistically diverse learners and families. She started the first bilingual special education programs for the Navajo Nation and the White Mountain Apache. She is currently the director of the national professional development project Curriculum Integration for Responsive, Cross-Cultural, Language Education (CIRCLE) at Western Washington University. She works extensively with school districts on professional and program development for at-risk diverse learners. Dr. Collier provides technical assistance to university, local, and state departments of education regarding programs serving at-risk cognitively, culturally, and linguistically diverse learners. She works with national organizations to provide professional development in the intersection of cross-cultural, multilingual, diversity, and special needs issues in education.

Introduction

Teachers are asked to do many things besides teach. They are responsible for identifying and addressing emerging learning and behavior problems within their classrooms as well as assisting in problem solving. Some of these problem-solving processes are referred to as multi-tiered support systems or multi-tiered systems of support and some as response to instruction and intervention or response to intervention. Education professionals in and out of the content classroom find themselves having to answer the question of what to do with specific student learning and behavior issues. All students deserve a chance to learn to the best of their abilities, but sometimes it requires efforts beyond basic instruction to facilitate that happening. As President Obama said about the Every Student Succeeds Act (ESSA), *"With this bill, we reaffirm that fundamentally American ideal—that every child, regardless of race, income, background, the zip code where they live, deserves the chance to make of their lives what they will."*

The ESSA was signed by President Obama on December 10, 2015, and represents the latest commitment to equal opportunity for all students. The new law builds on key areas of progress in recent years, made possible by the efforts of educators, communities, parents, and students across the country. The ESSA represents moving from the overreliance on high-stakes standardized testing to measure student success to the call for a more nuanced system that includes "Fewer, Better Assessments," and an "Investment in Innovation." This includes MTSS. The improvements offered under ESSA support the effort of schools to build capacity around MTSS in individual schools. MTSS represents a way for an entire school or school system to develop a data-driven, prevention-based framework for improving learning outcomes through a tiered or layered continuum of evidence-based practices and procedures.

In essence, MTSS is about using data (including standardized, authentic, and formative assessments) to identify struggling students and to make a plan to resolve the students' specific challenges. An MTSS student plan includes a problem statement, goals, interventions, and a schedule for monitoring student progress. Data are tracked over a period of time (typically 6–8 weeks) and then revisited to see if the MTSS plan should be continued, modified, or changed to another approach. RTI is a type of multi-tiered system of support based upon data about a student's specific presenting concern, specific goals for resolution, specific interventions to resolve the presenting concern, and data collection concerning the student's response to these interventions.

Within MTSS, support for the student at issue is thought of as tiers of support or as layered like a cake. The bottom tier is a universal tier called Tier 1, meaning that all students receive it. Tier 1 encompasses all the components of general classroom management and instruction in core curricula. An example of a universal support might be the class rules or behavioral expectations that a teacher hangs on the wall. This Tier 1 strategy is an effective means of providing students with consistent guidance about how one should behave in class. Another would be for the teacher to post the specific objectives for the day's lesson on the wall, spelling out what the goals are and the achievement expectations for the content being taught. This particular example of a Tier 1 strategy is part of typical Sheltered Instruction Observation Protocol (SIOP) instruction where the classroom has mixed language and culture students.

For students who are not succeeding with Tier 1 supports, Tier 2 is applied. A typical Tier 2 support might be creating a small group where some of the students review key vocabulary words related to specific content in English and in their more proficient language prior to rejoining the class for the main content lesson. The tiered supports become more intensive and focused as they are layered upon the instruction. These supports can be highly individualized with daily check lists for self-monitoring or with weekly one-on-one management strategies.

In theory, MTSS should be basic common sense, and as several teachers have said to me, it is just good teaching. However, not all teachers feel ready to take on the degree of differentiation required of this type of instruction, continual progress monitoring, documentation, and modification of instructional approach. One of the main comments I hear is "Well fine, but what do I actually do?"

The purpose of this book is to summarize evidence-based, positive, proactive, and responsive classroom learning and behavior intervention and support strategies for teachers. These strategies should be used classroomwide, intensified to support small group instruction, or amplified further for individual students. These tools can help teachers capitalize on instructional time and decrease disruptions, which is crucial as schools are held to greater academic and social accountability measures for all students.

Strategies used in instruction and intervention should not be selected at random or in a shotgun manner. It is important that they be selected and implemented with strategy fitness, that is, to target specific, identified learning and behavior problems of concern to the teacher. Additionally, instructional interventions are best when used in a differentiated instructional approach when using targeted interventions within an inclusive or integrated classroom setting. General suggestions for using differentiated instruction are to be (1) inclusive not exclusive, (2) developmental not remedial, (3) comprehensive but focused, and to focus on (4) building skills and strengths.

The effectiveness of these strategies arises maximized when (1) implemented within a schoolwide multi-tiered framework, such as schoolwide positive behavioral interventions and supports (PBIS), MTSS, or RTI type models; (b) classroom and schoolwide expectations and systems are directly linked; (c) classroom strategies are merged with effective instructional design, curriculum, and delivery; and (d) classroom-based data are used to guide decision making.

STRATEGY FITNESS

The purpose of any strategy used in instruction and intervention is to attempt to address identified learning or behavior problems. Many schools now require some form of intervention prior to referral for formal assessment, for example, MTSS, PBIS, RTI, or so on. Figure 0.1 illustrates the problem-solving model involved in this process. Selecting and implementing specific strategies that will effectively address specific learning and behavior problems is the heart of problem solving. It is critical that the strategy selection be narrowly defined and targeted on achieving an objective with specificity. Good instructional strategies are sometimes ineffective when used to address a problem only remotely related to their purposes. As shown in the problem-solving model, it is important to identify with as much specificity as possible exactly what the presenting concern is first. Upon identifying the nature and extent of the issue, a plan of action can be initiated including a specific strategy to use, the context within which to use it, the length of time and intensity to employ, the criteria for identifying success or resolution, and the method or methods of monitoring and measuring this success or resolution.

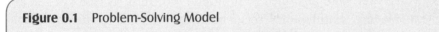

Figure 0.1   Problem-Solving Model

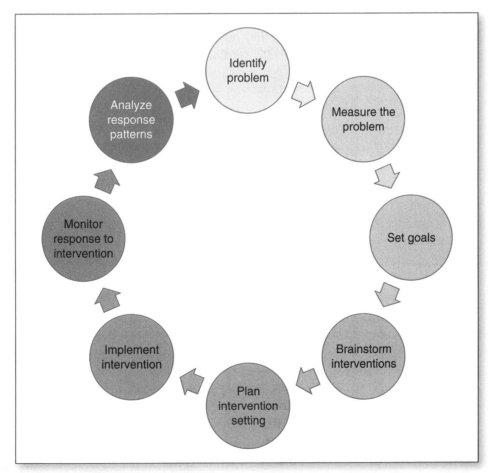

Source: Collier (2010b).

The steps for achieving strategy fitness are summarized as follows:

- Identify student's principal learning or behavior issues and prioritize
- Take the top two or three, and write specific objectives to be achieved for these student needs
- Look at the online Strategy Selection for these objectives, and identify the strategies that fit
- Plan for the duration of implementing the strategy within specific instructional contexts in light of your criteria for success
- Plan how you will monitor student response
- Plan how and when you will analyze your progress monitoring and criteria for when to tweak or stop

MONITORING STRATEGY EFFECTIVENESS

As shown in Figure 0.1, besides selecting appropriate strategies, another part of the problem-solving process is monitoring the student's response to the implementation of the strategy and determining if there is change or growth. Progress monitoring is used to assess student progress or performance in those areas in which they were identified by universal screening as being at risk for failure (e.g., reading, mathematics, social behavior). It is the method by which teachers or other school personnel determine if students are benefitting appropriately from the typical (e.g., grade level, locally determined, etc.) instructional program, identify students who are not making adequate progress, and help guide the construction of effective intervention programs for students who are not profiting from typical instruction (Fuchs & Stecker, 2003). Although progress monitoring is typically implemented to follow the performance of individual students who are at risk for learning difficulties, it can also follow an entire classroom of students (Fuchs & Fuchs, 2006).

To be effective, progress monitoring measures must be available in alternate forms, comparable in difficulty and conceptualization, and representative of the performance desired at the end of the year (Fuchs, Compton, Fuchs, & Bryant, 2008). Measures that vary in difficulty and conceptualization over time could possibly produce inconsistent results that may be difficult to quantify and interpret. Likewise, using the same measure for each administration may produce a testing effect, wherein performance on a subsequent administration is influenced by student familiarity with the content.

Within an average instructional intervention team period of eight weeks, several specific learning issues or behaviors may be addressed. The instructional intervention or RTI process usually takes at least six weeks and may last as long as the intervention team observes and documents positive responses to each successive or concurrent intervention. The instructional intervention team designs an instructional intervention plan that specifies the responsibilities of each member to address

a. any academic areas impacted by language difficulties;

b. learning and behavior problems arising from culture shock;

c. improvement of verbal skill in one or both languages;

d. improvement of writing skill in one or both languages;

e. any medical, behavioral, or emotional needs or adaptive behavior skills;

f. any cognitive learning strategies that would enhance students' ability to engage in learning; and

g. community services needed and outside agencies to access (food, clothing, employment, protective services, counseling).

Frame for Progress Monitoring of Specific Tasks

This frame can be used by any teacher or paraprofessional to monitor the ongoing progress of a student's response to a particular lesson or task. I provide a blank copy and then examples from lessons.

Beginning = 1   Developing = 2   Proficient = 3   Advanced = 4

Student	Objective	Objective	Objective	Objective	Objective	Objective
1						
2						
3						
4						
5						

Beginning = 1   Developing = 2   Proficient = 3   Advanced = 4

Data Collection for Monitoring: __ *Quick Write Activity* ____

Student	Following directions	Provided information about the country	Able to come up with predictions about story	Able to say what he or she wants to learn from the story	Able to share what he or she already knows about stories like this
Sam	2	3	2	1	2
Maria	3	3	2	3	2
Petre	1	3	1	1	1
Ali	4	3	3	3	4

Beginning = 1   Developing = 2   Proficient = 3   Advanced = 4

Data Collection for Monitoring: ____ Krypto Activity _____

Student	Following directions	Used addition	Used subtraction	Used higher level	Able to solve	Able to help others
Jose	2	3	2	2	3	3
Katra	2	3	3	2	2	1
Emil	3	3	3	2	3	3
Vlado	2	3	3	2	2	2

The strategies presented in this book are all offered in reference to the goals or objectives to be achieved by implementing them. Educators may locate a favorite strategy they are familiar with and which they have found useful and use the identified objectives listed under "Purpose" to design targeted lessons or interventions as part of the MTSS or RTI process. They may also look on the online Strategy Selection Grid and find the particular goals or objectives they wish to accomplish with the student and locate the strategy or strategies that will facilitate that purpose.

For each strategy there is also an explanation of how to do the strategy and often an example from one of our classrooms of how another teacher used it in a lesson or unit. Also included for each strategy are considerations for using the strategy with culturally and linguistically diverse (CLD) learners, including English language learners. I am intentionally using the term CLD without getting into a discussion of social justice, marginalization, or other issues common with these unique students. My purpose is to give the classroom teacher practical tips or suggestions to keep in mind when working with students who come from cultures different from their own, who speak languages or dialects different from their own, who come from backgrounds or experiences that diverge from those with which the teacher is familiar, or who are in any way very different from what the teacher is used to. This can also include economic and living situation factors, gender identity issues, health and mobility issues, and any other form of diversity from the teacher's common frame of reference. I hope that all teachers take into account how these different modes, identities, and experiences may have added challenges to the students' lives and learning within mainstream American schools and educate themselves about how oppression, poverty, injustice, and marginalization play a role in our school curriculum, rules, administration, system, and language use. I will not, however, include that discussion in this book beyond the notes on each strategy with advice for teachers working with CLD students within the context of their classroom.

ABCDEFGHIJKLMOPQRSTUVW

ACADEMIC LANGUAGE TRANSITION

Purpose of the Strategy

i. Build foundation for learning

ii. Build and develop cognitive academic language

iii. Develop and improve confidence in academic interactions

iv. Expand and elaborate on learning

v. Facilitate language development

vi. Build academic transfer skills

vii. Reduce code switching and culture shock

How to Do It

i. The teacher works with student peers or an assistant and overtly discusses the language of learning and the classroom. They engage in open discussions about what is going to occur and the language to describe what is going to occur before each lesson.

ii. Vocabulary words about instruction and content are put up around the room and pointed out before each lesson. Bilingual posters and signs about academic language are posted and referred to regularly.

iii. Periodically, the teacher will stop a lesson in various content areas and ask students what is being discussed and how the material is being presented, as well as about expected academic behaviors.

Research Base

Echevarria, Vogt, & Short (2007)

Law & Eckes (2000)

Zweirs (2008)

Zweirs (2014)

What to Watch for With ELL/CLD Students

i. Proficiency in using and understanding academic language will develop and grow with exposure and practice.

ii. Some English language learner/culturally and linguistically diverse (ELL/CLD) students will have limited or no prior experience in classrooms, instructional settings, or school buildings and will need step by step guidance in the vocabulary and language of instruction and the classroom environment.

Example of Spanish/English Academic Language Vocabulary Supports

accent	*acento*	**context**	*contexto*
action	*acción*	**contrast**	*contrastar*
action verb	*verbo de acción*	**definition**	*definición*
adjective	*adjetivo*	**demonstrative**	*demostrativo*
adverb	*adverbio*	**denotation**	*denotación*
alphabetical order	*orden alfabético*	**description**	*descripción*
analogy	*analogía*	**dialogue**	*diálogo*
analyze	*analizar*	**dictionary**	*diccionario*
antecedent	*antecedente*	**direct**	*directo*
antonym	*antónimo*	**effect**	*efecto*
apostrophe	*apóstrofe*	**evaluate**	*evaluar*
article	*artículo*	**event**	*evento*
author	*autor*	**example**	*ejemplo*
cause	*causa*	**exclamation**	*exclamación*
classify	*clasificar*	**figurative**	*figurativo*
combine	*combinar*	**fragment**	*fragmento*
compare	*comparar*	**future**	*futuro*
complex	*complejo*	**generalization**	*generalización*
comprehension	*comprensión*	**generalize**	*generalizar*
conclusion	*conclusión*	**glossary**	*glosario*
confirm	*confirmar*	**homophone**	*homófono*
conjunction	*conjunción*	**prefix**	*prefijo*
connotation	*connotación*	**preposition**	*preposición*
consonant	*consonante*	**prepositional**	*preposicional*

Cognates

idea	*idea*	**present**	*presente*
identify	*identificar*	**problem**	*problema*
illustration	*ilustración*	**pronunciation**	*pronunciación*
indirect	*indirecto*	**punctuation**	*puntuación*
introduction	*introducción*	**relationship**	*relación*
irregular	*irregular*	**sequence**	*secuencia*
language	*lenguaje*	**singular**	*singular*
myth	*mito*	**solution**	*solución*
negative	*negativo*	**structure**	*estructura*
object	*objeto*	**subject**	*sujeto*
order	*orden*	**suffix**	*sufijo*
paragraph	*párrafo*	**syllable**	*sílaba*
part	*parte*	**synonym**	*sinónimo*
perspective	*perspectiva*	**technique**	*técnica*
phrase	*frase*	**text**	*texto*
plural	*plural*	**theme**	*tema*
possessive adjective	*adjetivo posesivo*	**verb**	*verbo*
predicate	*predicado*	**visualize**	*visualizar*
prediction	*predicción*	**vowel**	*vocal*

ACCOUNTABILITY

Purpose of the Strategy

    i. Build foundation for learning

    ii. Build awareness of academic expectations

    iii. Develop association skills

    iv. Build awareness of appropriate academic behaviors

    v. Develop field independent skills

    vi. Ensure student is familiar with specific academic and behavioral expectations

    vii. Develop independence in learning situations

    viii. Eliminate or minimize inappropriate behavior

    ix. Build and develop awareness of cause and effect

    x. Ensure students are aware of and responsible for their own actions

    xi. Facilitate individualization

    xii. Improve confidence and self-esteem

xiii. Prevent minor inappropriate behaviors from escalating

xiv. Reduce specific attention to students misbehaving

How to Do It

i. This strategy may be done within the general education classroom with mixed groups of students or in an integrated classroom. It is especially helpful with students needing assistance in connecting their actions and the consequences of these actions.

ii. The teacher or assistant works with a particular student to establish an agenda or plan with a personalized list of tasks to be completed within a specified time. They also agree upon appropriate rewards and consequences for completion of work. This can also be done for specific behavior outcomes. See also Chapter C, Contracting.

iii. The teacher or assistant must ensure that these rewards and consequences are consistently implemented.

Example

Teacher and student meet together to identify specific tasks student is struggling to complete, for example, reading a passage and answering questions. The discussion includes why the task is necessary as well as steps to complete it and the consequences of completion and incompletion. Teacher provides a checklist or guide format for the student to complete.

a. What is the task?
b. When is the task to be completed?
c. What elements am I looking for?
d. What will a completed _____ look like?
e. What will I learn/earn by completing the task?

Example

Teacher or assistant issues a "pink slip" for specific task or behavior problems. Students receive a form when they do not meet a classroom expectation, such as following directions after a teacher request. In addition to increasing personal responsibility, the form also serves as documentation that can be used by the teacher during parent-teacher conferences or administrative meetings.

Research Base

Hamilton, Stecher, & Klein (2002)

Hoover & Collier (1987)

Tomlinson (1999)

What to Watch for With ELL/CLD Students

i. Particular social groups and cultures have different expectations of adults and children when it comes to being accountable for task completion. This is a learned difference between cultures. The teacher needs to be aware that the expectations in an American school may need to be taught directly to CLD students and not just assumed to be understood.

ii. One way to introduce the idea of your classroom rules is to ask students about any rules their parent have for them at home or rules they have learned about crossing the street or playing games. This can then be expanded to the idea of rules for completing tasks and acting appropriately in a classroom.

Figure A.1   Example of a Pink Slip

Date: _____
Name: _____
Class Section: _____

You've been *Pink-Slipped*!
Completing your homework or assignment is your responsibility as a student.

Missing Assignment:_____

I do not have my homework today because:

____ I did the assigned homework, but I did not bring it to class.
____ I chose not to do my homework.
____ I forgot to do my homework.
____ I did not have the appropriate materials at home.
____ Other – Please explain below

_____
_____
_____

Signature_____

ACTIVE PROCESSING

Purpose of the Strategy

i. Improve access of prior knowledge

ii. Build appreciation that everyone has a contribution to make

iii. Build awareness of academic expectations

iv. Facilitate student assuming responsibility for learning

v. Build awareness of learning

vi. Improve comprehension

vii. Recognize importance of working together

viii. Develop academic language and basic interpersonal communication

ix. Develop higher persistence

     x.   Develop personal control of situations

    xi.   Facilitate access of prior knowledge

    xii.   Facilitate student ownership in education

   xiii.   Reduce low-persistence behaviors

   xiv.   Develop problem-solving skills

    xv.   Facilitate discussion about new learning

   xvi.   Facilitate language development

   xvii.   Reduce off-task behaviors

  xviii.   Reduce impulsivity

   xix.   Strengthen language development

How to Do It

i.   This strategy is done with all students in the general education setting. Take caution: It can become quite noisy in a large classroom, so be prepared. (Set your expectations clearly with the Movement/Expectation/Talk Level [MET technique].) You can also use active processing in smaller groups and even in one-on-one sessions as a way to gauge what the students are thinking as they engage in a task. Using active processing reduces impulsive tendencies and naturally illustrates how a student can use reflection in answering questions and completing tasks.

ii.   The essence of active processing is that students work through a task aloud, naming and completing all steps by talking through them. This can involve asking themselves the appropriate questions for the task and then describing what they are doing during each step in the task. This is similar to "self-talk" activities in preschool and other early childhood development classes.

iii.   We recommend several demonstrations with modeling and role-playing of the steps and process for clarification of the expectations. I have also made small posters of each step and placed them around the room as reminders of the steps to follow.

iv.   The following are steps for students to follow in implementing this strategy:

    1.   What is my task?

    2.   What do I need to do to complete my task?

    3.   How will I know my task is done correctly?

    4.   How will I monitor the implementation?

    5.   How do I know the task is correctly completed?

When applying the active processing strategy, students work through problems or tasks using the sequence of self-monitoring questions provided.

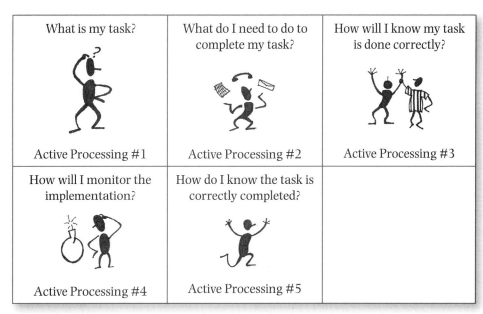

Source: Collier (2008).

Example With Standardized Tests

i. Your students must prepare for the state administered achievement tests required at this grade level, but several of your diverse learners have never taken such tests before and are unfamiliar with this type of evaluation. They have heard stories of something scary that happens to schoolchildren every year and are bracing themselves to endure this external event. You could modify your preparation for this event by integrating the active processing strategy into the lessons preceding the testing period.

ii. *Start* by having the students in your class speak out loud with one another in small groups about the content and process of lessons they are learning following the steps in active processing. Do this in every content area until the students are familiar with the process itself. Then a few weeks before the state assessments, introduce the concept of standardized achievement tests to your class.

iii. *(Step 1)* Have your students discuss how group and norm measures differ from individual and curriculum based assessments and the implications of this for each participant (Step 1 of active processing, "What is my task?").

iv. *(Step 2)* Have the groups discuss what they will need to have with them and what the setting is like. Have those students who have taken tests like this describe the process and what it was like for them. Talk about the expectations of test administrators regarding notes, whispering, looking at others, pencils, calculators, and so on. (Step 2 of active processing, "What do I need to do to complete my task?").

v. *(Step 3)* Discuss what an acceptable performance might be for various levels of completion and knowledge. Explain some of the test strategies that help successful test takers even when they are unsure of the answer. Clarify the expectations of parents, teachers, and others about the test activity (Step 3 of active processing, "How will I know my task is done correctly?").

vi. *(Step 4)* Provide suggestions for relieving stress during the test and ideas for self-monitoring progress through the different sections of the test (Step 4 of active processing, "How will I monitor the implementation?").

vii. *(Step 5)* Discuss how timekeepers work and what the timelines will be on this test. Discuss ways to identify when it is time to move to another section and what to do when students are finished with the test (Step 5 of active processing, "How do I know the task is completed?").

Example About a Thematic Unit

i. Suppose you want your students to complete a new unit in language arts about bears in fact and fiction. Some of your diverse learners are not familiar with the concept of fact versus fiction as used in our society and have no words in their native language for this distinction; also several of them have little or incomplete prior schooling. You could modify your preparation for this unit by integrating the active processing strategy into the lessons.

ii. *Begin* having the students in your class speak out loud with one another in small groups about what they know about bears and other animals following the steps in active processing. Do this within the context of reinforcement and review of prior content the students have successfully accomplished until the students are familiar with the active processing process itself.

iii. *(Step 1)* Introduce the concept of fact versus fiction to your class. Have the students discuss how these differ using real life experiences from their homes or communities. Use visual and physical examples of the concept, such as a photograph of a car and a sketch or drawing of a car, a realistic portrait of a child and an abstract painting of a child, a picture of astronauts on the moon and a picture of children playing on the moon, and so on, to ensure that students are aware of what is involved. Have students discuss examples from their own communities or lives. Discuss how to tell the difference and what is involved in the process (Step 1 of active processing, "What is my task?").

iv. *(Step 2)* Have the groups discuss what they will need to compare and contrast fact from fiction and what actions are involved. Have those that are more successful describe the process and what it was like for them to learn it. Talk about the importance of learning this skill and discuss the steps involved. Have your students work in groups to develop a set of "rules" outlining the steps to follow (Step 2 of active processing, "What do I need to do to complete my task?").

v. *(Step 3)* Discuss what an acceptable performance might be for various levels of skill and knowledge. Explain some of the strategies that help students be successful at separating fact from fiction. Discuss how to check for the accuracy and the steps involved (Step 3 of Active Processing, "How will I know my task is done correctly?").

vi. *(Step 4)* Provide suggestions for relieving stress during the lesson and ideas for self-monitoring progress through the different steps of the process (Step 4 of active processing, "How will I monitor the implementation?").

vii. *(Step 5)* Discuss ways to identify when it is time to move to another question or example and what to do when they have finished each set of comparisons (Step 5 of active processing, "How do I know the task is completed?").

Research Base

Cole (1995)

Collier (2002)

Law & Eckes (2000)

Tovani (2000)

What to Watch for With ELL/CLD Students

i. The strategy preparation can be done in the native language or dialect of the students to assure their understanding of your expectations and their task prior to carrying the assignment out in English or other communication mode.

ii. Students who are less proficient in English will need guidance in using the steps of active processing; the process can be explained and practiced in the students' most proficient language before going on in English.

iii. Active processing can be used in any language of instruction and in any content area or age level.

ADVANCED ORGANIZERS

Purpose of the Strategy

i. Access prior knowledge

ii. Build awareness of learning

iii. Develop analytical skills

iv. Develop categorization skills

v. Develop cognitive academic language

vi. Expand and elaborate on learning foundation

vii. Build first language to English transfer skills

viii. Build awareness of the appropriate content language

ix. Develop thinking and planning skills

x. Reduce response fatigue

xi. Improve mnemonic retrieval

xii. Increase students generating a correct response

How to Do It

i. This strategy may be done within an integrated classroom with all students or in small groups.

ii. The teacher or assistant previews lesson content, outlining key issues, rehearsing vocabulary and reviewing related prior knowledge using a graphic organizer to provide a focal point for the students. Graphic organizers appropriate for use as an advanced organizer are such things as KWL+ charts, Picture This!, W-Star, Mind Map, or PEARL frames.

iii. This advance front loading should be done in the most proficient language of the students, that is, in the first language for beginning English learners when possible or bilingually or using sheltered English when needed.

iv. The teacher or assistant may use the "analogy" strategy to teach one or more of the advanced organizer tools.

Examples

i. KWL+ is done by asking the students to discuss the following questions before beginning the lesson: What do you already know about this content? What do you want to know about this content? What will we learn about this? Why should we learn this? How will we learn this content? This may be done on a chart and student answers can be posted on the chart.

ii. W-Star is done by asking the students to brainstorm before beginning a reading: Who do you think this story/event is about? Where do you think the story/event is located? When do you think the story/event occurs? How do you think the story/event turns out? The answers are written onto the points of a star diagram, each point of which represents one of the "w" questions.

iii. Mind mapping has various forms, but the basic idea is to put the central concept or vocabulary word related to what will be in the lesson in a circle on the board or on a piece of paper. Students then generate other words or concepts related to that main idea and connect them to the center like spokes on a wheel. For each of these ideas or words another set of connections may be made and so on and so on outward from the center concept.

Example With a Read-Aloud

i. When applying the advanced organizer strategy, students work through problems or tasks using a sequence of ordering, sequencing, and connecting techniques. Suppose you want your students to write a short personal reflection about the story, *Everyone Cooks Rice* by Norah Dooley, that the class reads together.

ii. *(Step 1)* Start by having your students work in small groups of similar ability level. Show a copy of a graphic organizer form outline on the overhead projector/document camera or drawn on the whiteboard.

iii. *(Step 2)* Assign each group two or three of the boxes in the graphic organizer. For example, you might assign the most challenged group to fill in the box about title, author, location, and country. Another group would be responsible for the main and supporting characters. Another group would be responsible for identifying the sequence of events in the story and a summary statement about these. Another group could be assigned to identify the main problem faced by the main character.

iv. *(Step 3)* After reading the story through the first time, the groups complete their tasks, and you or they write down their answers on the large or projected graphic organizer.

v. *(Step 4)* As a group, you ask about how this main problem (finding Anthony) was resolved, the barriers to resolution that Carrie faced, and things in the story that helped Carrie solve her problem.

vi. *(Step 5)* The students can now discuss the final resolution (everyone is home for dinner) and what the moral of the story might be from their perspectives.

vii. You can expand this activity by comparing and contrasting the story with others like it or with happenings in the students' own lives.

viii. You might now step back from the lesson and discuss the metacognitive learning that you have provided students, the learning to learn lesson that is represented by the strategy you had them use.

Teaching Advanced Organizers

You might now step back from the lesson and discuss the metacognitive learning that you have provided students, the learning to learn lesson that is represented by the strategy you had them use.

i. Steps for Teaching Advanced Organizers

1. *Inform* the students what advanced organizers are, how they operate, when to use them, and why they are useful. Begin by saying that advanced organizers are a way to help them (the students) plan and remember. They work by previewing or putting information concerning the lesson or assignment they are working on into graphic form. Once the students learn how to use advanced organizers, they can use them anytime and with any content or lesson you give them to do.

2. *Use cues*, metaphors, analogies, or other means of elaborating on a description of advanced organizers combined with visual cues. One way to do this is to have the students look at a blueprint of a house or other building they are familiar with. Have them see how the architect had to plan for everything ahead of time and create a preview or graphic image of what everyone was going to have to do to complete the construction. Explain that almost anyone could help construct the house or building by reading the blueprint and the ability to read and understand it is a special and critical skill that will be useful to them later in life.

3. *Lead group discussions* about the use of advanced organizers. Have students start with talking about a lesson they have just successfully completed. They can go back through the lesson or book using different advanced organizer tools to see how they work and what is required. Encourage them to ask you anything about the learning process they want clarified.

4. *Provide guided practice* in applying advanced organizers to particular tasks. Work directly with student groups demonstrating and modeling how to identify elements. Have more skilled students demonstrate for the class.

5. *Provide feedback* on monitoring use and success of advanced organizers. While students use advanced organizers in small groups, you should move around the room listening and supplying encouragement for consistent use of the tools. As students get more comfortable using these tools, you can have them monitor one another in the use of the strategy.

Research Base

Collier (2002)

Harwell (2001)

Heacox (2002)

Moore, Alvermann, & Hinchman (2000)

Opitz (1998)

What to Watch for With ELL/CLD Students

i. There are cultural differences in cognitive/learning style, and some ELL/CLD students may not respond to the brainstorming construct behind most advanced organizers.

ii. By keeping the graphic design of the advanced organizer as close as possible to the illustrations in the text or some aspect of the lesson, the teacher can more tightly connect the concepts being studied with the what/who/where questioning that precedes the lesson.

iii. This is another activity that works best with preparation in the students' most proficient language and relevance to their culture before proceeding.

ALTERNATE RESPONSE METHODS

Purpose of the Strategy

    i. Improve access to prior knowledge

    ii. Adapt to meet individual or unique student needs

    iii. Adapt the mode of response required of students

    iv. Facilitate access of prior knowledge

    v. Eliminate or minimize inappropriate responses

    vi. Enhance ability of student to focus on learning

    vii. Expand and elaborate on learning

    viii. Facilitate school adaptation

    ix. Increase time on task

    x. Lower anxiety levels

    xi. Reduce anxiety and stress

    xii. Reduce fears associated with assignments

    xiii. Reduce response fatigue

    xiv. Strengthen awareness of learning process

How to Do It

    i. This strategy is an application of universal design principles and is effective within multi-tiered support systems, including response to intervention (RTI).

    ii. It works well in mixed general education classrooms where a few students with special response needs have been mainstreamed or where there is a great variation in student preparedness.

    iii. The teacher introduces the alternate response strategy by illustrating, demonstrating, and explaining alternate acceptable responses to the task at hand. For example, oral, written, drawn, electronic, cut-out images, or so on modes of answering a question or completing an assignment may be acceptable. A poster or other visual reminder of appropriate ways to respond within a variety of activities may be posted on the wall and reviewed regularly with students.

    iv. In essence, students are encouraged to respond to assignments, tasks, or questions in a manner compatible with their needs. For example, you could allow a student who has difficulty with writing activities to dictate his or her answers through a tablet or other voice-to-writing tool. Students are allowed to express their understanding of a task, question, or issue in varied ways to meet their individual needs. This practice ensures that students have the best possible chance to show that they have acquired and retained skills and knowledge.

v. Keep in mind Howard Gardner's (1993) work on "multiple intelligences." What other forms might be available to the student to express her or his understanding? If the topic is westward expansion, the student could find musical examples illustrating the various cultures that came into contact with each other and could make a mixed sound recording to demonstrate the culture clashes and consequences of expansion. The student could draw a map or other illustration supporting the musical representation and her or his understanding of the geographic concept of the movement of populations from one location to another.

Example

Students may record their oral responses to questions given in class. For the geography unit, provide the questions in writing for the students to take home and practice responding. Some names of American states are very difficult to pronounce: Provide time for the students to work alone or with a peer to write the difficult state names on tag board cards that they can hold up during class discussion rather than say aloud.

Research Base

Cole (1995)

Gardner (1993a)

What to Watch for With ELL/CLD Students

i. Some CLD students have had previous schooling in situations where students have no choice in their responses and teachers are authority figures who direct every action in the classroom.

ii. When the teacher wishes to make student empowerment an instructional goal, this strategy is an excellent direction to take.

iii. The teacher should demonstrate how the various responses can be made, including color, modeling, illustrating, and so on.

iv. Some role play in the process from initial choice to final task completion may be helpful.

ANALOGY

Purpose of the Strategy

i. Facilitate connections between known and new

ii. Improve access to prior knowledge

iii. Strengthen retention and application abilities

iv. Strengthen learning to learn skills

v. Develop higher tolerance

vi. Build awareness of learning process

vii. Develop cognitive learning strategies

viii. Develop problem-solving skills

ix. Enhance ability of students to learn new things

x. Expand and elaborate on learning

xi. Facilitate access of prior knowledge

xii. Develop association skills

xiii. Develop analytical skills

xiv. Build academic transfer skills

xv. Build foundation for learning

xvi. Build metacognition skills

xvii. Develop categorization skills

How to Do It

i. This cognitive strategy can be done in the general education class-room with all students participating. Students may be paired with culture and language peers at first and then mixed pairs of diverse students as they become comfortable with the strategy.

ii. The teacher or assistant models making analogies by using physical items or visual representations of animals, tools, or other objects. They hold up a familiar object and ask students to describe it and what they know about it already. Next a new item that is related in some way to the older item is held up. The teacher leads students through a discussion of how the items are similar or different from one another. She introduces the sentence frame "X is to Y, as Y is to Z" where X is the new item and Y and Z are familiar items. For example, a ratchet is similar to a hammer just as a hammer is similar to a screwdriver; they are all tools.

iii. The teacher brings up this idea of analogies between known and new when they introduce a new topic. He or she asks students to share something they already know about the lesson topic, something that is meaningful to them. They go through the steps of analogy in pairs as they share their items/ideas with one another.

iv. I recommend several demonstrations with modeling and role-playing of the steps and process for clarification of the expectations. I have also made small posters of each step and placed them around the room as reminders of the steps to follow.

    v. The following are steps for students to follow in implementing this analogy strategy:

      1. What do I already know about this item or concept?

      2. How does what I already know about this idea or item compare with the new idea or item?

      3. Can the known idea or item be substituted for the new item or idea and still make sense?

      4. How can I elaborate on these comparisons through analogies?

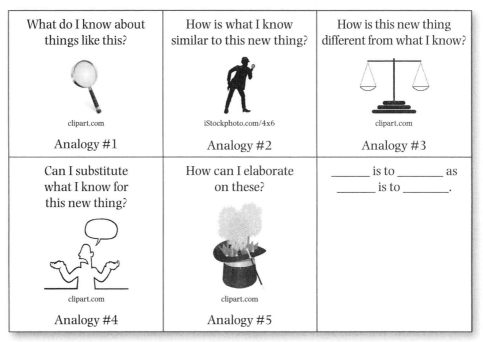

Source: Collier (2008).

    vi. A basic description of analogy is that you have students work through a task describing, comparing, and contrasting things that are meaningful to them. They go through the steps of analogy in pairs or groups as they share their items with one another, asking one another five specific questions that guide them through the application of the steps involved in analogy. Eventually they ask themselves these five self-guiding questions silently as they complete tasks.

    vii. An example of a content application of analogy that I have used is having students compare an object representing a new subject we are going to study with an object they are familiar with, describing the objects and making analogies between the two items. For example, I brought examples of different "dragons" (Chinese, Japanese, English, Javanese, and Scandinavian) to share with students after we had read *The Reluctant Dragon* by Kenneth Grahame and when we were about to move into a unit on Asia. I had them make analogies between and among the various types of dragons, discussing cultural and linguistic manifestations of these different impressions of and perspectives on a mythological figure. I then had them do expansions related to our Asian unit. The students were to all bring something they had that was meaningful to them and that was from Asia to share it with others using the analogy strategy. They created Venn diagrams showing the many ways their various objects were similar and different from each other.

viii. The following are steps for teaching analogy:

1. *Inform* the students what analogy is, how it operates, when to use it, and why it is useful. Begin by saying that analogy is a tool for learning and remembering. It works by asking and answering a series of five questions concerning the lesson or assignment they are working on. Once they learn how to use analogy, they can use it anytime and with any content or lesson you give them to do.

2. *Use cues,* metaphors, or other means of elaborating on a description of analogy combined with visual cues. One way to do this is to have the group compare their jackets or shoes or something else everyone in the class has with them. Have them see how although everyone has the same object, there are many ways these are different and many ways they are similar to one another. You can also use favorite stories or activities, anything where a fundamental similarity exists along with distinct differences.

3. *Lead group discussions* about the use of analogy. Have students start with talking about a lesson they have just successfully completed. They can go back through the lesson using the analogy question steps to see how they work and what information is required. Encourage your students to ask you anything about the learning process they want clarified.

4. *Provide guided practice* in applying analogy to particular tasks. Here is an example of guided practice as the teacher leads the students through the use of analogy. Examples of both teacher and student comments are shown.

   a. Teacher: The first step is to see if you can recall something from your own language or experiences that is similar to this item?

   b. Student: What do I know that is like this item? Is there something in my background, language, or experiences that is similar to the item?

   c. Comparison

   d. Teacher: Second, examine how these items are similar or different. Do they have similar uses?

   e. Student: How are these items similar and different? Are they used in similar ways?

   f. Teacher: Third, identify the items or parts of items that might be substituted for these items. Why would this substitution work? Why might it not work?

   g. Student: Can I use these similar elements interchangeably? What other items might be substituted for these items?

   h. Elaboration

   i. Teacher: Fourth, think about other experiences, words, or actions from your life, language, or culture that are similar to elements of English or your life here in this community. In what ways are they similar and different? How could you use your prior knowledge effectively in new situations?

   j. Student: When the teacher asks for examples, I can provide them based upon my own experiences and do not have to use American examples. I know that aspects of a new situation may be similar to something I know from my previous experiences.

5. *Provide feedback* on monitoring use and success of analogy. While students use analogy in small groups, you should move around the room listening and supplying encouragement for consistent use of the question and answer steps. As students get more comfortable using this strategy you can have them monitor one another in the use of the strategy, encouraging each other to ask and answer the questions.

6. *Provide generalization* activities. Have your students use analogy for a variety of lessons and tasks. You should be sure to identify the strategy by name and point to the poster or visual cues about the strategy whenever you have students use it. Hold enhanced cognitive discussions about the use of analogy in these different lesson settings and encourage discussion of how useful or not useful students found this strategy in particular tasks.

ix. When applying the analogy strategy, students work through problems or tasks using the above sequence of self-monitoring questions. Suppose that you are about to have your students begin a new unit in social studies about immigration nationally and in your state and your local community. You have several students who are newcomers to your community, from a different part of the world and from a culturally and linguistically diverse background. You could modify your usual instructional approach by building in an opportunity for your students to compare and contrast their personal experiences with current immigration and refugee policies and procedures with those in their past experience. You would have them first discuss the difference between *immigrant, colonist, settler, emigrant,* and *refugee* using examples from current news stories on television. You could also have them watch dvd/videotapes or actually visit an immigration office or a center where particular groups of newcomers to America receive services. You could then have them share what they know about these terms and services from their personal, current experience (Step 1 of analogy, "What do I know about things like this?"). They could then share how these experiences are similar to others they are familiar with or others in the classroom (Step 2 of analogy, "How is what I know similar to this new thing?"). Then they would discuss the differences between their personal or familiar experiences and what is new to them about the policies, procedures, services, and experiences (Step 3 of Analogy, "How is this new thing different from what I know?"). The students could explore how different people's experiences might change if certain elements of their circumstances were substituted for another (Step 4 of Analogy, "Can I substitute what I know for this new thing?"). Now the students would be ready to expand this knowledge to identifying ways to improve current models of service and how they might help other newcomers to the community (Step 5 of Analogy, "How can I elaborate on this?"). Discussions will naturally arise out of these lessons about comparing and contrasting based upon high versus low tolerance characteristics.

Example

i. Students are shown an object that looks familiar, such as a metal rod used to connect two wheels on a toy car. They generate words describing the rod such as *long, shiny, manufactured, connects, an axle,* and so on. They then are shown another metal rod that is unfamiliar to them. They generate more words describing the new object. Some of the words will be similar, some different. Example words might be *long, shiny, threaded ends, connects something, pointy, heavy, metallic,* or so on. They may actually try to substitute the new rod for the toy axle, or they may make guesses about substitution and conclude that it could be done but won't work exactly. They generate sentences such as "The axle is smaller than the new rod." "The new rod is larger than the axle of the toy car." "The new rod has threaded ends while the axle does not." "The axle is to a car as the new rod is to something else." "The axle is as shiny as the new rod is shiny."

Research Base

Cole (1995)

Collier (2002)

Tovani (2000)

What to Watch for With ELL/CLD Students

i. Be sure students are matched with peers with whom they can communicate comfortably while they are all learning the strategy and steps in the process.

ii. After students learn the process and steps, posters or cards with reminder illustrations and the words of the steps can be placed around the room.

iii. Once students can use analogy without prompting, they can be paired up with nonbilingual peers for more applications.

ASSESSMENT

Purpose of the Strategy

   i. Build awareness of academic expectations

   ii. Build awareness of learning process

   iii. Clarify responsibilities and consequences

   iv. Measure performance and set goals and objectives

   v. Improve retention of content

   vi. Ensure student is familiar with specific academic and behavioral expectations

   vii. Facilitate student assuming responsibility for learning

   viii. Improve student ability to organize and prioritize information

   ix. Strengthen retention and application abilities

How to Do It

   i. Use the assessment strategy to establish baseline performance levels as well as achievement target goals for individual students.

   ii. This strategy may be conducted with the entire classroom in the general education setting to monitor the needs and strengths of all students and establish baseline expectations and norms.

   iii. When used in multi-tiered small group support and intervention, this strategy is done with small groups to monitor the needs and strengths of the students in the content being studied, consistently taking into consideration questions of language development and culture shock. It may also address questions of language development and level of acculturation.

   iv. An example would be, for a geography lesson on the United States, determining an individual student's general knowledge of the North American continent, countries bordering the United States, the difference between states and countries, how these boundaries are demarcated, and so on. What does the student know about the geography of his or her country of origin or city or state? Determine key vocabulary and sentence structures the student needs to master for the lesson, building on structures and vocabulary that the student has already mastered.

| Beginning = 1 | Developing = 2 | Proficient = 3 | Advanced = 4 |

Student	Objective	Objective	Objective	Objective	Objective	Objective
1						
2						
3						
4						
5						

Research Base

Shores & Chester (2009)

Walker, Carta, Greenwood, & Buzhardt (2008)

What to Watch for With ELL/CLD Students

i. Non-English-speaking or very limited English proficient students will need interpreters and lots of modeling and demonstration of how to take a test and how to respond in assessment activities.

ii. Explanations and example products should be given in the students' most proficient language before moving into English-only assessment situations. If this is not done, all assessments will become essentially measures of language proficiency and not assessments of content achievement.

ABCDEFGHIJKLMOPQRSTUVW

BELONGING

Purpose of the Strategy

  i. Build awareness of school culture expectations

 ii. Clarify responsibilities and rewards

iii. Enhance ability to resolve conflicts

 iv. Recognize the importance of working together

  v. Appreciate that everyone belongs, everyone is needed, and everyone has a contribution to make

How to Do It

  i. In this activity, students will recognize the importance of working together as a team to accomplish a common goal. They will become aware of the relationship between personal success and group or team success and will realize that when they shift from personal self-interest to concern for the needs of others, their own needs get taken care of in the process. In advance, prepare sets of broken square puzzles as diagrammed.

 ii. Divide the class into groups of five students. (If there are extra students, have them function as "observers." The observers' job is to watch the process, notice how the team approaches putting together the puzzle, and be prepared to report during the debriefing.)

iii. Tell the students in the groups, "The purpose of this activity is for you to experience the interrelationship of everyone and the connection between personal success and group success. The goal of this activity is for each of you to put together a square that is equal in size to the square of everyone else on your team."

iv. Players may not talk, point, or communicate in any way with the other people in the group. Players may give pieces to other participants but may not just take pieces from another person. Players may not throw their pieces into the center for others to take; they must give the pieces directly to an individual. Players may give away pieces to their puzzle, even after they have already formed a square.

v. In order for this game to work, each player must make a commitment to the purpose, goal, and operating instructions. Ask, "Is there anyone not willing to follow the operating instructions?" (Answer questions or concerns. If there are some unwilling to participate, assign these students as observers.) Tell them, "Those of you who are observers are to watch the process, notice how the team approaches putting the puzzles together, and be prepared to report back to us."

vi. Allow enough time for each group to complete the activity. Ask groups who are finished to wait quietly until the others are done. Let the students who are finished talk among themselves about their experience of the activity. You might also ask them to give clues to the groups who are still working on the puzzle, without revealing too much and spoiling the fun of discovery.

vii. Bring the class together to debrief:

"What worked?"

"What got in the way of success?"

"Based on this experience, what would you say is important for individual success and group success?" (Responses to the last question can be written on the board under the heading "Guidelines for Individual and Group Success.")

viii. You may want to make the following concluding remarks:

"This exercise serves as a model for how we can create a classroom, school, and society where everybody wins. Recognizing that there is no scarcity, there are no missing pieces, we realize that the universe already has everything that any of us could need or want.

We each have a contribution to make to the whole. We can each look at what other people need and give what we have to give. We can be open to what other people have contributed to us. Then, like magic, it all comes together.

What is needed is a commitment to our own personal success and also a commitment to contribute to the success of everyone else in the class."

What to Watch for With ELL/CLD Students

i. Students with limited English will need modeling of what is intended. The teacher can demonstrate through actions and have an aide or bilingual student assist with interpreting the actions needed.

ii. The teacher could also have students grouped into homogeneous language groups and then have them work together to create the belonging actions.

iii. If using mixed language or culture groups, the teacher must assure that at least one member of the group is able to explain and assist all to participate.

Supplementary Activity

A nice way to end this activity is to read *Horton Hears a Who* by Dr. Seuss (1954) to the class. This delightful book stresses this same theme—that everyone's contribution is important, that we are all indispensable pieces to the overall puzzle.

Making the Puzzle Pieces

To make the puzzle pieces for this activity, use poster board or heavy coated paper. For each group of five or six students, cut five 6-inch squares. Using the following patterns, cut each of the squares into pieces. (Note: All the As are the same size.) In order to mix the pieces up, put them in envelopes as follows:

Envelope A: pieces I, H, E

Envelope C: pieces A, J

Envelope E: pieces G, B, F, C

Envelope B: A, A, A, C

Envelope D, D, F

BILINGUAL AIDE

Purpose of the Strategy

i. Improve and facilitate access of prior knowledge

ii. Reduce stress for new students

iii. Build upon family language and culture

iv. Build upon existing language strengths of students

v. Improve and develop confidence in school culture interactions

vi. Develop self-esteem

vii. Improve motivation

viii. Improve retention of content

ix. Increase and improve time on task

x. Facilitate acquisition of content knowledge

Figure B.1 Belonging Activity Puzzle Pieces

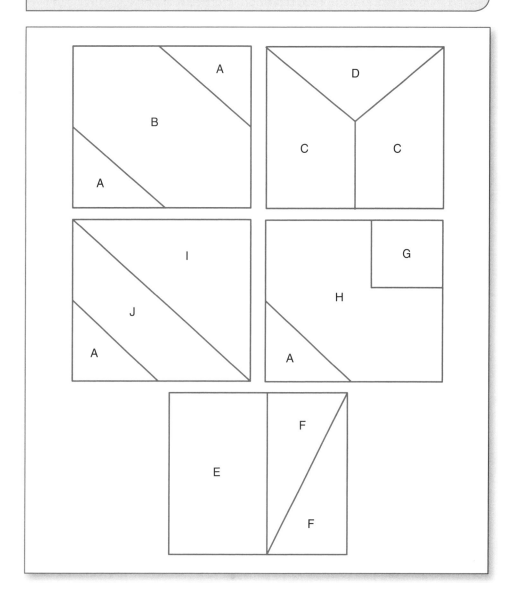

   xi. Facilitate discussion about new learning

   xii. Encourage pride in home language and culture

   xiii. Enhance ability of student to learn new things

   xiv. Develop cognitive academic language

   xv. Build transfer skills

   xvi. Ensure students are familiar with specific academic and behavioral expectations

   xvii. Build upon diverse language foundations of students

   xviii. Reduce anxiety and stress

   xix. Reduce culture shock

xx. Reduce frustration

xxi. Reinforce and improve retention of content lessons

xxii. Reduce off-task behaviors

xxiii. Build awareness of appropriate academic behavior

xxiv. Strengthen knowledge of academic content

How to Do It

i. This strategy is done within the general education classroom with a bilingual adult working in coordination with the classroom teacher. An instructional assistant or aide fluent in both English and the native or home language of English language learner (ELL) students is available within the classroom to assist ELL/limited English proficiency (LEP) students when possible, regarding content instruction, academic behavior, and communication.

ii. The bilingual instructional assistant coordinates with the teacher in presenting content area instruction to all students. The aide must be trained in providing bilingual assistance and must plan lessons with the teacher.

iii. When used in multi-tiered small group support and intervention, this strategy is done with small groups. An instructional assistant or aide works with a small group of linguistically similar students, though they may speak English to some extent. This can also be done with non-English speaking students who are new to the classroom.

iv. In settings with speakers of many different languages, bilingual aides can rotate among several rooms providing assistance to mixed groups as well as linguistically matched groups of students.

v. The bilingual aide may assist speakers of languages they are not fluent in by their example and modeling of how to learn and transition between languages.

vi. Materials may be provided in both English and another language, in as many languages as necessary for the population of the classroom. The assistant and teacher who are bilingual may draw upon these materials to supplement their explanation or interpretation of classroom content and situations.

Research Base

Cole (1995)

Collier (2003a)

Garcia (2005)

Kovelman, Baker, & Petitto (2008)

What to Watch for With ELL/CLD Students

    i. When this strategy is used for sequential translation, that is, the teacher speaks and then the aide speaks, ELL/LEP students may become dependent upon the bilingual aide and remain unengaged while the teacher speaks in English, waiting for the interpretation and explanation by the bilingual aide.

    ii. Better use would be for the aide to prepare the ELL/LEP students for the English lesson by reviewing key vocabulary words, explaining what will be occurring, and discussing what the teacher's expectations will be for the students' performance. This would then be followed by the teacher presenting the lesson in English. Students would be given the opportunity to ask for specific clarification only during the lesson.

    iii. Students could work on their projects subsequent to the English lesson with the assistance of the bilingual aide as needed. Content discussion and clarification should be in the students' most proficient language while they are preparing their task or project for presentation in English with the rest of the class.

BILINGUAL PEERS

Purpose of the Strategy

    i. Improve and facilitate access of prior knowledge

    ii. Build appreciation that everyone belongs, is needed

    iii. Develop confidence in academic interactions

    iv. Develop confidence in school culture interactions

    v. Build appreciation that everyone has a contribution to make

    vi. Build foundation for learning

    vii. Develop positive peer relationships

    viii. Encourage pride in home language and culture

    ix. Encourage pride in student's personal history

    x. Expand comprehension

    xi. Facilitate access of prior knowledge

    xii. Facilitate acquisition of content knowledge

    xiii. Lower anxiety levels

    xiv. Reduce culture shock

    xv. Reduce anxiety and stress responses

xvi. Strengthen learning to learn skills

xvii. Build upon existing language skills

xviii. Build upon family language and culture

xix. Build upon the diverse language foundations of students

xx. Build upon existing language strengths of students

xxi. Develop cognitive academic language

xxii. Develop basic interpersonal communication

xxiii. Build transfer skills

xxiv. Develop content knowledge foundation

How to Do It

i. This strategy is done by pairing linguistically similar students within an integrated classroom, preferably a more advanced, emerging bilingual student with a beginner or newcomer or less advanced.

ii. When used within multi-tiered support systems, including response to intervention (RTI), this strategy may be done in small groups with teams of matched pairs of students.

iii. In essence, home and community language peers who are more proficient in English assist home and community language students in specific content area lessons and activities. The peer assistants are given training or guidance in being a language partner or tutor, with guidelines about how to facilitate learning without doing another's work, how to translate appropriately, and how to monitor for understanding.

iv. This can be part of a general classroom buddy system where students are matched up with partners of differing skills for specific activities.

Research Base

Cole (1995)

Garcia (2005)

Kovelman, Baker, & Petitto (2008)

What to Watch for With ELL/CLD Students

i. With specific first generation refugee, indigenous, migrant, and immigrant groups, the teacher must be careful about pairing students based on his or her own perceptions of them coming from similar language backgrounds. There can be cultural and class differences which will make the partners uncomfortable with one another.

    ii. The teacher must be prepared to deal with prejudice between populations where language is the same, but culture, class, or racial issues may impede comfort and communication. American "all togetherness" may come in time, but the teacher must proceed slowly and not push.

   iii. Students may interact more as they become more comfortable in the classroom or more trusting that they are accepted and valued.

BILINGUAL TEXTS

Purpose of the Strategy

      i. Facilitate access to prior knowledge

     ii. Build upon existing language skills of students

   iii. Build academic transfer skills

   iv. Build upon existing language strengths of students

    v. Build upon family language and culture

   vi. Build upon the diverse language foundations of students and parents

  vii. Build vocabulary

 viii. Develop confidence in school culture interactions

   ix. Develop content area skills

    x. Develop content knowledge foundation

   xi. Develop cognitive academic language

  xii. Expand and elaborate on learning

 xiii. Expand comprehension

 xiv. Facilitate access of prior knowledge

  xv. Facilitate acquisition of content knowledge

 xvi. Improve access to prior knowledge

 xvii. Improve comprehension

xviii. Improve confidence and self-esteem

 xix. Reduce and lower anxiety

  xx. Encourage pride in home language and culture

 xxi. Enhance ability of students to learn new things

 xxii. Build home and community language to English transfer skills

xxiii. Strengthen knowledge of academic content

xxiv. Develop confidence in academic interactions

How to Do It

i. This strategy facilitates understanding content area instruction within the integrated general education classroom by allowing students of various linguistic backgrounds to access content-related materials in their more proficient language.

ii. When used within multi-tiered support systems or during RTI interventions, this strategy facilitates content clarification, vocabulary, and specificity without interrupting the flow and direction of the lesson for other students.

iii. Duplicate or parallel texts are made available in English and home and community language of students for all content areas. Reference texts are made available in English, bilingual, or home and community language format. Students are shown how and when to access the texts.

iv. One source for bilingual materials in Spanish is the Colorín Colorado website and organization, http://www.colorincolorado.org. Multiple Asian language source materials may also be found at asiaforkids .com.

v. Another source is the National Council for Lifelong Learning and Work Skills (CONEVyT). CONEVyT was created in 2002 in Mexico to provide primary and secondary education and training to adults (15+) left behind in education in that country as well as migrant populations living in the United States. Through an online portal and a network of Plazas Comunitarias where direct instruction, assessment, and varied materials can be found, both U.S. and Mexican governments make educational support available for anyone willing to learn or to teach. For more information, go to www.conevyt.org.mx.

Research Base

Cole (1995)

Garcia (2005)

Hu & Commeyras (2008)

Kovelman, Baker, & Petitto (2008)

Ma (2008)

What to Watch for With ELL/CLD Students

i. Not all ELL/CLD students are literate in their home or community language.

ii. Picture dictionaries with bilingual words and definitions are usually the most practical reference to use with younger, less educated students.

BUILDING CONNECTIONS

Purpose of the Strategy

i. Access prior knowledge

ii. Build learning foundation

iii. Build upon existing language skills of students

iv. Build upon existing language strengths of students

v. Build upon family language and culture

vi. Build upon the diverse language foundations of students and parents

vii. Develop positive peer relationships

viii. Enhance ability to resolve conflicts with others

ix. Enhance awareness of school adaptation process

x. Enhance student interaction with family during transition

xi. Facilitate students' comfort with learning environment

xii. Facilitate students' ownership in their education

xiii. Strengthen school/parent partnerships

xiv. Reduce anxiety and stress

xv. Reduce culture shock

xvi. Reduce response fatigue

xvii. Reduce stress for new students

xviii. Build transfer skills

xix. Develop self-esteem

xx. Encourage pride in home language and culture

xxi. Strengthen home/school relationship

How to Do It

i. This strategy may be done within an integrated classroom as well as in small groups of students needing extra assistance with a specific issue.

ii. The teacher or assistant sets up groups of students who are challenged by or are interested in a similar issue or situation. These can be groups around a specific problem, either academic or behavioral, or can be interest or focus groups that facilitate communication and a sense of identity among the students.

iii. For groups around a particular problem, behavior issue, or adaptation concern, the school counselor may select the target group and provide guidance to the group. Or other teachers or assistants may support the student group.

iv. Staff may give workshops to the students on learning how to cope with the specific problem or how to deal with emerging issues in new situations. These can become ongoing support groups for coping with culture shock, language transition, and so on.

v. The groups can also be focused around music, culture, and language or other identity concerns while students from diverse backgrounds bond with one another while learning to adapt to a multicultural environment in their new school.

vi. The groups may become school clubs for celebrating culture and language, preparing for particular holidays, or so on, which invite students from different backgrounds into the group to share heritage and build cross-cultural friendships.

Research Base

Carrigan (2001)

Brownlie & King (2000)

What to Watch for With ELL/CLD Students

i. Learning to survive and thrive in a new environment is challenging for anyone. This can be especially difficult for ELL and CLD learners and their families.

ii. Small social support groups within school and within the community can provide a "safe" group within which to ask questions and learn ways to succeed at tasks or in solving problems.

BUILDING CONNECTIONS— READING STRATEGY

Purpose of the Strategy

i. Enhance and improve access to prior knowledge

ii. Build learning foundation

iii. Build academic transfer skills

iv. Build awareness of appropriate cognitive academic language

v. Build awareness of appropriate social and academic language

vi. Build awareness of learning process

vii. Build vocabulary

viii. Develop content area skills

ix. Develop content knowledge foundation

x. Encourage questioning and exploration of new learning

xi. Enhance ability of students to learn new things

xii. Expand and elaborate on learning

xiii. Expand comprehension

xiv. Facilitate access of prior knowledge

xv. Facilitate acquisition of content knowledge

xvi. Improve reading comprehension

xvii. Improve retention of content

How to Do It

i. All readers bring to the reading/writing process their own growing knowledge of language, the world, and their understandings of how print is used to convey meaning. A child who is often read to, or who regularly sees adults reading and writing for personal tasks and pleasure, will expect that reading and writing play useful roles in life and are valued activities. A child who has limited exposure to reading and writing will have very different expectations and understandings. Each of these situations, however, provides some of the background knowledge that children bring to the act of reading and writing.

ii. The building connections strategy for reading fosters students' expectations of reading and writing as purposeful and meaningful acts and honors and builds on learners' diverse areas of knowledge through thoughtful selection of reading materials and activities.

iii. The teacher or assistant activates students' background knowledge before a reading activity. To assist in activating background knowledge or prior experiences similar to what is depicted in the reading selection, the teacher introduces the topic or general content of the reading and asks students to create pictures or images they may have when they hear the title or topic. Or the teacher may ask for descriptive words about the topic.

iv. The teacher may use KWL+ charts or other advanced organizers to introduce a new reading selection and deliberately make connections between the new materials and prior information or readings the class has engaged in or knows about. If students do not have any background knowledge on the topic of the reading material that is to be used, then every effort should be made to build that knowledge through prior discussion, looking at pictures or objects, or through other means before introducing the new text. That will lead to much greater success with the reading experience.

Example

The teacher flashes a picture of a dinosaur upon the wall or takes the class through a "virtual walk" through a natural history museum with skeletons of dinosaurs prior to having the students read a book about dinosaurs. Beginning readers, too, need to learn to use their own background knowledge. Helping them activate and extend this knowledge and selecting texts that build on what they already know or understand about their world supports their attempts to make sense of what they are reading.

Research Base

Carrigan (2001)

Brownlie & King (2000)

What to Watch for With ELL/CLD Students

i. ELL and CLD students may not have much depth of knowledge in what is considered "usual" among typical school students. They may have experienced extensive disrupted learning opportunities or may have gaps in their prior learning.

ii. Never assume your diverse learners know what you are talking about. Always have pictures or objects for the students to look at and handle that can activate learning or prior learning about the topic under discussion.

ABCDEFGHIJKLMOPQRSTUVW

CAN-DO—RETENTION STRATEGY

Purpose of the Strategy

 i. Improve access to prior information

 ii. Develop higher tolerance

 iii. Build academic transfer skills

 iv. Develop higher persistence

 v. Build academic transfer skills

 vi. Develop problem-solving skills

 vii. Build awareness of learning process

 viii. Build foundation for learning

 ix. Develop analytic skills

 x. Develop higher tolerance

 xi. Develop thinking and planning skills

 xii. Improve mnemonic retrieval

 xiii. Improve retention

 xiv. Use prior knowledge

xv. Develop thinking and planning skills

xvi. Improve mnemonic retrieval

xvii. Improve retention

xviii. Use prior knowledge

How to Do It

i. This is in essence a mnemonic retrieval strategy for retaining information, particularly an itemized list. CAN-DO provides the learner with a structure for organizing items to be learned or remembered.

ii. These could be the steps in a process or elements in a unit or assignment. They could be vocabulary words in a selection of current reading or in a content area, for example, math or science terms.

iii. CAN-DO may be done in mixed, integrated classrooms or as part of small group focused interventions within a tiered support program such as response to intervention (RTI).

iv. The teacher makes a poster or other visual aid illustrated with the steps to CAN-DO and shows students how to organize the information or vocabulary list they are working on in the CAN-DO framework.

v. The following are the visualization steps in CAN-DO:

1. **Create** list of items to learn
2. **Ask** self if list is complete
3. **Note** details and main ideas
4. **Describe** components and their relationships
5. **Overlearn** main items followed by learning details

Research Base

Derwinger, Stigsdotter Neely, & Baeckman (2005)

Eskritt & McLeod (2008)

Jutras (2008)

Lee (2005)

What to Watch for With ELL/CLD Students

i. Newcomers will need to have the CAN-DO steps modeled and explained in their most proficient language before they can proceed independently.

ii. Students can be paired with partners who are slightly more bilingual than themselves to facilitate their learning this process.

C Create list of items to learn	
A Ask self if list is complete	
N Note details and main ideas	
D Describe components and their relationships	
O Overlearn main items followed by learning details	

CHOICES

Purpose of the Strategy

    i. Develop self-esteem

    ii. Adapt the mode of response required of students

    iii. Alleviate power struggles between teacher and student

    iv. Clarify responsibilities, assignments, and rewards

    v. Develop confidence in school culture interactions

    vi. Enhance ability of student to focus on learning

    vii. Facilitate individualization

    viii. Improve motivation

    ix. Lower anxiety levels

    x. Strengthen ability to discuss what is happening

    xi. Strengthen awareness of learning process

    xii. Enhance student focus on learning

    xiii. Alleviate power struggles between teacher and student

    xiv. Reduce fears associated with assignments

How to Do It

i. The teacher arranges the learning environment such that students have several activities to choose from. The students have the opportunity to select one or more activities developed by the teacher, all of which arise out of the focus or content being covered.

ii. Another way choices can be provided is for there to be a range of modalities for students to choose from as they do follow up work related to a topic introduced by the teacher such as slide shows on their tablets, books to read, music to listen to, and so on.

iii. The room could be arranged into learning centers or other configurations with focus areas available for students to choose inquiry or listening or reading activities all related to the content under consideration.

iv. The readings can be leveled as well as be different takes on the same subject. National Geographic and Hampton Brown have excellent leveled reading materials on a wide variety of topics.

Example

The teacher provides two different reading selections of interest to the student, both of which address the same desired objective. Allow the student to choose one of the selections for the assignment. If student does not choose either of the selections, introduce a third selection or ask student to choose a content-appropriate reading selection.

Research Base

Ainley (2006)

Cordova & Lepper (1996)

Flowerday & Schraw (2003)

Flowerday, Schraw, & Stevens (2004)

Kragler & Nolley (1996)

Sanacore (1999)

What to Watch for With ELL/CLD Students

i. Some culturally and linguistically diverse (CLD) students have had previous schooling in situations where students have no choice and teachers are authority figures who direct every action in the classroom.

ii. When the teacher wishes to make choice and student empowerment an instructional goal, this strategy is an excellent direction to take.

iii. Demonstrate how the choice has to be made, including color coding or otherwise graphically illustrating the different choices.

iv. Some role-play in the process from initial choice to final task completion may be helpful.

CHUNKING

Purpose of the Strategy

i. Assist students to learn information through paraphrasing

ii. Build academic transfer skills

iii. Build awareness of learning process

iv. Build foundation for learning

v. Build metacognition skills

vi. Build transfer skills

vii. Build vocabulary

viii. Develop analytical skills

ix. Develop extended time on task

x. Develop problem-solving skills

xi. Develop thinking and planning skills

xii. Expand and elaborate on learning foundation

xiii. Facilitate reading process

xiv. Facilitate writing process

xv. Improve reading comprehension

xvi. Improve sequencing skills

xvii. Improve writing strategies

xviii. Increase focus on reading

xix. Improve students' ability to organize and prioritize information

xx. Reduce low-persistence behaviors

xxi. Strengthen awareness of learning process

xxii. Strengthen language development

xxiii. Strengthen learning to learn skills

xiv. Strengthen retention and application abilities

xv. Sustain engagement

xvi. Sustain engagement with reading and writing

How to Do It

i. The teacher explains that the students will learn a strategy that helps to comprehend challenging texts. Chunking is an example of a strategy that helps students break down difficult text into more manageable pieces. Dividing content into smaller parts helps students identify key words and ideas, develops students' ability to paraphrase, and makes it easier for students to organize and synthesize information.

ii. The teacher or aide can illustrate chunking of individual sounds, words, sentences, and more as a general cognitive learning strategy. Evidence that chunking works is all around us: Phone numbers and credit card numbers are typically chunked. Both types of numbers are usually chunked in groups of three or four numbers. When you encounter a phone number (or other familiar grouping) that is chunked differently than the way you are used to, it can be much harder to remember it. For example, memorizing the letters XOICTE may be difficult, but converting them to the word "EXOTIC" makes the task much easier.

iii. The teacher can also extend chunking to writing more complicated sentences and paragraphs. He or she explains that chunking can be done with individual words into sound parts or sentences into meaningful phrases.

iv. The teacher illustrates chunking by writing sentences on the board and showing how to break the sentences up into chunks of meaning. The teacher can also use a graphic organizer to show how each chunk has a place in the whole sentence or paragraph.

v. The teacher takes one sentence and shows how to use slash marks to separate the phrases. The teacher can also write the separate phrases on different lines, like a poem.

Example

The rain came down, stronger and stronger with each peal of thunder, so that all the horses twitched their ears and hunkered under the trees.

The rain came down,/ stronger and stronger/ with each peal of thunder,/ so that all the horses twitched their ears/ and hunkered under the trees.

i. Before having students work on chunking the text, it is helpful to go over specific decoding strategies. You may want to post the following "reading reminders" on the board:

1. Circle words that are unfamiliar.
2. Use context clues to help define.
3. Look up the meaning of unknown words.
4. Write synonyms for these new words in the text.
5. Underline important places and people and identify.
6. Read aloud.
7. Read multiple times.

ii. The teacher or aide reminds students that chunking the text simply means breaking the text down into smaller parts. Sometimes teachers chunk the text in advance for students, especially if this is the first time students have used this strategy. Other times, teachers ask students to chunk the text.

ii. Students can work on chunking texts with partners or on their own. Depending on students' reading level, the lengths of chunks can vary. A struggling reader may work with phrases, rather than sentences. A stronger reader can often work with longer chunks.

iii. Another part of chunking is to assist students in paraphrasing their reading and writing. The teacher directs the students to rewrite chunks in their own words. By the end of this activity, students should have a paraphrased version of the original text.

iv. The teacher can also use paraphrasing and chunking to assess students' understanding and reading ability. You can also have students compare their versions of the text. This step often leads to interesting discussion about interpretation—how people can often find different meaning in the same words.

Expansions

i. Identify and define key words: To help students move from reading the text to paraphrasing, you can ask them to first identify and define the key words found in that chunk. You can add a space on a graphic organizer for this step.

ii. Create a visual: To improve comprehension and retention of ideas, have students visually represent the selected chunk as a picture or symbol. They can create the symbol or image, or they can find one in a magazine or online.

iii. Paragraph shrinking: To help students clarify main ideas, ask them to summarize the meaning of a paragraph in ten words or less.

iv. Identifying significance and connections: After students summarize a portion of the text, you can ask them to respond to these ideas. Questions you might use to prompt their thinking include the following: What do these ideas remind you of? What questions do they raise? Why is this idea important? To whom is it important?

v. Jigsaw chunking: You can divide a longer text into sections and have small groups work on summarizing a paragraph or two each. Groups can share the meaning of their section with the rest of the class by using the jigsaw strategy or by having small group presentations. This variation works well with a text that has clearly divided parts, such as the Bill of Rights, because students need to be able to paraphrase their section without having read prior sections.

Research Base

Carver (1970)

Casteel (1988)

Jeffries & Mikulecky (2009)

Nishizawa, Yoshioka, & Fukada (2010)

What to Watch for With ELL/CLD Students

  i. If students are literate in their primary language, the teacher can illustrate chunking with examples in that language.

 ii. Chunking can also be done orally, out loud, with familiar phrases, such as the typical morning greeting or directions given in the classroom.

iii. Songs frequently have words and phrases chunked and can be used to illustrate this technique.

CLASS BUDDIES/PEER HELPERS/ PEER TUTORS

Purpose of the Strategy

     i. Build transfer skills

    ii. Build academic transfer skills

   iii. Build appreciation that everyone belongs and is needed

    iv. Build appreciation that everyone has a contribution to make

     v. Build awareness of school culture expectations

    vi. Build awareness of appropriate communication behaviors for school language and rules

   vii. Enhance awareness of school adaptation process

  viii. Enhance ability of student to focus on learning

    ix. Facilitate discussion about new learning

     x. Expand comprehension

    xi. Develop basic interpersonal communication

   xii. Develop cognitive academic language

  xiii. Improve access to prior knowledge

   xiv. Lower anxiety levels

    xv. Minimize ambiguity in classroom

   xvi. Recognize the importance of working together

  xvii. Reduce confusion in locus of control

 xviii. Reduce culture shock

   xix. Reduce distractibility

    xx. Reduce fears associated with assignments

   xxi. Reduce frustration

  xxii. Reduce frustration in students due to unclear expectations

xxiii. Develop content knowledge foundation

xxiv. Develop higher tolerance

xxv. Develop positive peer relationships

xxvi. Develop thinking and planning skills

xxvii. Improve retention

xxviii. Use prior knowledge

How to Do It

i. The teacher and assistant create matched pairs or small teams of students who work together on various tasks or assignments. Students may be matched by language or culture background or other similarity of experience. For example, a newcomer student is paired with a more experienced student of similar background.

ii. Students assist in the classroom by working with other students. Tutors may receive training about objectives, reinforcement, or so on. A student who has mastered a list of sight words or math facts presents these items on flash cards to another student needing assistance in this area. Students help other learners of similar or different ages in the classroom to complete assignments or other responsibilities. This strategy has been shown to provide learning gains for both the tutor and the tutee and allows for the teacher to work closely with more students. The teacher should always be clear about the objectives of the tutoring session and hold the students accountable for their work.

iii. Home and community language peers who are more proficient in English assist home and community language students in specific content area lessons and activities. The peers are given training in being a tutor, with guidelines about how to facilitate learning without doing another's work, how to translate appropriately, and how to monitor for understanding.

iv. As students become more comfortable, they may be paired with more diverse peers and tutors.

Example

The tutoring student shares he or /his report with the tutee. In preparation, the tutor identifies key concepts and vocabulary used in the report and presents these on tag board cards to the tutee. The tutee tells the tutor in his or her own words what he or she understood from the report.

Expansion

Peer helpers develop code of ethics and their own guidelines for tutoring.

Research Base

Carrigan (2001)

Cole (1995)

What to Watch for With ELL/CLD Students

i. With specific first generation refugee, indigenous, migrant, and immigrant groups, the teacher must be careful about pairing students based on his or her own perceptions of them coming from similar language backgrounds. There can be cultural and class differences that make the partners uncomfortable with one another.

ii. The teacher must be prepared to deal with prejudice between populations where language is the same, but culture, class, or racial issues may impede comfort and communication. American "all togetherness" may come in time, but the teacher must proceed slowly and not push.

iii. Students may interact more as they become more comfortable in the classroom or more trusting that they are accepted and valued.

CLASS CONTRACTS

Purpose of the Strategy

i. Build appreciation that everyone belongs and is needed

ii. Build appreciation that everyone has a contribution to make

iii. Build awareness of academic expectations

iv. Build awareness of adaptation process

v. Facilitate nondirective guidance about student misbehavior

vi. Build foundation for learning

vii. Develop higher persistence

viii. Develop self-monitoring skills

ix. Facilitate student assuming responsibility for learning

x. Facilitate student self-evaluation skills

xi. Increase the frequency of appropriate responses or behaviors

xii. Minimize ambiguity in classroom

xiii. Minimize behavior problems

xiv. Alleviate power struggles between teacher and students

xv. Build students self-awareness of behavior

xvi. Develop personal control of situations

   xvii. Improve confidence in school interactions

   xviii. Reduce distractibility

   xix. Reduce acting out behaviors

How to Do It

i. The teacher introduces the idea of a contract with lists of rules and responsibilities for teachers and learners. The teacher leads a discussion on rules in the classroom and the need for everyone to understand the rules as well as have a say in the rules.

ii. Key points of discussion involve the idea of creating a culture in the classroom that is inclusive of all students and allows both the teacher and students to feel comfortable, a sense of belonging, and safe.

iii. The teacher has students start by thinking of particular behaviors that upset them or help them learn. A list can be generated. Some role-play of the behaviors may assist in understanding.

iv. The students talk about these behaviors in a small group.

v. On a large poster or paper, have the students share what they talked about in the group. Try to have everyone represented on the paper.

vi. Once the paper is complete, have each student sign if he or she agrees with the class contract. You can relate the contract to the constitution for older students to help with a social studies connection.

Research Base

Herrera (2010)

What to Watch for With ELL/CLD Students

i. Ensure that all students understand the value in this. The teacher may need to translate this purpose to the home language.

ii. This process can also be related to family rules and how they are important.

CLASSROOM AND SCHOOL SURVIVAL STRATEGIES

Purpose of the Strategy

i. Build academic transfer skills

ii. Develop personal control of situations

iii. Build awareness of learning process

iv. Build foundation for learning

    v.   Clarify responsibilities, assignments, and rewards

    vi.   Ensure student is familiar with specific academic and behavioral expectations

    vii.   Ensure that students are aware of and responsible for their own actions

    viii.   Improve confidence and self-esteem

    ix.   Improve confidence in academic interactions

    x.   Lower anxiety levels

    xi.   Minimize ambiguity in classroom

    xii.   Minimize behavior problems

    xiii.   Improve confidence in school interactions

    xiv.   Reduce distractibility

    xv.   Reduce acting out behaviors

    xvi.   Reduce anxiety and stress

    xvii.   Reduce anxiety and stress responses

    xviii.   Reduce anxiety in social/academic interactions

    xix.   Reduce misperceptions

    xx.   Reduce number of conflicts with other students

    xxi.   Reduce off-task behaviors

    xxii.   Reduce resistance to change

    xxiii.   Reduce response fatigue

    xxiv.   Develop confidence in cognitive academic interactions

    xxv.   Strengthen retention

    xxvi.   Sustain engagement

How to Do It

    i.   This strategy may be done prior to school starting with new incoming students or during the beginning days of school depending upon setting and types of students.

    ii.   Teacher and assistant demonstrate how to get around the school and what is expected of students in various school and learning interactions. This is done by taking students around, modeling appropriate interactions in various settings, videos or other visual reminders, and posting graphic or other reminders in appropriate positions.

    iii.   The teacher or assistant provides explicit guidance about school rules for moving around the building and about behavior expectations. They provide examples of appropriate phrases or words to use for requesting assistance or permission to go to particular places. This may involve physically taking students into particular rooms or settings and demonstrating how to use pieces of equipment in common use.

iv. A student, peer, or specialist demonstrates how to act in a given school or school culture situation. The situation is explained, in home and community language when possible, and each stage is modeled. Students then practice each stage of the interaction with familiar participants until comfortable and successful in appropriate behaviors.

Research Base

Becker & Hamayan (2008)

Brownlie & King (2000)

Law & Eckes (2000)

What to Watch for With ELL/CLD Students

i. Particular social groups and cultures have different expectations of adult and children when it comes to learning. This is a learned difference between cultures. The teacher needs to be aware that the expectations in an American school may need to be taught directly to CLD students and not just assumed to be understood.

ii. One way to introduce the idea of behavior and strategies specific to your classroom is to ask students about how their parents have them behave at home or learn by playing games. This can then be expanded to the idea of acting appropriately in a classroom.

iii. Demonstrate all of the desired behaviors and strategies. Some role-play may be helpful. Examples of bad behaviors may be used with caution.

COGNITIVE CONTENT PICTURE DICTIONARY

Purpose of the Strategy

i. Build foundation for learning

ii. Build home and community language to English transfer skills

iii. Build learners' confidence in their control of the learning process

iv. Access and use prior knowledge

v. Adapt to meet unique student needs

vi. Develop content knowledge foundation

vii. Expand and elaborate on learning

viii. Expand comprehension

ix. Facilitate access of prior knowledge

x. Facilitate acquisition of content knowledge

xi. Improve retention of content

xii. Improve vocabulary

xiii. Strengthen ability to discuss what is happening

xiv. Strengthen knowledge of academic content

xv. Strengthen language development

xvi. Strengthen learning to learn skills

xvii. Strengthen retention and application abilities

xviii. Sustain engagement

xix. Sustain engagement with reading and writing

xx. Use prior knowledge

xxi. Build awareness of appropriate cognitive academic language

xxii. Build awareness of learning process

xxiii. Develop cognitive academic language

xxiv. Build metacognition

xxv. Build vocabulary

xxvi. Improve comprehension

How to Do It

i. The teacher and assistant create dictionaries of vocabulary words with illustrations, photographs, or other visual examples of the meaning and use of the word. They may also use published picture dictionaries in English and other languages. Although many of these are more often used with English language learner (ELL) students, they also work well with any student with limited vocabulary.

Example

i. Using the frame provided below, the teacher posts a large piece of paper or projects the image on the wall. The teacher selects a word from the unit vocabulary and writes it in the first column of the strategy frame. This word becomes the special word for the day. The teacher asks the students to predict what the word means in the day's lesson. The teacher or assistant may guide this discussion by sharing pictures from the reading passage, book, or existing picture dictionary.

ii. The students then read the passage or book under discussion and sketch something that will help them remember the meaning of the word. The group votes on the illustration that best represents the word, and it is placed on the dictionary frame along with an updated "final meaning." The class may also add an example from another language that means the same thing as the English word.

iii. The dictionary gradually gets filled in with more vocabulary words chosen by the teacher, assistant, or voted on by the students as needing to be included in the dictionary.

iv. An expansion activity would be to have the students use the word in a sentence.

Research Base

Brechtel (2001)

What to Watch for With ELL/CLD Students

i. Limited English speaking students will need more structured guidance with this through the use of picture dictionaries in their most proficient language or with the assistance of bilingual peers or aides.

ii. Students with limited experiences or exposure to the content being discussed in the reading passage will benefit from more graphic examples. Additionally, field trip or real living examples of what is discussed in the reading will help broaden the students' grasp of what is meant by the vocabulary words.

Word	Prediction	Final Meaning	Illustration	Other Language

COGNITIVE STRATEGIES IN HOME AND COMMUNITY LANGUAGE

Purpose of the Strategy

i. Improve motivation

ii. Facilitate access to prior knowledge

iii. Adapt to meet individual or unique student needs

iv. Build academic transfer skills

v. Build appreciation that everyone belongs and is needed

vi. Develop confidence in school culture interactions

vii. Build appreciation that everyone has a contribution to make

viii. Build awareness of adaptation process

ix. Facilitate student comfort with learning environment

x. Facilitate school adaptation process

xi. Build awareness of learning process

xii. Build awareness of school culture expectations

xiii. Build first language to English transfer skills

xiv. Build foundation for learning

xv. Build home and community language to English transfer skills

xvi. Minimize behavior problems

xvii. Develop independence in learning situations

xviii. Develop personal control of situations

xix. Develop problem-solving skills

xx. Develop self-esteem

xxi. Develop thinking and planning skills

xxii. Eliminate inappropriate behavior

xxiii. Encourage pride in home language and culture

xxiv. Enhance ability of students to focus on learning

xxv. Enhance awareness of school adaptation process

xxvi. Enhance student interaction with family during transition

xxvii. Ensure students are familiar with specific academic and behavioral expectations

xxviii. Build transfer skills

xxix. Build upon existing language skills of students

xxx. Build upon existing language strengths of students

xxxi. Build upon family language and culture

xxxii. Build upon the diverse language foundations of students and parents

xxxiii. Build vocabulary

xxxiv. Strengthen language development

xxxv. Strengthen learning to learn skills

xxxvi. Develop cognitive academic language

xxxvii. Reduce code switching

xxxviii. Reduce frustration

xxxix. Reduce anxiety and stress

How to Do It

i. This strategy facilitates the transition of ELL/CLD students from their primary language base to bilingualism and helps with their interaction with all students in the general education classroom.

ii. The teacher works with student language peers or with the aid of a bilingual assistant to explain and illustrate academic terms and various cognitive academic strategies that will be used or expected to be used in the classroom.

iii. Students may be asked for examples of "teacher talk" from their previous schools. A list of these words can be developed comparing the terms in both English and other languages.

iv. The teacher discusses the academic language of learning in both English and in the home and community language. Examples of classroom terms and vocabulary of learning are provided in the home language of the students, and charts showing both the English and the term in the home language are created with students' assistance.

v. The bilingual posters and signs about cognitive academic language and strategies are posted and referred to regularly. Graphics that illustrate the actions that are expected with specific words are included.

Expansion

Periodically, the teacher will stop a lesson in various content areas and ask students to discuss what is being presented and how and what academic behaviors are expected.

Research Base

Collins Block & Mangieri (2003)

Roessingh, Kover, & Watt (2005)

Strickland, Ganske, & Monroe (2002)

Walter (2004)

What to Watch for With ELL/CLD Students

i. Not all ELL/CLD students are academically fluent in their home or community language.

ii. Graphics and illustrations representing the cognitive strategies may be used on posters or individual cue card sets for the students. These can be bilingual but must be very explicit in what and how strategies are represented.

CONCURRENT LANGUAGE DEVELOPMENT/ACQUISITION SESSIONS

Purpose of the Strategy

i. Build awareness of appropriate communication behaviors for school language and rules

ii. Access prior knowledge

iii. Adapt to meet individual or unique student needs

iv. Build academic transfer skills

v. Build first language to English transfer skills

vi. Build foundation for learning

vii. Build home and community language to English transfer skills

viii. Build upon existing language skills of students

ix. Build upon existing language strengths of student

x. Build upon family language and culture

xi. Encourage pride in home language and culture

xii. Encourage pride in home language and culture

xiii. Enhance student interaction with family during transition

xiv. Expand comprehension

xv. Facilitate access of prior knowledge

xvi. Improve confidence in home and community culture/school culture interactions

xvii. Build upon the diverse language foundations of students and parents

xviii. Strengthen school/parent partnerships

xix. Reduce culture shock

xx. Reduce anxiety and stress

How to Do It

i. This strategy is an effective way to improve readiness among students while building communication with their parents.

ii. Adults bring their children with them, and both attend language development support classes held concurrently in different rooms.

iii. School personnel and community outreach personnel work with parents and community leaders to identify appropriate locations and times for classes and presentations.

    iv. Arrangements for holding concurrent classes with adult learners in one space or room and student learners in another need to be worked out ahead of time.

    v. Classes are provided at a time selected by parents or primary caregivers.

    vi. Parents, caregivers, and other adults participate in English as a second language instruction in one room while their children receive home and community language instruction (when possible) in another room. Academic content support may also be provided with computers.

    vi. After the formal class period, the groups reunite and parents practice bilingual educational games they can play at home with their children.

Example

Russian speaking families come to the school on Saturday and split into two rooms with bilingual teachers. In one room a Russian/English speaking English as a second language (ESL) teacher works with community adults in English as an additional language, including information about school structure, expectations and rules, community resources, and so on. The Russian speaking youngsters go to another room with bilingual high school students and an adult monitor. They watch a video in Russian about adapting to life in America and refugee/immigrant experiences. They have an activity where they make posters or flyers with tips in Russian for assisting their grandparents or other community members who are not there to learn things about America that might help with their adjustment. After an hour and a half, the two groups reconvene together, adults and youngsters. The Russian/English ESL teacher shows the group a language game, a typical classroom activity used to support English acquisition in the regular ESL program during the school day and explains how it is used. The teacher has the adults and youngsters divide up in small groups and play the language game just like they do it in the classroom.

Research Base

Brownlie & King (2000)

Cole (1995)

Law & Eckes (2000)

What to Watch for With ELL/CLD Students

    i. This is most effective with large communities of one language and more difficult to implement where there are separate families or small groups speaking various and diverse languages.

    ii. In multi-language family communities, focus can remain on English as a second language with first language support offered for as many languages as you have access to bilingual personnel. You can also bring in bilingual students from the high school, and these students can assist with these activities.

CONSEQUENCE WHEEL

Figure C.1 Example of the Consequence Wheel Strategy

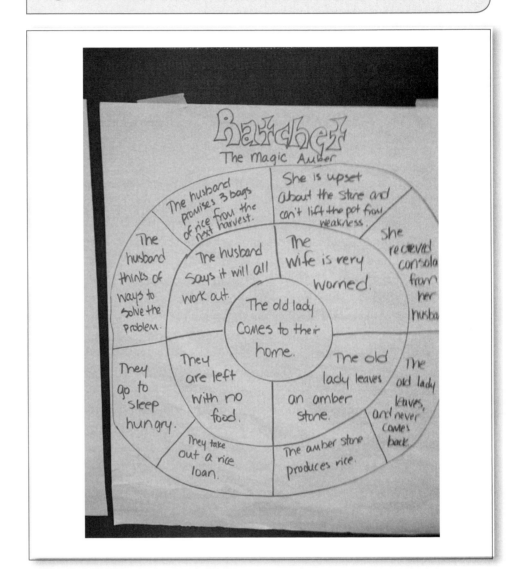

Purpose of the Strategy

- i. Build awareness of relation between cause and effect
- ii. Build academic transfer skills
- iii. Build awareness of learning process
- iv. Develop extended time on task
- v. Develop field independent skills
- vi. Develop thinking and planning skills
- vii. Expand and elaborate on learning
- viii. Expand comprehension

ix. Facilitate acquisition of content knowledge

x. Facilitate analogy strategies

xi. Build awareness of learning

xii. Builds metacognitive skills

xiii. Improve comprehension

xiv. Develop analytical skills

xv. Improve retention of content

xvi. Improve sequencing skills

xvii. Increase time on task

xviii. Strengthen learning to learn skills

xix. Strengthen retention and application abilities

xx. Retention of content

xxi. Strengthen ability to discuss what is happening

xxii. Strengthen awareness of learning process

xxiii. Develop awareness of the connection between actions and the consequences of these actions

xxiv. Develop problem-solving skills

xxv. Reduce confusion in locus of control

How to Do It

i. The consequence wheel (also called ripple effect activity) demonstrates a graphic model of cause and effect. I have used this for both behavioral and academic concerns with students of all ages. With primary students, I keep the wheel smaller with only one or two consequences, but with older students including graduate students, the wheel has sometimes extended to eight to ten circles. You can make your wheel go out as far as you wish and be as large as your space allows. For classrooms, you could make a very large extended wheel upon a wall and have students keep adding consequences outward. I have also created individual wheels on sheets of paper for students to work on a personal level.

ii. Write an event or question or happening in the center circle.

iii. In the five spaces immediately encircling the center write five separate direct consequences of this event or issues that arise from the question.

iv. Take each of these five direct consequences separately and write at least two things that might (or did or will) happen because of this direct consequence. This is illustrated in Figure C.2.

v. These two effects or consequences will have their own ripple effects in turn.

vi. The cycle of cause and effect, the ripple, continues outward as far as you wish to go.

vii. If the effects of a central action are primarily negative, at least one ripple should represent possible positive consequences and vice versa.

Example

Suppose we put a single behavioral event in the center, for example, Joe hit Mary outside the classroom. The direct consequences of this may be that (1) Mary cries, (2) Joe hurts his hand, (3) Joe feels better about what Mary said, (4) Mary drops her jacket, or (5) Joe drops his books. We can now take each direct effect and show how they have their own set of consequences. In #1 two effects might be (1.1) a teacher hears Mary crying and (1.2) Mary's friend hits Joe. At this point you can either keep going around the circle of events adding consequence layers or you can keep going out one extended ripple. Going outward, 1.1 results in (1.1a) teacher puts Joe in detention and (1.1b) teacher calls Joe's parents. 1.2 results in (1.2a) Joe cries and (1.2b) Joe gets a bloody nose. And so on and so on.

The circles can be used for historical events or hypothetical questions as well. In the center might be hypothetical questions: What if the moon exploded? What if Quebec seceded from Canada? In the center might be historical or literary questions: What if the Russians did not sell Alaska to the United States? What happened when the American colonies defeated the British in the eighteenth century? What happened when Harry Potter discovered he was a wizard? What is the consequence of the chemical reaction xxxx (choose a formula or a biological process)?

Research Base

Collier (2012a)

Heacox (2002)

Moore, Alvermann, & Hinchman (2000)

What to Watch for With ELL/CLD Students

i. There are cultural differences in how children are expected to understand and act upon cause and effect. Some ELL/CLD students may need structured demonstrations and modeling to understand the idea of sequential events and how to see each subsequent step or event as related. Simple stories with illustrations can build up the idea of a string of related events that can be indicated on the wheel.

ii. By keeping the step-by-step sequence of events as close as possible to the illustrations and story line in the text, the teacher can more tightly connect the cause and effect aspect of the consequence wheel.

iii. This is another activity that works best with preparation in the students' most proficient language and relevance to their culture before proceeding.

Figure C.2 Directions for a Consequence Wheel

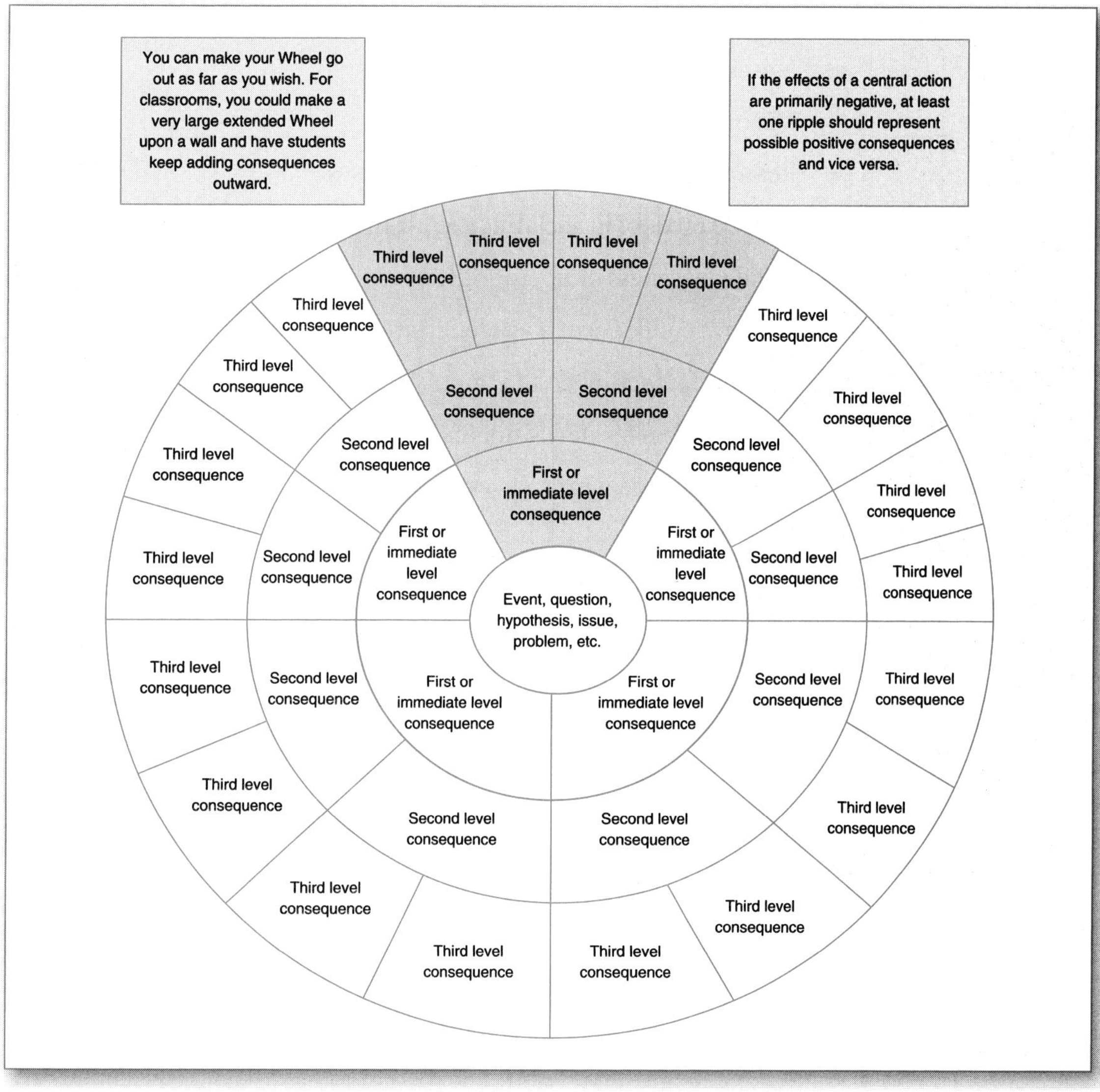

CONSISTENT SEQUENCE

Purpose of the Strategy

   i. Build academic transfer skills

  ii. Build awareness of learning process

 iii. Build awareness of relation between cause and effect

 iv. Build awareness of school culture expectations

   v. Develop association skills

 vi. Develop confidence in academic interactions

 vii. Develop higher persistence

viii. Develop independence in learning situations

 ix. Enhance ability of students to focus on learning

 x. Improve sequencing skills

 xi. Increase students' time on task

 xii. Lower anxiety levels

 xiii. Minimize ambiguity in classroom

 xiv. Reduce anxiety and stress and responses

 xv. Reduce anxiety in social/academic interactions

 xvi. Build awareness of appropriate academic behaviors

 xvii. Improve confidence in academic and school interactions

 xviii. Reduce distractibility and impulsivity

 xix. Reduce stress for new students

 xx. Sustain engagement

How to Do It

 i. This can be more challenging to do than you think. The teacher must consciously and overtly stick to the same instructional language and sequence as much as possible. She can have a regular pattern of set up and approach for each topic and lesson even without using rote phrases, but a routine is important for diverse learners.

 ii. The teacher may post a lesson outline on the wall and have posters around the room with the lesson process.

 iii. The teacher may point to each step as she or he goes through every lesson and especially when introducing any new topic.

Expansion

Students can role-play giving the directions themselves, using the routine pattern and phrases the teacher has established.

Research Base

Mathes, Pollard-Durodola, Cárdenas-Hagan, Linan-Thompson, & Vaughn (2007)

Vaughn & Linan-Thompson (2007)

What to Watch for With ELL/CLD Students

 i. This strategy is consistent with the Sheltered Instruction Observation Protocol (SIOP) model used in many ELL programs as well as universal design.

ii. Newcomers who have never attended school may become confused if every lesson and activity occur in seemingly random patterns. They do not know what is expected of them at various stages of the lesson. They do not know what to attend to and what is less important. Consistency and routine are their security!

iii. This is also going to impact students with undiagnosed attention deficit disorders that they have not yet learned to accommodate.

iv. It is better to start out with simple consistent steps and slowly add new steps to the process as students become comfortable and familiar with what is going to happen in the classroom.

CONTENT LANGUAGE GAMES

Purpose of the Strategy

i. Access and use prior knowledge

ii. Develop cognitive academic language

iii. Develop basic interpersonal communication

iv. Build upon existing language skills and strengths of students

v. Build upon family language and culture

vi. Build upon the diverse language foundations of students and parents

vii. Expand and elaborate on learning

viii. Expand comprehension

ix. Facilitate access of prior knowledge

x. Facilitate acquisition of content knowledge

xi. Facilitate connections between known and new

xii. Facilitate discussion about new learning

xiii. Improve vocabulary

xiv. Improve retention of content

xv. Reduce anxiety in social/academic interactions

xvi. Reduce code switching

xvii. Strengthen knowledge of academic content

xviii. Strengthen language development

xix. Strengthen learning to learn skills

xx. Strengthen retention and application abilities

xxi. Build transfer skills

xxii. Develop content knowledge foundation

How to Do It

i. The teacher or assistant guides small groups of students through language and content games that support the content of the current unit, lesson, or theme. These games are structured to match what is being offered in English to the body of the class but done in the language of the limited English speaking students in each group.

ii. This strategy can be done in the general education classroom with all students participating. Students may play in groups with culture and language peers at first and then mixed groups of diverse students as they become comfortable with the games activities.

iii. Students play language games that reinforce specific content. The games are structured to reinforce and elaborate on content knowledge while developing home and community language and English language skills including turn taking, asking questions, giving appropriate responses, giving directions, and other game, communication, and interaction skills.

iv. Examples of game structures are memory games like Concentration, rummy games such as Go Fish, and matching games such as Old Maid.

v. The content topics of the games can be chosen and developed to match a specific topic or lesson in the classroom and to reinforce the vocabulary words of that lesson. Some examples might be terms from the rainforest, historical events, types of animals, mathematical equations, visits to community locations, workers in the community, and so on.

vi. These are also useful in illustrating second language learning strategies. All of the three basic games, Sets, Pairs, and Memory, can be played to reinforce receptive and expressive language, visual and auditory memory, or content literacy.

vii. The games can be played periodically during the school year to provide a review of foundation concepts when making a transition to a new topic or subject matter. The cards may also be used individually as flashcards to review the vocabulary words and language content.

viii. The games may be used as an alternate assessment process. By watching the students play the card games, especially when a lot of expressive and receptive language is required, the teacher will be able to observe the extent to which individual students have acquired the learning concepts and content or how well they have retained previously presented information.

ix. All of the games can be played to reinforce receptive and expressive language, visual and auditory memory, or content literacy. If students are nonverbal, the games can be played through cognitive visual matching. If students do not speak English or are limited English proficient, the games can be played in their native language or bilingually. They can play using as much English as they have acquired or wholly in English.

Example

The teacher introduces the game of Weather as a follow up to a unit on seasons and weather. The teacher introduces the cards in the Weather game by flashing illustrations of the images on the wall of each card and saying the name of the card in all languages represented in the group. She models how to ask and respond to the cues in the cards. The cards in Weather consist of nine sets of four cards per set illustrating common weather conditions in English. These are the weather words most often used in calendar activities in the classroom.

  i.   Players: Two to six in each group playing.

  ii. Object: To collect the most sets of four of a kind.

  iii. Deal: Cards are dealt one at a time. Each player receives five cards. The rest of the pack is placed face down in the center of the table to form the draw pile.

  iv. Play: Have the students choose the first player by names alphabetically, ages, or other device. Starting with the first player, each player calls another by name and requests cards of a specific type, such as, "David, do you have any sunny days?" The player asking must hold at least one of the types of card requested. The player asked must give up the card requested, saying, "Yes, Kala, I have a sunny day." Another variation of this is to have the player ask for a category first. If Kala successfully identifies the picture, "cloudy day," then she gets the card. The player asked does not have to say she has more of the set of cards if she has more than one of the same set of cards. The player requesting has to ask for each individual card. For example, "David, do you have another cloudy day?" If the player asked does not have any cards of the type requested, then he says "Draw!," and the asker draws the top card from the draw pile. A player's turn to ask continues as long as she is successful in getting the cards requested. If she is told to draw and happens to draw a card of the type requested, the player may show this card, name it, and continue the turn. As soon as any player gets a set of all four cards of one type, he or she must show them and give the names of the cards out loud, placing them on the table in front of him or her. If played competitively, the player who collects the most sets by the end of the game wins.

Research Base

Ajibade & Ndububa (2008)

Law & Eckes (2000)

Padak & Rasinski (2008)

Wright, Betteridge, & Buckby (2006)

What to Watch for With ELL/CLD Students

i. Be sure to establish consistent game playing rules and phrases that all students are to use when playing the game. At first, these can be as simple as "Do you have an xxx?" "Is this an xxx?" Here are xxx." These phrases may need to be reinforced regularly and monitored to see if the students are using them consistently in both English and the home language in their groups.

ii. The phrases can become more complex and more natural as students become more comfortable playing the games.

CONTENT MODIFICATION

Purpose of the Strategy

i. Adapt content to meet individual or unique student needs

ii. Build awareness of appropriate academic behaviors

iii. Build a foundation for learning

iv. Develop confidence in academic interactions

v. Develop confidence in school culture interactions

vi. Develop content knowledge foundation

vii. Reduce anxiety and stress and responses

viii. Expand and improve comprehension

ix. Lower anxiety levels

x. Adapt mode of response to content

xi. Improve motivation and response

xii. Improve retention of content and information

xiii. Reduce frustration

How to Do It

i. The teacher or assistant uses specific content elements of the lesson to create modified activities and units of instruction. The modifications do not change the goals or aims of the lesson but break the content into smaller pieces for the struggling learner.

ii. This differentiation may include several levels or variations in the way the same core content is presented to a group of students with widely varying levels of preparation or prior learning experience.

iii. Students should also be allowed to modify their responses, for example a student who has difficulty with writing activities could tape-record his answers.

Example

The teacher uses social studies subject matter to teach a group of limited English speakers how to interact in the local grocery store. For instance, how a store is laid out and the meaning of the signs and symbols used in the store may become a vocabulary lesson as well as a lesson in math, greetings, behavior expectations, and so on.

Research Base

Arkoudis (2005)

Brinton, Wesche, & Snow (2003)

Echevarria & Graves (2006)

McIntyre, Kyle, Chen, Kraemer, & Parr (2009)

Weisman & Hansen (2007)

What to Watch for With ELL/CLD Students

i.   This can be done in any language and content lesson but will need to be explained in students' most proficient language.

ii. Provide lots of practice and modeling.

iii. When presenting a topic, the teacher can ask students for what specifically they would like to learn about this topic.

CONTEXT EMBEDDING

Purpose of the Strategy

i.   Build academic transfer skills

ii.   Develop content knowledge foundation

iii.   Build awareness of appropriate cognitive academic language

iv.   Build foundation for learning

v.   Expand and elaborate on learning

vi.   Expand comprehension

vii.   Facilitate acquisition of content knowledge

viii. Facilitate language development

ix.   Strengthen knowledge of academic content

x.   Strengthen language development

xi.   Improve comprehension

xii.   Improve retention of content

xiii. Develop cognitive academic language proficiency

xiv.   Develop content area skills

How to Do It

i. The teacher presents lessons with concrete, physical models and demonstrations of both content and expected performance. He or she uses graphics, signs, pictures, and objects to clarify exactly what is being discussed.

ii. The teacher and assistant use language that is simplified and content focused, reducing slang or idioms. Lessons address real life situations and learning.

iii. Students are encouraged to work in small groups on content-focused activities and to discuss lessons in home and community language.

Research Base

Cummins (1984)

Cummins, Baker, & Hornberger (2001)

Cole (1995)

Donaldson (1978)

Echevarria & Graves (2006)

Echevarria, Vogt, & Short (2007)

Roessingh, Kover, & Watt (2005)

What to Watch for With ELL/CLD Students

i. Vocabulary may be previewed with fluent speakers in the students' most proficient language.

ii. Building familiarity is critical for the success of this strategy. Not all ELL/CLD students will know what the objects or models represent.

iii. The teacher will need to introduce the models or objects in full scale representations or use the actual items to build a true understanding. Only after students have actually seen, felt, smelled, and possibly tasted an apple will they respond to a picture of an apple.

iv. Different cultures may have strictures against children handling or being too close to certain objects. Always screen items ahead of time with knowledgeable community members.

CONTRACTING

Purpose of the Strategy

i. Adapt to meet individual or unique student needs

ii. Alleviate power struggles between teacher and student

iii. Clarify responsibilities, assignments, and rewards

iv. Build awareness of relation between cause and effect

v. Build awareness of school culture expectations

vi. Build students' self-awareness of behavior

vii. Develop awareness of cause and effect

viii. Develop extended time on task

ix. Develop field independent skills

x. Develop higher persistence

xi. Develop self-monitoring skills

xii. Enhance ability of students to focus on learning

xiii. Ensure that students are aware of and responsible for their own actions

xiv. Facilitate students assuming responsibility for learning

xv. Facilitate student regaining control over self

xvi. Facilitate students' ownership in their education

xvii. Facilitate student self-evaluation skills

xviii. Minimize ambiguity in classroom

xix. Minimize behavior problems

xx. Improve motivation

xxi. Reduce confrontations over minor misbehaving

xxii. Reduce confusion in locus of control

xxiii. Reduce frustration in students due to unclear expectations

xxiv. Reduce impulsivity

xxv. Reduce inappropriate behaviors

xxvi. Reduce low-persistence behaviors

xxvii. Reduce misperceptions

xxviii. Reduce number of conflicts with other students

xxix. Reduce off-task behaviors

xxx. Build awareness of academic expectations

xxxi. Build awareness of appropriate behaviors for school language and rules

xxxii. Adapt the mode of response required of students

How to Do It

i. Establish a verbal or written mutual agreement between teacher and student.

ii. These can be formal or informal contracts in a standard format or checklists of expectations or both. A contract usually details specific minimum expectations that are understood by the student and teacher or assistant. If those expectations are met over a specified period of time, a predetermined reward is earned.

iii. A checklist is a tool to help students self-monitor their behavior or performance throughout the lesson or during the day under the terms of the contract. The behaviors or steps in the academic task are listed out, and the students are responsible for checking or crossing off items after they complete them. The checklist helps *guide* task completion, achievement, or behavior while the more formal contract attempts to *change* certain learning performance or behaviors.

iv. Contracts can be developed for behavior goals, academic goals, specific content benchmarks, or other objectives. They can also be used as a frame for having students reflect on their behavior or their learning efforts. I call this a "look back" activity and include it in my PEARL strategy.

v. There are lots of examples of contracts to be found online for all kinds of goals, including behavior before and during the school day, homework completion, personal organization, time management, following directions, classroom rules, routine, specific content achievement outcomes, benchmarks for unit completion, and so on. I have included three examples below.

vi. The goal of a contract or checklist is to make students aware of the desired outcome, performance, or behavior so they can modify their own performance or behavior. You want them to be more self-aware and to take charge of paying attention to what they are doing. Contracts should be formally recognized as completed once the students have the gist of what you want them to do. When behaviors do not change, it may be necessary to involve the school assistance team to help determine what further interventions may be needed.

Example

The teacher discusses a student's struggle with math problems and the need to improve the student's completion and accuracy in these types of problems. The teacher has already modified the content to a level achievable by the student. Between the two of them, they come up with a written document that the student signs that the student will complete twenty math problems with 80 percent accuracy during the regular math period, and that the student will receive ten minutes of extra free time if these contract conditions are met. The teacher and the student keep copies of the contract in their desks in case they need to revise or return to the contract.

Research Base

Harwell (2001)

Tomlinson (1999)

What to Watch for With ELL/CLD Students

i. Contracts will need to be explained in the students' most proficient language.

ii. Examples should be provided from their own family or community experience. Each desired outcome can be written in simple language and illustrated with a graphic prompt that shows exactly what is expected.

Name:	Date:					
I want to be able to:						
Work quietly during cooperative group activities.						
Listen to the teacher's directions and take notes of what I need to do.						
Put the materials away in their proper boxes when I am done using them.						

Name:		Date:	
I am missing the following homework assignments:			
Assignment	**Date Due**	**Turned In**	**Comments**

I understand if I do not have my homework the day after it is due, I will need to do one lap around the track. If I do not have it the next day, I will spend one recess completing the missing work.

Signed x/x/x	Signed x/x/x
(Student signature)	(Parent signature)

Name:		Date:			
My goal this week is to improve my writing.					
How did I do on:	**Monday**	**Tuesday**	**Wednesday**	**Thursday**	**Friday**
I am working on:					
1) Take time to think before each sentence.					
2) Stay on the line.					
3) Spell each word correctly.					
4) Capitalize each sentence.					
5) Put a period at the end of each sentence.					
6) Read through what I wrote to be sure it makes sense or says what I want it to say.					

CONTROL AND ATTENTION STRATEGY—STAR

Purpose of the Strategy

   i. Build transfer skills

   ii. Build awareness of appropriate academic behaviors

   iii. Develop extended time on task

   iv. Develop field independent skills

   v. Develop thinking and planning skills

   vi. Develop higher persistence

   vii. Expand and elaborate on learning

   viii. Expand comprehension

   ix. Facilitate access of prior knowledge

   x. Facilitate acquisition of content knowledge

xi. Build awareness of and foundation for learning

xii. Increase students' probability of generating a correct response

xiii. Increase students' time on task

xiv. Develop personal control of situations

xv. Improve access to prior knowledge

xvi. Reduce off-task behaviors

xvii. Strengthen language development

How to Do It

i. The teacher introduces students to the use of the STAR for assisting in regaining control over their actions, paying attention to what is going on, and as a way to take time during reading and writing or other lessons.

ii. The teacher can make a poster or chart showing STAR and what is to be done at each step. He or she can also model each action and tell students that whenever he or she stops a lesson and says "what does the STAR say," they are to stop and think about what is happening or what they are doing and then act appropriately. The teacher can have review points during the day as students become more familiar with this technique.

iii. This strategy can be used for all content areas and for behavior modification. Students can make cue cards for each step.

iv. The following are the steps in STAR:

1. Stop
2. Think
3. Act
4. Review

Research Base

Agran, King-Sears, Wehmeyer, & Copeland (2003)

Carpenter (2001)

Lee et al. (2006)

What to Watch for With ELL/CLD Students

i. Newcomers will need to have the STAR steps modeled and explained in their most proficient language before they can proceed independently.

ii. Students can be paired with partners who are slightly more bilingual than themselves to facilitate their learning this process.

STAR Elements	What am I to do at this step?	What did I do about it?	How many times did I do this?
Stop			
Think			
Act			
Review			

COOPERATIVE LEARNING STRATEGIES

Purpose of the Strategy

i. Build transfer skills

ii. Build appreciation that everyone belongs and is needed

iii. Build appreciation that everyone has a contribution to make

iv. Build upon existing language strengths of student

v. Develop basic interpersonal communication

vi. Develop higher persistence

vii. Enhance ability of students to focus on learning

viii. Enhance ability of students to learn new things

ix. Expand and elaborate on learning

x. Expand comprehension

xi. Facilitate discussion about new learning

xii. Facilitate acquisition of content knowledge

xiii. Improve comprehension

xiv. Improve vocabulary

xv. Increase students' time on task

xvi. Increase the frequency of appropriate responses or behaviors

xvii. Increase time on task

xviii. Lower anxiety levels

xix. Recognize the importance of working together

xx. Reduce off-task behaviors

xxi. Reduce resistance to change

xxii. Reinforce content lessons

xxiii. Reinforce school/parent partnership

xxiv. Retention of content

xxv. Strengthen ability to discuss what is happening

xxvi. Strengthen awareness of learning process

xxvii. Build foundation for learning

xxviii. Build awareness of learning

xxix. Reinforce content lessons

xxx. Develop confidence in cognitive academic interactions

xxxi. Develop higher tolerance

xxxii.   Improve access to prior knowledge

xxxiii. Sustain engagement

xxxiv. Strengthen learning to learn skills

xxxv.   Strengthen knowledge of academic content

xxxvi. Reduce distractibility

How to Do It

i.   The teacher establishes small groups for accomplishing particular objectives and provides group members with guidelines for completing their group task.

ii. The teacher or assistant works with students who are familiar with group process or more experienced with working with a team to model what is expected and how cooperative learning activities occur.

iii. The teacher facilitates various cooperative learning activities, varying setting and content of focus only after students have a clear understanding of what they are to do in the different approaches. Home and community language explanations of what is expected are provided when possible.

iv. These group learning experiences may be adjusted for differing ability or readiness levels.

Example

The teacher splits the class into six groups after introducing the topic of the Amazon Rain Forest. A group of beginning level students looks through books and magazines for graphics or illustrations that show what different areas of the rain forest look like. Another ability group looks in books for information to post under the pictures. Higher ability groups research online about the different tiers within the forest, animal types, botanical information, and so on. All groups work together with their pieces to put together a program with illustrations explaining the Rain Forest to another class at the same grade level.

Research Base

Cole (1995)

Collier (2002)

What to Watch for With ELL/CLD Students

i.   The teacher should not assume students will understand what is called for within cooperative learning groups. Role-play or videos illustrating cooperative learning will assist in clarifying what is expected.

ii. Cultural groups have differing norms for with whom children should interact and when they can do such interaction. Appropriate interactions can be based on age, gender, religion, and so on. Group assignments should keep these cultural differences in mind when first introducing this strategy.

iii. Gradually introduce the American model of cooperative learning through role-play and modeling. Provide lots of guided practice of the roles and performance expectations.

COPING/PROBLEM SOLVING

Purpose of the Strategy

i. Build awareness of learning and adaptation process

ii. Facilitate access of prior knowledge

iii. Build foundation for learning

iv. Build learners' confidence in their control of the learning process

v. Develop awareness of cause and effect

vi. Develop self-monitoring skills

vii. Develop thinking and planning skills

viii. Eliminate inappropriate behavior

ix. Facilitate students assuming responsibility for learning

x. Facilitate students regaining control over self

xi. Facilitate student self-evaluation skills

xii. Improve access to prior knowledge

xiii. Increase students' time on task

xiv. Increase the frequency of appropriate responses or behaviors

xv. Increase time on task

xvi. Reduce anxiety and stress

xvii. Reduce anxiety and stress responses

xviii. Reduce anxiety in social/academic interactions

xix. Reduce confusion in locus of control

xx. Develop extended time on task

xxi. Reduce inappropriate behaviors

xxii. Reduce low-persistence behaviors

xxiii. Strengthen awareness of learning process

xxiv. Reduce off-task behaviors

xxv. Develop higher tolerance

xxvi. Develop higher persistence

xxvii. Develop problem-solving skills

xxviii. Lower anxiety levels

xxix. Develop personal control of situations

How to Do It

i. The teacher leads the class through the steps of the coping strategy using illustrations and role-play, demonstrating how all people sometimes need to stop and think about how to solve a problem.

ii. The steps of the coping strategy apply to both academic and social/ behavior problems. The teacher directs students to identify a specific problem they want to solve as a group. Each group follows the coping steps as they address their problem, writing down their answers and ideas for each stage.

iii. The teacher can provide a list of typical social or behavior problems that students have and want to solve, or he or she may use simple math problems to introduce the academic application.

iv. The teacher or assistant posts a sign with the coping strategy steps and graphics illustrating the steps on the wall in the room as a reminder.

v. Once the students have all learned the steps to the coping strategy and are familiar with the steps, the teacher just needs to refer to the poster to remind students once in a while how they can use the strategy within various situations in the classroom.

vi. Some example situations for students to think about solving either individually or in a small group could be social studies research problems, essay writing problems, science or math problems, social conflict or family issues, or so on.

vii. The following are the steps for students to follow in implementing the coping strategy:

1. What is the problem?

2. What are possible solutions?

3. Where can I go for help?

4. How will I deal with setbacks?

5. What is my outcome?

viii. When applying the coping strategy, students work through problems or tasks using the above sequence of self-monitoring questions. Suppose that you are about to have your students begin a new unit in social studies about your local community services and service people. You tend to enjoy challenges and usually teach these lessons

What is the problem?	What are possible solutions?	
clipart.com	clipart.com	
Coping #1	Coping #2	
Where can I go for help?	How will I deal with setbacks?	What is my outcome?
iStockphoto.com/Alex Belomlinsky		clipart.com
Coping #3	Coping #4	Coping #5

Source: Collier (2008).

by having students discover local resources and people on their own, but you have several students who are new to your community and from a culturally and linguistically diverse background. You could modify your usual instructional approach by building in an opportunity for your students to examine what your expectations are and identify any problems they may have in meeting your expectations (Step 1 of coping, "What is the problem?"). The student groups then would identify what they will do to successfully complete the lesson (Step 2 of coping, "What are possible solutions?"), discussing ahead of time who they might see, where they might go, and what might happen. This might include identifying vocabulary words and discourse patterns they will need to use and possibly some practice ahead of time in speaking with adults from different speech communities from their own. The students identify ahead of time where sources of information and assistance are available to them (Step 3 of coping, "Where can I go for help?") including people at the school, church, or other community groups. During this planning time, they also discuss what might happen to prevent them getting information or achieving parts of your outcomes. They come up with a supportive group plan for dealing with barriers in accomplishing their tasks (Step 4 of coping, "How will I deal with setbacks?"). Finally, they create a clear idea in their minds of what exactly an acceptable outcome of this activity will be (Step 5 of coping, "What is my outcome?"). By following these steps and keeping all of this in mind while working on the lesson you have for them, they will greatly reduce their anxiety level about the task and will increase their likelihood of completing the task successfully.

Research Base

McCain (2005)

Reid, Webster-Stratton, & Hammond (2007)

What to Watch for With ELL/CLD Students

i. The strategy preparation can be done in the native language or dialect of the students to assure their understanding of your expectations and their task prior to carrying the assignment out in English or other communication mode.

COPS—WRITING STRATEGY

Purpose of the Strategy

i. Build awareness of learning

ii. Build awareness of adaptation process

iii. Facilitate and access prior knowledge

iv. Build transfer skills

v. Build vocabulary

vi. Develop academic language

vii. Develop analytical skills

viii. Develop cognitive academic language

ix. Develop cognitive learning strategies

x. Develop extended time on task

xi. Develop field independent skills

xii. Facilitate student writing

xiii. Facilitate student self-evaluation skills

xiv. Improve access to prior knowledge

xv. Facilitate language development

xvi. Sustain engagement with reading and writing

xvii. Use prior knowledge

xviii. Strengthen learning to learn skills

xix. Strengthen retention and application abilities

xx. Improve mnemonic retrieval

xxi. Improve test taking

xxii. Reduce impulsivity

xxiii. Improve writing strategies.

How to Do It

i. This strategy provides a structure for proofreading written work prior to submitting it to the teacher.

ii. The teacher introduces COPS by writing the steps on the board next to a passage from a hypothetical student written paragraph or sentence depending upon the grade level of the class. The teacher then has the class walk through the steps in COPS pointing out and correcting elements in the writing sample.

iii. The teacher can provide a large COPS frame as a poster or as a projection on the screen and walk through the steps with the class.

iv. The poster can remain up on the wall as a reminder of the COPS process during any writing activity, and students should be reminded to check it periodically as they work on writing assignments.

v. Students can also be given worksheets with the COPS format to accompany desk work.

vi. The following are the steps in COPS:

1. Capitalization correct
2. Overall appearance
3. Punctuation correct
4. Spelling correct

Research Base

Cole (1995)

What to Watch for With ELL/CLD Students

i. Newcomers will need to have the COPS steps modeled and explained in their most proficient language before they can proceed independently.

ii. Students can be paired with partners who are slightly more bilingual than themselves to facilitate their learning this process.

COPS Elements to Check	Correct?	Corrections Made
Capitalization		

(Continued)

(Continued)

COPS Elements to Check	Correct?	Corrections Made
Overall Appearance		
Punctuation		
Spelling		

CROSS-CULTURAL COMMUNICATION STRATEGIES

Purpose of the Strategy

i. Build academic transfer skills

ii. Adapt to meet individual or unique student needs

iii. Adapt the mode of response required of students

iv. Build awareness of appropriate communication behaviors for school language and rules

v. Build first language to English transfer skills

vi. Build transfer skills

vii. Build upon existing language skills of students

viii. Build upon existing language strengths of students

ix. Build upon family language and culture

    x. Build upon the diverse language foundations of students and parents

    xi. Encourage pride in home language and culture

    xii. Encourage pride in students' personal history

    xiii. Improve confidence in academic interactions

    xiv. Improve confidence in home and community culture/school culture interactions

    xv. Improve confidence in school interactions

    xvi. Reduce anxiety and stress and responses

    xvii. Reduce anxiety in social/academic interactions

    xviii. Reduce code switching

    xix. Build upon existing language strengths of students

    xx. Develop confidence in school interactions

    xxi. Reduce culture shock

    xxii. Strengthen ability to discuss what is happening

    xxiii. Strengthen awareness of learning process

    xxiv. Strengthen home/school relationship

    xxv. Develop confidence in school language

How to Do It

    i. The teacher models cross-cultural communication strategies such as reflection, proximics, latency, and active listening.

    ii. Reflection is positioning yourself in an almost mirror image to the posture of the other person, using similar rate of speech and level of language. It is not mimicry or imitation, however; it is reflecting back and adapting one's own communication to be in tune with the other.

    iii. Proximics is paying attention to how close you are to the person you are speaking with and stepping back if necessary to remain within each other's area of comfort and understandability.

    iv. Latency is the culturally learned length of time between one speaker's turn and the next speaker's turn to speak. Practicing being aware of these differences in listening before speaking is a useful technique for anyone to truly attend to what others are saying and meaning. With older students, they can practice with stop watches or other actual measurement of time and practice waiting before answering. This is sometimes hard for teachers to do as most want immediate responses.

    v. Active listening is showing that you are paying attention and responding in culturally appropriate ways to indicate your attention. This may include repeating some portion of what was said.

vi. The teacher has the students practice using these strategies in a variety of interactions. The teacher can model, have videos of the interactions, and set up interaction scenarios or role-plays for everyone to practice.

Research Case

Croom & Davis (2006)

Gibbons (2002)

Trudeau & Harle (2006)

What to Watch for With ELL/CLD Students

i. All cultures have different morés about how close you can stand or sit next\to another person (proximics), who or what you may touch, how much time should elapse before you speak after another person (latency), and so on. The teacher should become familiar with these differences regarding the students in his or her classroom.

ii. The strategy of reflection can look like mockery if not done with sensitivity. The goal is to reflect, not to imitate, the mode of the speaker.

CROSS-CULTURAL COUNSELING

Purpose of the Strategy

i. Build awareness of adaptation process

ii. Adapt to meet individual or unique student needs

iii. Build awareness of appropriate academic behaviors

iv. Build awareness of school culture expectations

v. Build students' self-awareness of behavior

vi. Build transfer skills

vii. Develop confidence in academic interactions

viii. Develop confidence in school culture interactions

ix. Develop self-esteem

x. Develop self-monitoring skills

xi. Facilitate school adaptation process

xii. Facilitate student regaining control over self

xiii. Facilitate student self-concept as a successful person

xiv. Facilitate students' comfort with learning environment

xv. Improve confidence in academic interactions

xvi. Improve confidence in home and community culture/school culture interactions

xvii. Improve confidence in school interactions

xviii. Lower anxiety levels

xix. Reduce anxiety and stress responses

xx. Reduce anxiety in social/academic interactions

xxi. Reduce culture shock

xxii. Strengthen school/parent partnerships

xxiii. Facilitate family adaptation to new community

xxiv. Enhance student interaction with family during transition

xxv. Enhance awareness of school adaptation process

xxvi. Reduce anxiety and stress

xxvii. Develop personal control of situations

How to Do It

i. Education staff, including teachers, assistants, counselors, and clerical and administrative members, all assists with this strategy in the context of their opportunities and situations in the school.

ii. There are a variety of ways to provide cross-cultural counseling assistance to students and their families. We recommend that education professionals receive training and demonstrations from specialists to ensure a consistent level of proficiency with these, but most folks will be able to implement the strategy within the context of their teaching or service setting.

iii. The following are the principle elements of this strategy:

- Identify and focus on resiliency
- Provide a safe place to share and openly discuss cross-cultural adaptation issues and culture shock responses
- Respect and empower the student and family members as they acculturate to new school and community
- Recognize situations that may trigger a heightened sense of alienation and culture shock
- Listen with empathy

  ○ Acknowledge that you are listening
  ○ Show empathy (nod, smile, touch)
  ○ Face the person speaking and maintain appropriate eye contact
  ○ Maintain open, available posture
  ○ Acknowledge what you heard and ask clarifying questions

iv. Teachers and assistants receive training in cross-cultural stress response patterns and interventions for use in the classroom. Specialist with training in cross-cultural stress responses and culture shock provides counseling and guidance.

Research Base

Brownlie & King (2000)

Burnham, Mantero, & Hooper (2009)

Carrigan (2001)

Johnson (1995)

Landis, Bennett, & Bennett (2004)

Law & Eckes (2000)

McAllister & Irvine (2000)

Wolpow, Johnson, Hertel, & Kincaid (2009)

What to Watch for With ELL/CLD Students

i. Many cultures have adverse reactions to official personnel getting involved with the family and particularly with someone telling them how to raise their children.

ii. The specialist facilitating the counseling must be trained not only in cross-cultural techniques but also familiar with the particular culture and language of the family being assisted.

DEFENDS—WRITING STRATEGY

Purpose of the Strategy

i. Assist learners to defend a particular position in a written assignment

ii. Build academic transfer skills

iii. Build awareness of appropriate cognitive academic language

iv. Develop analytical skills

v. Develop extended time on task

vi. Develop field independent skills

vii. Develop problem-solving skills

viii. Improve retention of content

ix. Improve writing strategies

x. Increase students' time on task

xi. Improve student's ability to organize and prioritize information

xii. Reduce confusion in locus of control

xiii. Reinforce content lessons

xiv. Retention of content

xv. Strengthen ability to discuss what is happening

xvi. Strengthen awareness of learning process

xvii. Facilitate writing process

xviii. Build awareness and foundation of learning

xix. Develop cognitive academic language

xx. Develop thinking and planning skills

xxi. Strengthen knowledge of academic content

xxii. Strengthen language development

xxiii. Strengthen learning to learn skills

xxiv. Strengthen retention and application abilities

xxv. Expand and improve comprehension

How to Do It

i. The DEFENDS writing strategy framework provides a structure for completing initial and final drafts of written reports and may be used with any group of students including mixed language groups.

ii. The teacher reads an example of a passage that defends a particular position on a topic or area of interest to the students. The teacher or assistant introduces the students to the vocabulary words: decide, examine, form, expose, note, drive, and search. He or she explains how the example passage "defends" a position and shows how points are made to support the position or idea. He or she shows how the position is "driven" home.

iii. Students are asked to read the passage and note each reason and its associated points, creating a list of points. The teacher then has students try writing their own version of the passage using DEFENDS.

iv. The vocabulary words, decide, examine, form, expose, note, drive, and search, may be printed on posters with space for posting examples or on the chalkboard. As the teacher explains each term, he or she asks for examples from the example passage or a familiar previous reading.

v. The teacher writes these examples under the word on the poster or chalkboard. Then students can combine them into a composition as an example.

vi. When used within multi-tiered support systems, including response to intervention (RTI), this strategy may be done with small groups or one-on-one for focused intensive periods of time. It is also useful with whole classrooms where all students are working on their writing assignments at varied levels.

vii. You can combine DEFENDS effectively with the COPS proofreading strategy structure.

viii. To help the students remember the steps in DEFENDS, the teacher can provide the students with a printed form with the letters D, E, F, E, N, D, and S down the left side and their meaning under each letter.

ix. The following are the steps in DEFENDS:

1. Decide on a specific position

2. Examine own reasons for this position

3. Form list of points explaining each reason

4. Expose position in first sentence of written task

5. Note each reason and associated points

6. Drive home position in last sentence

7. Search for and correct any errors

Research Base

Ellis & Colvert (1996)

Ellis & Lenz (1987)

Goldsworthy (2003)

What to Watch for With ELL/CLD Students

i. Newcomers will need to have the DEFENDS steps modeled and explained in their most proficient language before they can proceed independently.

ii. Students can be paired with partners who are slightly more bilingual than themselves to facilitate their learning of this process.

DEFENDS Step	DEFENDS Outcome
D Decide on a specific position	
E Examine own reasons for this position	
F Form list of points explaining each reason	
E Expose position in first sentence of written task	

(Continued)

(Continued)

DEFENDS Step	DEFENDS Outcome
N Note each reason and associated points	
D Drive home position in last sentence	
S Search for and correct any errors	

DEMONSTRATION

Purpose of the Strategy

    i. Build awareness of learning

    ii. Adapt the mode of response required of students

    iii. Build academic transfer skills

    iv. Build awareness of academic expectations

    v. Build awareness of adaptation process

    vi. Build awareness of appropriate academic behaviors

    vii. Build awareness of appropriate behaviors for school language and rules

    viii. Build awareness of appropriate communication behaviors for school language and rules

    ix. Build awareness of learning process

    x. Build awareness of school culture expectations

    xi. Build foundation for learning

    xii. Clarify responsibilities, assignments, and rewards

    xiii. Enhance ability of students to focus on learning

    xiv. Enhance ability of students to learn new things

    xv. Expand comprehension

    xvi. Facilitate acquisition of content knowledge

    xvii. Improve comprehension

    xviii. Increase students' probability of generating a correct response

    xix. Reassure frustrated students

xx.   Reduce anxiety and stress

xxi.   Reduce anxiety and stress responses

xxii.   Reduce anxiety in social/academic interactions

xxiii.   Reduce misperceptions

xxiv.   Strengthen awareness of learning process

xxv.   Strengthen learning to learn skills

xxvi.   Sustain engagement

xxvii.   Facilitate language development

xxviii.   Improve confidence in academic interactions

xxix.   Reduce distractibility

xxx.   Build academic transfer skills

xxxi.   Develop content knowledge foundation

How to Do It

i.   This strategy can be used in any lesson and in any classroom by teachers, peer tutors, instructional assistants, and volunteers.

ii.   The teacher, assistant, or peer demonstrates the content of the lesson. The content is explained in the home and community language when possible, and each aspect of the lesson is demonstrated.

iii.   Demonstration is more than just pointing out what is expected of the students. The teacher needs to do a complete walk through of the actions, words, and outcomes that are expected for an appropriate implementation and completion of the lesson. It is best to use real examples, models, or materials for the demonstration, not just pictures.

iv.   You can also have students demonstrate their understanding of the lesson and content.

v.   The teacher should carefully select activities and assessment that are designed to facilitate demonstration of understanding.

Research Base

Asher (1980)

Echevarria, Vogt, & Short (2007)

Gibbons (2006)

What to Watch for With ELL/CLD Students

i.   This strategy is consistent with both Sheltered Instruction Observation Protocol (SIOP) and the guided language acquisition design (GLAD) process used in many English language learner (ELL) programs.

ii.   Students who have never attended school before will not know what is expected and will benefit from concrete direct demonstrations of content elements and activity expectations.

DIFFERENTIATION

Purpose of the Strategy

    i. Adapt content to meet individual or unique student needs

    ii. Adapt the mode of response required of students

    iii. Build appreciation that everyone has a contribution to make

    iv. Build awareness of academic expectations

    v. Build foundation for learning

    vi. Build transfer skills

    vii. Develop association skills

    viii. Develop content area skills

    ix. Develop content knowledge foundation

    x. Develop extended time on task

    xi. Develop independence in learning situations

    xii. Enhance ability of students to learn new things

    xiii. Expand and elaborate on learning

    xiv. Expand comprehension

    xv. Facilitate students' comfort with learning environment

    xvi. Facilitate students' ownership in their education

    xvii. Facilitate acquisition of content knowledge

    xviii. Improve confidence in academic interactions

    xix. Improve retention of content

    xx. Increase students' probability of generating a correct response

    xxi. Increase students' time on task

    xxii. Increase the frequency of appropriate responses or behaviors

    xxiii. Increase time on task

    xxiv. Reduce anxiety and stress and responses

    xxv. Reduce anxiety in social/academic interactions

    xxvi. Reduce off-task behaviors

    xxvii. Reduce resistance to change

    xxviii. Reduce response fatigue

    xxix. Strengthen learning to learn skills

    xxx. Strengthen retention and application abilities

    xxxi. Sustain engagement

    xxxii. Build learners' confidence in their roles in the learning process

    xxxiii. Develop confidence in academic interactions

    xxxiv. Enhance ability of students to focus on learning

    xxxv. Establish baseline performance levels

    xxxvi. Facilitate students assuming responsibility for learning

    xxxvii. Facilitate student self-concept as a successful person

    xxxviii. Improve comprehension

    xxxix. Lower anxiety levels

How to Do It

i. The teacher designs instruction so individual needs and abilities are addressed. This strategy can be used in any lesson and in any classroom by teachers, peer tutors, instructional assistants, and volunteers.

ii. A basic premise of differentiation is that one type of instruction does not necessarily work for all students, that is, one size does not fit all. Teachers are advised to begin where their students are, with their learning differences and their learning strengths.

iii. Learners are motivated and complete tasks appropriate to their needs, interests, and abilities. Individual Education Plan (IEP) may state that student will be able to use or respond to specific cues or reinforcements.

Example

The class is working on a unit about the Lewis and Clark expedition, and the teacher has prepared reading selections and field trips about various aspects of this for the class. After a visit to Fort Clatsop, the teacher has a group of students with good visual and manual skills work on posters and diagrams illustrating the fort. Another group of students who are good at writing work with students who are good at storytelling to develop a set of short stories about events that happened at the fort. A different group of students, who are more familiar with technology use, does research online about the expedition and locates apps and games where reference to the expedition are part of the challenge. Students in the classroom who come from local tribal communities may want to interview the elders in their community to see if there are any old stories about "the first White man" or the government explorers. The students bring all their different efforts into small work groups within the classroom to design a walk-through experience they can share with classes of other students.

Research Base

Benjamin (2003)

Ferris & Hedgcock (2005)

Herrera & Murry (2004)

Krumenaker, Many, & Wang (2008)

Murrey (2008)

What to Watch for With ELL/CLD Students

i. For ELL and CLD students, instructional personnel are to build upon learners' cultural and linguistic differences and strengths by developing instructional activities based on essential topics and concepts, significant processes and skills, and multiple ways to display learning while providing flexible approaches to content, instruction, and outcomes.

ii. In-depth differentiation for ELL and culturally and linguistically diverse (CLD) students would involve bilingual, multilingual, and multicultural materials as well as leveled readers and units. As this would be challenging to do with today's school financial issues, I suggest involving community organizations and other resources to provide as much variety of materials as possible. In the end, however, differentiation is recognizing that each student responds and works best in his or her own manner regardless of the breadth of resources, that is, breadth of approach and expectation are the heart of differentiation.

iii. The teacher needs to keep in mind that different groups of folks have different opinions about events and their impact upon various communities. I used the Lewis and Clark expedition activity as an example because it illustrates both a strength and a caution for using historical events as instructional content. While you may focus on the raw facts of the historical event, you will also need to be conscious of how the event is perceived from a variety of perspectives.

DOUBLE-ENTRY

Purpose of the Strategy

i. Build awareness of academic expectations

ii. Develop analytical skills

iii. Develop association skills

iv. Develop categorization skills

v. Develop cognitive academic language

vi. Develop problem-solving skills

vii. Develop thinking and planning skills

viii. Expand and elaborate on learning

ix. Expand comprehension

x. Build awareness of appropriate cognitive academic language

xi. Build transfer skills

xii. Facilitate language development

xiii.   Facilitate acquisition of content knowledge

xiv.   Facilitate writing process

xv.   Improve reading comprehension

xvi.   Strengthen language development

xvii.   Strengthen learning to learn skills

xviii.   Strengthen retention and application abilities

xix.   Build vocabulary

xx.   Improve reading and writing strategies

xxi.   Enhance ability of students to focus on learning

xxii.   Improve reading strategies

How to Do It

i.   Double entry is a method of taking comprehensive notes as well as reflecting on what is read.

ii.   The teacher illustrates the strategy by making a large version out of chart paper and demonstrates how to use double entry while reading a selection of text. He or she folds the chart paper in half so it looks like the individual sheet that all the students have at their desks. Depending upon the focus the teacher intends, he or she makes headings on the top of the two columns, for example, "sentence" and "part of composition" or "summary of passage" and "inference."

iii.   The whole group then reads through the selection, and the teacher writes down selected sentences from the reading in the left hand column. He or she has the students identify what the sentence in the left hand column represent and writes that in the right hand column.

iv.   There are several applications of double entry: identifying parts of a composition or sentence, using paraphrasing to summarize, locating specific examples of persuasion or dialogue, generalizing meanings or implications, generating individual interpretations of passages, locating elements of new content, and so on.

v.   When reading a book, article, passage, or so on, students divide a piece of paper in half, lengthwise. In the left hand column, they copy sentences or summarize a passage. In the right hand column, they write down their interpretation, inferences, and critical thinking about the passage. This activity can also be done as a journal in which the pages are divided into the two columns.

vi.   Students can also use the double entry form as a writing strategy. In other words, in reverse, that is, identifying the elements of composition they wish to use and then adding their own key sentences. After doing this, they can then pull the whole together as a written passage.

Example

The teacher tells the students they are to identify the key parts of composition in an article about owning a pet. After reading the whole, he or she has the students write key sentences from the article down the left hand column of their individual double entry sheets. The teacher then has the students identify which part of the composition each sentence represents and write that in the right hand column. The students compare and discuss their answers, clarifying why or why not each part of the composition is included in the element of composition.

Research Base

Strickland, Ganske, & Monroe (2002)

Tovani (2000)

What to Watch for With ELL/CLD Students

i.   This is an easy strategy to assist students who are beginning to do more reading and writing to organize and think about what they are reading.

ii. This can be done in any language in which the students are literate.

Double-Entry Example for Writing or Reading

Sentences From Article	What Part of the Composition Is This?
Pets can be a lot of hard work, but they are a lot of fun, too.	Introduction
Lots of people think pets are more trouble than they are worth, but I think they are a joy to have.	Main idea
Sometimes dogs make neighbors upset by barking at night.	Supporting comments
Sometimes dogs chase cats, or cats catch birds.	
My dog rolled in oil one time, and I had to bathe him. When I dried him off, he curled up next to me and licked my hand to thank me.	Examples
So, now you can see why I like having pets.	Conclusion

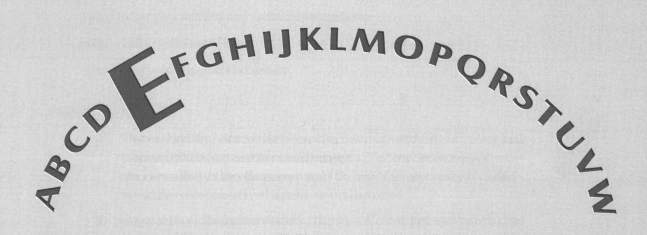

EASY (READING COMPREHENSION)

Purpose of the Strategy

    i. Develop analytic skills

    ii. Build confidence in independent work

    iii. Build academic transfer skills

    iv. Build awareness of academic expectations

    v. Develop extended time on task

    vi. Develop field independent skills

    vii. Develop cognitive learning strategies

    viii. Develop thinking and planning skills

    ix. Enhance ability of student to focus on learning and to learn new things

    x. Improve comprehension

    xi. Improve confidence and self-esteem

    xii. Build awareness of learning

    xiii. Develop higher persistence

    xiv. Develop self-monitoring skills

xv. Improve sequencing skills

xvi. Improve test-taking skills

xvii. Increase focus on reading

xviii. Increase students' probability of generating a correct response

xix. Increase students' time on task

xx. Improve students' ability to organize and prioritize information

xxi. Reduce confusion in locus of control

xxii. Strengthen awareness of learning process

xxiii. Strengthen learning to learn skills

xxiv. Sustain engagement

xxv. Sustain engagement with reading and writing

xxvi. Facilitate student self-concept as a successful person

xxvii. Facilitate students' comfort with learning environment

xxviii. Facilitate students' ownership in their education

How to Do It

i. This strategy helps students organize and prioritize information within their reading by focusing on questions designed to identify important content.

ii. The teacher introduces EASY by pointing to the steps on a large poster or projection. It is best to have graphics that serve as cues for what each step in EASY stands for. As the teacher points to the step, he or she says the phrase and explains the meaning of each step and provides examples of the action to take at each step of EASY using a current reading selection as an illustration.

iii. Posters with the EASY framework are posted around the room for reference during reading activities.

iv. The teacher reviews this strategy several times before students are to read articles or passages in a content lesson.

v. Students can create cue cards to remember each step. Students follow steps while reading passages or thematic elements. The following are the steps in EASY:

1. Elicit questions (who, what, where, when, why, and how)

2. Ask self which information is least difficult

3. Study easy content initially, followed by difficult

4. Yes! Provide self-reinforcement through rewards or points for self

Research Base

Lapp, Flood, Brock, & Fisher (2007)

Moore, Alvermann, & Hinchman (2000)

What to Watch for With ELL/CLD Students

i. Much like the other mnemonics provided in these strategy lists, English language learner (ELL)/culturally linguistically diverse (CLD) students need bilingual explanations of the teacher's expectations and guided practice in implementing the steps in the strategy.

ii. Newcomers will need to have the EASY steps modeled and explained in their most proficient language before they can proceed independently.

iii. Students can be paired with partners who are slightly more bilingual than themselves to facilitate their learning this process.

EASY Element	What am I to do at this step?	What did I do about it?	Notes
Elicit questions (who, what, where, when, why, and how)			
Ask self which information is least difficult			
Study easy content initially, followed by difficult			
Yes! Provide self-reinforcement through rewards or points for self			

EMBEDDING

Purpose of the Strategy

i.   Adapt to meet individual or unique student needs

ii.   Develop content knowledge foundation

iii. Build awareness of appropriate cognitive academic language

iv.   Develop cognitive academic language proficiency

v.   Adapt the mode of response required of students

vi.   Build awareness of the appropriate content language in English culture/language

vii. Build first language to English transfer skills

viii. Develop cognitive academic language

ix.   Develop field sensitive skills

x.   Develop higher persistence

xi.   Enhance ability of students to focus on learning and to learn new things

xii. Expand comprehension

xiii. Facilitate acquisition of content knowledge

xiv. Facilitate language development

xv.   Facilitate discussion about new learning

xvi. Facilitate acquisition of content knowledge

xvii. Improve comprehension

xviii. Reduce code switching

xix. Reduce misperceptions

xx.   Reinforce and improve retention of content

xxi. Strengthen ability to discuss what is happening

xxii. Strengthen awareness of learning process

xxiii. Develop content area skills

xxiv. Reduce distractibility

xxv. Build learners' confidence in their control of the learning process

xxvi. Strengthen awareness of language development

xxvii. Develop personal control of situations

How to Do It

i.   The teacher presents lessons with concrete, physical models and demonstrations of both content and expected performance. Language is simplified and content focused. Lessons address real life situations and learning. Use graphics, signs, pictures, and objects to clarify exactly what is being discussed.

ii. Embed all instruction in context-rich activities. Embed instruction in concrete, explicit structures or models, making sure that concrete context is used. This may involve using real objects, models, and demonstrations or the use of specific cues and guide structures.

iii. Students are encouraged to work in small groups on content-focused activities and to discuss lessons in their most proficient language. They are encouraged to use models, guides, and frames for completing their work.

Example in Writing/Reading

As students become more familiar with specific vocabulary or content through embedded examples, the teacher can introduce graphic frames for creating or understanding sentences. Three examples are included below for guiding students in reading and writing sentences using selected vocabulary words embedded in a guiding structure. Two of the examples provide all the words students could choose from to write their own sentences. The words are embedded in a frame that follows the preferred sentence structure. Students can choose the words they wish but should keep to the recommended word order in the frame. The blank example is one that can be used as a frame for students to generate their own sentences, but it still provides a frame for how the words should be ordered in the sentence.

Expansion

Students are encouraged to discuss lessons in home and community language and work in small groups on content activities.

Research Base

Cole (1995)

Cummins (1984)

Cummins, Baker, & Hornberger (2001)

Donaldson (1978)

Echevarria & Graves (2006)

Echevarria, Vogt, & Short (2007)

Roessingh, Kover, & Watt (2005)

What to Watch for With ELL/CLD Students

i. Vocabulary may be previewed with fluent speakers in the students' most proficient language. Building familiarity is critical for the success of this strategy. Not all ELL/CLD students will know what the objects or models represent.

ii. Some cultures may have strictures against children handling or being too close to certain objects. Always screen items ahead of time with knowledgeable community members.

iii. The teacher will need to introduce the models or objects in full scale representations or use the actual items to build a true understanding. Only after students have actually seen, felt, smelled, and possibly tasted an apple will they respond to a picture of an apple.

Example: Sentence Building Frame Activity

Subject Clause	Verb Clause		Object Clause			
Subject Pronoun	Adverb	Verb	Article	Noun	Preposition	Object Pronoun

Subject Clause		Verb Clause				Object Clause					
Article	Adjective	Adjective	Noun	Adverb	Verb	Article	Noun	Preposition	Article	Adjective	Noun
The	wrinkled	hairy	cat	quickly	ate	a	rabbit	in	an	ancient	barn.
An	ugly	bald	dog	hastily	fetched	the	bone	to	a	simpering	girl.
A	pretty	young	frog	quietly	jumped	an	eel	under	the	gleaming	water.
The	sweet	merry	girl	gently	sang	the	aria	about	an	aching	heart.
An	old	cranky	boy	avidly	threw	an	egg	over	the	bending	bough.
A	green	supple	fish	eagerly	leaped	a	puddle	near	a	flowering	tree.

Subject Pronoun	Adverb	Verb	Article	Noun	Preposition	Object Pronoun
You	badly	bashed	an	apple	behind	her.
We	vastly	underestimated	the	cost	to	them.
They	quietly	sang	a	song	about	me.
She	meanly	washed	the	floor	under	him.

ENTRY POINTS

Purpose of the Strategy

    i. Build awareness of learning process

    ii. Adapt to meet individual or unique student needs

    iii. Adapt the mode of response required of students

    iv. Build awareness of academic expectations

    v. Build awareness of adaptation process

    vi. Build confidence in independent work

    vii. Build foundation for learning

    viii. Develop self-esteem

    ix. Enhance ability of students to focus on learning

    x. Enhance ability of students to learn new things

    xi. Expand and elaborate on learning

    xii. Expand comprehension

    xiii. Facilitate students assuming responsibility for learning

    xiv. Facilitate student self-concept as a successful person

    xv. Facilitate students' comfort with learning environment

    xvi. Facilitate students' ownership in their education

    xvii. Improve confidence and self-esteem

    xviii. Improve confidence in academic interactions

    xix. Improve motivation

    xx. Improve retention of content

    xxi. Increase students' probability of generating a correct response

    xxii. Increase students' time on task

    xxiii. Increase the frequency of appropriate responses or behaviors

    xxiv. Reduce fears associated with assignments

    xxv. Reduce frustration

    xxvi. Reduce frustration in students due to unclear expectations

    xxvii. Reduce anxiety and stress and responses

    xxviii. Reduce anxiety in social/academic interactions

    xxix. Retention of content

    xxx. Strengthen ability to discuss what is happening

    xxxi. Strengthen awareness of learning process

xxxii. Build appreciation that all can contribute

xxxiii. Build transfer skills

xxxiv. Develop independence in learning situations

xxxv. Develop extended time on task

xxxvi. Develop personal control of situations

How to Do It

i. The teacher ensures that students with different abilities work with the same essential ideas and use the same key content but provides different points of entry for a variety of skills and abilities. For example, a student having difficulty with reading still needs to make sense of the basic concepts and ideas of a story. Simultaneously, a student who is advanced in the same subject needs to find genuine challenge in working with these same concepts and ideas. Providing different entry points to the content of the lesson facilitates students focus on essential understandings and skills but at different levels of complexity, abstractness, and open endedness. This is done by keeping the focus of activity the same but providing routes of access at varying degrees of difficulty.

ii. This is also related to the idea of multiple intelligences developed by Howard Gardner, wherein the teacher adapts lesson to students' varied intelligence preferences or strengths. For example, a student who is strong spatially may take in information, solve problems, and express learning differently than a student whose strength is verbal-linguistic. Teachers can facilitate the learning process by considering these differences when planning and carrying out instructions.

Research Base

Gardner (1993a)

Heacox (2002)

Tomlinson (1999)

What to Watch for With ELL/CLD Students

i. A basic premise of differentiation is that one type of instruction does not necessarily work for all students, that is, one size does not fit all. Teachers are advised to begin where their students are with their learning differences and their learning strengths.

ii. For ELL and CLD students, instructional personnel are to build upon learners' cultural and linguistic differences and strengths by developing instructional activities based on essential topics and concepts, significant processes and skills, and multiple ways to display learning while providing flexible approaches to content, instruction, and outcomes.

EVALUATION

Purpose of the Strategy

    i. Build awareness of learning process

    ii. Access prior knowledge

    iii. Adapt to meet individual or unique student needs

    iv. Adapt the mode of response required of students

    v. Build awareness of adaptation process

    vi. Build awareness of appropriate academic behaviors

    vii. Build awareness of school culture expectations

    viii. Build confidence in independent work

    ix. Build foundation for learning

    x. Develop analytical skills

    xi. Develop association skills

    xii. Develop awareness of cause and effect

    xiii. Develop personal control of situations

    xiv. Develop problem-solving skills

    xv. Develop self-esteem

    xvi. Develop self-monitoring skills

    xvii. Develop thinking and planning skills

    xviii. Ensure students are familiar with specific academic and behavioral expectations

    xix. Ensure that students are aware of and responsible for their own actions

    xx. Expand and elaborate on learning

    xxi. Facilitate access of prior knowledge

    xxii. Facilitate acquisition of content knowledge

    xxiii. Improve access to prior knowledge

    xxiv. Improve comprehension

    xxv. Improve confidence and self-esteem

    xxvi. Improve confidence in academic interactions

    xxvii. Reduce anxiety and stress responses

    xxviii. Reduce anxiety in social/academic interactions

    xxix. Reinforce content lessons

    xxx. Retention of content

xxxi. Strengthen awareness of learning process

xxxii. Strengthen home/school relationship

xxxiii. Strengthen knowledge of academic content

xxxiv. Strengthen language development

xxxv. Strengthen learning to learn skills

xxxvi. Strengthen retention and application abilities

xxxvii. Sustain engagement

xxxviii. Use prior knowledge

xxxix. Develop categorization skills

xl. Develop extended time on task

xli. Develop personal control of situations

xlii. Strengthen awareness of learning process

xliii. Develop guidelines for strategy choice

xliv. Develop field sensitive skills

xlv. Develop higher persistence

xlvi. Strengthen learning to learn skills

xlvii. Lower anxiety levels

xlviii. Reduce confusion in locus of control

How to Do It

i. The teacher introduces the students to the strategy of evaluation by explaining that a strategy is a tool to help them learn, and evaluation is one of these tools or strategies.

ii. The teacher's goals in developing the students' evaluation strategy skills include increasing the students' awareness of what they need to do to complete a given task, providing the students with concrete guidelines for selecting and using appropriate specific strategies for achievement, and guiding the students in comprehensive monitoring of the application of the strategy. These goals are accomplished through modeling, demonstrating, and describing the purpose or rationale for using the strategy. This, in turn, assists students to become aware of the types of tasks or situations where the strategy is most appropriate, the range of applications and transferability, the anticipated benefits from consistent use, and the amount of effort needed to successfully deploy the strategy.

iii. The teacher takes the students through the steps, referring to a poster or diagram of the four steps. The first step is to think about how to identify what a problem consists of and how it can be measured and completed. The second step is to identify all the components of the problem and all the elements needed to solve it or to complete the task. The third step is to plan ahead for difficulties and to identify where and how to get feedback and assistance. The fourth and final step is to think about ways to generalize the lesson learned and how to apply the information in other settings and contexts.

iv. Students use index cards with the steps for the evaluation strategy on them to cue themselves for each step. They select a specific problem or task and use the cards as mnemonics as they proceed through the assignment.

v. The following are the steps for students to follow in implementing the strategy:

1. How will I analyze the problem?

2. What are the important elements of this problem?

3. How will I get feedback?

4. How can I generalize the information?

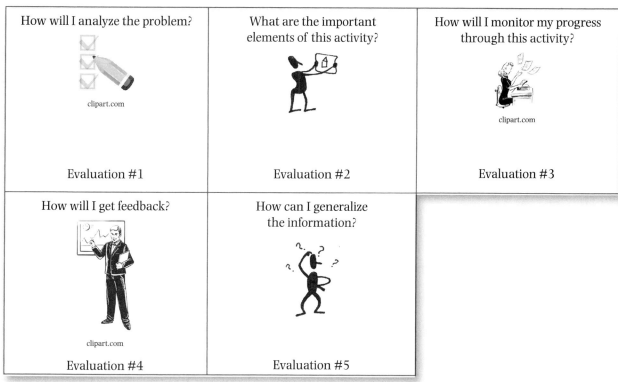

Source: Collier (2008).

vi. Steps for Teaching Evaluation

1. *Inform* the students what evaluation is, how it operates, when to use it, and why it is useful. Begin by saying that evaluation is a way to help them analyze and monitor their learning. It works by asking and answering the above series of four questions concerning a lesson they are working on. Once they learn how to use evaluation, they can use it anytime and with any content or lesson you give them to do.

2. *Use cues,* metaphors, analogies, or other means of elaborating on a description of evaluation combined with visual cues. One way to do this is to have the group watch a panel discussion or other presentation on television where a group is analyzing a problem or evaluating a proposal to do something. Another is to show a video of scientists working in a laboratory to evaluate whether a substance works effectively. Show how everyone can analyze, monitor, and control learning when he or she goes step by step.

3. *Lead group discussions* about the use of evaluation. Have students start by talking about a science or math lesson they have just successfully solved. They can go back through the lesson or interaction stopping to show how each step of the lesson can be analyzed and monitored using the evaluation steps to see how they work and what is required. Encourage them to ask you anything about the learning process they want clarified.

4. *Provide guided practice* in applying evaluation to particular tasks. Here is an example of guided practice as the teacher leads the students through the use of evaluation. Examples of both teacher and student comments are shown.

    a. Teacher: First, you must analyze the task to determine what it requires. This includes items such as materials, time, space, or types of actions. What is the expected outcome of the task? What steps must you follow in order to complete the task? Review other completed assignments to determine possible steps you might take to complete this task.

    b. Student: What do I need to do to complete this task, and do I have all necessary materials and resources? What should the expected outcome look like? What steps must I follow to effectively achieve the expected outcome?"

    c. Teacher: Second, after you have analyzed the task, you must identify possible strategies that might be used to accomplish the task. Think about strategies you have used in the past to complete similar tasks. One or more of these may be necessary to complete this task.

    d. Student: What strategies do I know that might be appropriate for this particular task? Why might these be useful in this particular situation?

    e. Strategy Implementation

    f. Teacher: Third, prior to using a selected strategy, review the steps in that strategy. Remember that one strategy may be used in several different situations and different situations may require the use of more than one strategy.

g. Student: I've selected these strategies for this task. I'll review the process associated with each strategy prior to implementation. I'll use these strategies while I complete this task.

h. Feedback

i. Teacher: Fourth, you must become aware of how useful it is to use the strategies you have selected. They assist you to complete the task accurately and efficiently. Periodically reflect upon how you are doing and how effective the strategy is for completing the task at hand.

j. Student: How useful is this strategy for this particular task? Is this strategy helping me to accurately and efficiently confront the assigned task? Do I need to use a different strategy?"

k. Teacher: Finally, think of other previously completed tasks where use of one or more of these strategies would have been beneficial to confronting the tasks. Could you have completed those tasks more efficiently had you used these strategies? Think of other types of tasks or future tasks where you might appropriately use one or more of these strategies.

l. Student: Why were these strategies useful to this particular task? In what other types of situations would the use of these strategies be beneficial?

5. *Provide feedback* on monitoring use and success of evaluation. While students use evaluation in small groups, you should move around the room listening and supplying encouragement for consistent use of the question and answer steps. As students get more comfortable using this strategy, you can have them monitor one another in the use of the strategy, encouraging each other to ask or answer the questions.

6. *Provide generalization* activities. Have your students use evaluation for a variety of lessons and tasks. You should be sure to identify the strategy by name and refer to the poster or visual cues about the strategy whenever you have students use it. Hold enhanced cognitive discussions about the use of evaluation in these different lesson settings, and encourage discussion of how useful or not useful students found this strategy in particular tasks.

Research Base

Brown & Palincsar (1987)

Cole (1995)

Opitz (1998)

Pressley, Borkowski, & O'Sullivan (1984)

What to Watch for With ELL/CLD Students

i. Since these students may be limited in English proficiency, the monolingual English-speaking teacher must increase the amount of demonstration and visual cues and rely less upon verbal descriptions and cues. If available, bilingual assistance from peers or other education personnel may be useful in translating what is discussed in the classroom. This is especially important in order to provide explicit information to students concerning the rationale and value of the strategy. In addition, analogy elaboration of the evaluation strategy may be drawn from the students' cultural and linguistic backgrounds. This reinforces the validity of the students' previous successful learning and increases the ability of the students to make associations that will strengthen their cognitive development.

ii. Students who have never been in school before will not know what is expected of them and what measuring, analyzing, and evaluating look like.

iii. Some translation and discussion in the ELL students' more proficient language may be necessary to clarify what is to be done and why.

EXPECTATIONS AWARENESS/REVIEW

Purpose of the Strategy

i. Alleviate power struggles between teacher and student

ii. Build awareness of academic expectations

iii. Clarify responsibilities, assignments, and rewards

iv. Build awareness of appropriate academic behaviors

v. Build foundation for learning

vi. Facilitate nondirective guidance about student misbehavior

vii. Facilitate student assuming responsibility for learning

viii. Facilitate student ownership in learning

ix. Minimize behavior problems

x. Reduce frustration in students due to unclear expectations

xi. Minimize ambiguity in classroom

How to Do It

i. This strategy can be used in any lesson and in any classroom by teachers, peer tutors, instructional assistants, and volunteers where there is a need to ensure that each student is familiar with specific academic and behavioral expectations.

ii. The teacher modifies or breaks down general classroom rules into specific behavioral expectations and demonstrates each rule or expectation through modeling or role play, to ensure that each student knows exactly what is meant by acceptable behaviors.

iii. Illustrations and demonstrations of the desired behaviors and rules should be posted around the room. If the expectation is for a specific level of neatness, correctness, or thoroughness of response on written assignments, actual examples of what the finished product should look like must be posted on the wall for review.

Research Base

Davis (2005)

Nelson, Martella, & Galand, B. (1998)

Rubenstein (2006)

What to Watch for With ELL/CLD Students

i. Particular social groups and cultures have different expectations of adult and children when it comes to being accountable for task completion. This is a learned difference between cultures. The teacher needs to be aware that the expectations in an American school may need to be taught directly to CLD students and not just assumed to be understood.

ii. One way to introduce the idea of your classroom rules is to ask students about any rules their parent have for them at home or rules they have learned about crossing the street or playing games. This can then be expanded to the idea of rules for completing tasks and acting appropriately in a classroom.

iii. Demonstrate all of the desired behaviors and rules. Some role-play may be helpful. Examples of bad behaviors may be used with caution.

EXPERIENCE-BASED LEARNING

Purpose of the Strategy

i. Access and use prior knowledge

ii. Build foundation for learning

iii. Build upon existing strengths of student

iv. Build awareness of learning process

v. Build awareness of relation between cause and effect

vi. Develop content area skills

vii. Develop content knowledge foundation

    viii. Develop field sensitive skills

    ix. Develop higher persistence

    x. Develop higher tolerance

    xi. Encourage questioning and exploration of new learning

    xii. Enhance ability of students to focus on learning

    xiii. Enhance ability of students to learn new things

    xiv. Expand and elaborate on learning

    xv. Expand comprehension

    xvi. Facilitate access of prior knowledge

    xvii. Facilitate acquisition of content knowledge

    xviii. Facilitate connections between known and new

    xix. Facilitate discussion about new learning

    xx. Improve comprehension

    xxi. Improve motivation

    xxii. Minimize ambiguity in classroom

    xxiii. Reduce misperceptions

    xxiv. Reduce culture shock

    xxv. Strengthen knowledge of academic content

    xxvi. Strengthen language development

    xxvii. Strengthen learning to learn skills

    xxviii. Strengthen retention and application abilities

    xxix. Sustain engagement

    xxx. Build and improve vocabulary

    xxxi. Build transfer skills

    xxxii. Develop cognitive academic language

    xxxiii. Develop content knowledge foundation

    xxxiv. Facilitate analogy strategies

How to Do It

    i. This strategy can be done in the general education classroom with all students participating. Students may be paired with culture and language peers at first and then mixed pairs of diverse students as they become comfortable with the strategy.

    ii. The first stage of this strategy is to have the students attend events, go to different places, see new or varied things, visit buildings or important locations related to lessons that will be coming up, or provide other opportunities for students to experience real world situations, people, structures, areas, or so on that will be featured in later lessons in the classroom.

iii. These actual experiences will then be followed by teacher-provided guided discussions about the experience answering questions, eliciting oral responses, and drawing comments from the students about the experience.

iv. Primary level: The teacher presents lessons with concrete reference to specific experiences in which students have participated. The activity may be paired with field trips or other shared experiences or may be in reference to prior life experiences of ELL/LEP students. Community members may make presentations about events significant to students' families. The teacher then has students tell what their illustrations depict and writes down verbatim what the students say. Students then read back to the teacher what has been written.

v. Intermediate and secondary levels: The teacher guides students to illustrate and write their own stories about their experiences. These stories can be put into collections and bound for use by other students. Stories can be kept in the classroom, library, or media center.

Research Base

Beckett (2002)

Beckett & Miller (2006)

Beckett & Slater (2005)

Coelho & Rivers (2003)

Cole (1995)

Echevarria, Vogt, & Short (2007)

Gibbons (2002)

Nessel & Nixon (2008)

Wasik (2004)

What to Watch for With ELL/CLD Students

i. Some shared experiences will be very novel for particular cultural members of a group, more so than for other members. Be sure to give those who have never before seen something extra preparation time and explanations of what they are going to see or do during the field trip or experience.

ii. Be sure students are matched with peers with whom they can communicate comfortably while they are all learning the strategy and steps in the process.

iii. Be sensitive to cultural mores about certain experiences and businesses. You may need to spend extra time discussing what is going to be seen and heard, or in some cases, prepared to have some students participate in a related but separate activity.

EXPLORATION—INQUIRY TECHNIQUE

Purpose of the Strategy

    i. Adapt to meet individual or unique student needs

    ii. Adapt the mode of response required of students

    iii. Build awareness of learning process

    iv. Develop analytical skills

    v. Develop association skills

    vi. Develop extended time on task

    vii. Develop field independent skills

    viii. Facilitate analogy strategies

    ix. Facilitate connections between known and new

    x. Strengthen learning to learn skills

    xi. Develop cognitive learning strategies

    xii. Improve comprehension

    xiii. Develop student understanding of prediction and confirmation

    xiv. Facilitate acquisition of content knowledge

    xv. Build learner confidence in their control of the learning process

    xvi. Facilitate student self-evaluation skills

How to Do It

    i. This strategy is usually used with mathematics or science lessons of new content related to previous lessons. It can, however, be used with social studies, music, and other content units where a question is to be answered or the teacher wants students to approach an issue to be resolved.

    ii. The gist of the exploration strategy is to present a puzzle, problem, or situation in such a way that students are to resolve it with a minimum of guidance, usually through group examination and trial.

    iii. The teacher actively engages students in constructing mathematical or scientific knowledge through the use of activities that encourage them to explore and investigate content principles or ideas. For example, students visit a garden and observe, count, and measure the different petals that are attached to different species of flowers. Students could also explore the different configurations in which leaves grow on each stem.

    iv. The National Science Education Standards call for students to do inquiry and to know about inquiry. When students do inquiry, they use the same ideas as scientists do when they are conducting research. Students become miniscientists.

v. Exploration or open learning has many benefits. It means students do not simply perform experiments in a routine fashion but actually think about the results they collect and what they mean. With traditional nonopen lessons there is a tendency for students to say that the experiment went wrong when they collect results contrary to what they are told to expect. In open lessons, there are no wrong results, and students have to evaluate the strengths and weaknesses of the results they collect themselves and decide their value. Because the path taken to a desired learning target is uncertain, open lessons are more dynamic and less predictable than traditional lessons

Research Base

Banchi & Bell (2008)

Bruner (1961)

Cole (1995)

Olson & Loucks-Horsley (2000)

What to Watch for With ELL/CLD Students

i. This strategy is not appropriate for newcomer or very limited English proficient students. Introduce it to ELL/CLD students only after they have spent some time in American classrooms and are comfortable with the expectations and processes used regularly in the science or math class.

ii. Many CLD students from other countries have been in educational systems that do not allow or encourage open exploration, inquiry, or free thinking about content material. These school systems teach students through routines and correct answers and often expect rote memorization and recitation by students to demonstrate their understanding of the lesson.

iii. Many indigenous and native populations have an observational approach to learning and do not encourage children to take action until after they have watched an elder or knowledgeable person complete a task multiple times successfully. They are actively discouraged from trial and error.

iv. CLD students may be very hesitant and uncomfortable about stepping outside of books and other information sources and may not initiate exploring by doing.

EXPLORATION TEAM

Purpose of the Strategy

i. Access and use prior knowledge

ii. Build appreciation that everyone belongs and is needed

iii. Build appreciation that everyone has a contribution to make

iv. Build awareness of appropriate academic behaviors

v. Build awareness of the appropriate content language in English culture/language

vi. Build foundation for learning

vii. Develop content knowledge foundation

viii. Develop student understanding of prediction

ix. Encourage questioning and exploration of new learning

x. Facilitate connections between known and new

xi. Facilitate discussion about new learning

xii. Improve access to prior knowledge

xiii. Improve comprehension

xiv. Recognize the importance of working together

xv. Strengthen language development

xvi. Strengthen learning to learn skills

xvii. Strengthen retention and application abilities

xviii. Facilitate acquisition of content knowledge

xix. Improve vocabulary

xx. Build awareness of academic expectations

xxi. Build awareness of learning process

xxii. Build upon existing language skills of student

xxiii. Provides opportunity to negotiate for meaning

xxiv. Develop academic language

xxv. Sustain engagement

xxvi. Develop thinking and planning

How to Do It

i. The exploration team is a strategy for scaffolding vocabulary and the meaning of various information for a lesson or unit

ii. The teacher introduces the use of the exploration team and their report as an introductory lesson to a unit of instruction.

iii. The teacher divides the class into exploration teams and hands out a variety of photographs or illustrations representing content in the upcoming unit of instruction, using real photos, in color, if possible. The teacher should choose high interest photos and give two to three photos to each team.

iv. The teacher asks each exploration team to look at the photos and decide on one photo to report on. The team should then decide on an observation, a question, and a prediction that they will report to the class

v. The teacher will then ask each team for their observation, question, and prediction. Sometimes the teacher color codes the responses to match each team on a large chart.

vi. The teacher uses the information generated and recorded on the chart to determine the students' background knowledge and specific areas to expand upon during the unit lessons. He or she can also use the charts as a formative monitoring chart for periodically revisiting with the class or one of the evaluation teams to check and review information learned.

vii. This strategy can be used as an advanced organizer for any new topic or unit of instruction.

Research Base

Brechtel (2001)

Collier (2002)

Heacox (2002)

Moore, Alvermann, & Hinchman (2000)

What to Watch for With ELL/CLD Students

i. This will need to be demonstrated and lots of guidance provided for newcomers as well as students from diverse schooling experiences.

ii. Students may need to be introduced to the idea of observation, questioning or wondering, and predicting. These cognitive academic vocabulary words should be added to those ELL students are learning as they learn the language of instruction.

Observations	What are you wondering?	What are your predictions?

FAMILY-CENTERED LEARNING ACTIVITY

Purpose of the Strategy

i. Access prior knowledge

ii. Build awareness of school culture expectations

iii. Build academic transfer skills

iv. Build appreciation that everyone belongs and is needed

v. Build appreciation that everyone has a contribution to make

vi. Build awareness of academic expectations

vii. Build foundation for learning

viii. Build home and community language to English transfer skills

ix. Develop cognitive learning strategies

x. Develop confidence in academic interactions

xi. Enhance ability of student to focus on learning

xii. Enhance ability of students to learn new things

xiii. Facilitate student self-concept as a successful person

xiv. Facilitate students' comfort with the learning environment

xv. Improve comprehension

xvi. Improve school/parent partnership

xvii. Increase the frequency of appropriate responses or behaviors

xviii. Increase time on task

xix. Lower anxiety levels

xx. Reduce culture shock

xxi. Develop confidence in school culture interactions

xxii. Encourage questioning and exploration of new learning

xxiii. Expand comprehension

xxiv. Retention of content

xxv. Reinforce school/parent partnership

xxvi. Build awareness of academic expectations

xxvii. Build awareness of appropriate school language and rules for academic and social behaviors

xxviii. Build upon family language and culture

xxix. Strengthen school/parent partnerships

How to Do It

i. This strategy is useful in building family involvement in school, strengthening the support at home for student learning, as well as reinforcing content and vocabulary learned during the school day.

ii. Learning activities are offered to families centered on specific content areas. For example, family math, family computer, and family literacy nights. School staff, with the assistance of community members, offer several interactive activities and provide an educational and fun setting for all. Parents benefit from home and community language explanations, when possible, about education outcomes and how they can help students at home.

iii. These activities can be done bilingually or wholly in the family language. For Spanish speakers, you can tie into the existing Spanish language computer, math, science, and language materials available online from CONEVyT.

Example

In one district *Libros Sin Fronteras* was established as an evening and weekend activity for Spanish speaking families. Parents and their children were invited to attend sessions where they received a copy of a bilingual or Spanish book and met the author of the book, for example Alma Flor Ada. She presented a discussion about her book, read sections aloud, and answered questions from parents in Spanish. School staff members gave lessons on how to use books at home, the importance of reading to your children, and demonstrating how to read to and discuss books in a comfortable family situation. *Libros Sin Fronteras* was held every other weekend, and families ended up with several books to keep and read at home.

Example

The teacher prepares simple worksheets that reflect what was learned that day or that week and sends them home with the student. The student is to go over the materials with their parents/caregivers in the home language. The worksheets can be in English and reflect what was learned in English, but the student is asked to explain the content in the home language and go through the worksheet items in the home language. The parent/caregiver signs off on the worksheet and the student brings it back to school the next day/week. This activity assists the student in transitioning back and forth in cognitive academic language and strengthens both content and language skills.

Research Base

Garcia, Hasson, Hoffman, Paneque, & Pelaez (1996)

Sink, Jr., Parkhill, Marshall, Norwood, & Parkhill (2005)

What to Watch for With ELL/CLD Students

i. It is important to tie these extracurricular activities into general classroom content areas. These can be a point of academic content support by offering the activities in the home language of participants as well as having bilingual personnel available.

ii. The Mexican government offers free materials and textbooks that can supplement these activities for Spanish speaking families. Contact the Mexican embassy or consulate closest to you to find out more. An example of what the Mexican government offers is National Council for Lifelong Learning and Work Skills (CONEVyT). CONEVyT was created in 2002 in Mexico to provide primary and secondary education and training to adults (15+) left behind in education in that country as well as migrant populations living in the United States. Through an online portal and a network of Plazas Comunitarias where direct instruction, assessment, and varied materials can be found, both U.S. and Mexican governments make educational support available for anyone willing to learn or to teach. For more information, go to www.conevyt.org.mx.

FIFTY GRID (MATH)

Purpose of the Strategy

i. Access prior knowledge

ii. Build academic transfer skills

iii. Build awareness of learning process

iv. Develop field independent skills

v. Develop academic language in math

vi. Develop extended time on task

vii. Develop problem-solving skills

viii. Improve retention of content

ix. Develop independence in learning math

x. Reinforce content lessons

xi. Strengthen awareness of learning process

How to Do It

i. This strategy has been used with students from third grade and up and works every time. For less prepared groups, use less random numbers. Calculators could be provided for individuals.

ii. You need this 10x5 grid. You can print it on paper or on an acetate transparency sheet for use with an overhead projector. The students will need to be able to mark off the numbers on the grid, so it should be projected onto a whiteboard.

1	2	3	4	5	6	7	8	9	10
11	12	13	14	15	16	17	18	19	20
21	22	23	24	25	26	27	28	29	30
31	32	33	34	35	36	37	38	39	40
41	42	43	44	45	46	47	48	49	50

1. The numbered squares on the grid need to be randomly colored either white, blue, yellow, lavender, or green. There should be ten squares of each of the five colors in the grid.

2. The pupils are placed in five teams. Each team is given five random numbers generated by rolling a variety of dice. This is best recorded in a table on a flipchart or on the board:

Team	Dice-Generated Numbers					Score
1	8	7	11	12	10	
2	3	7	2	1	6	
3	10	6	1	4	3	
4	10	2	5	14	4	
5	6	8	7	2	13	

3. The teams take turns using their random numbers to make a number from one to fifty using any mathematical operation. The object is to capture one of the cells on the colored board by making the number inside it. Once a cell has been captured, it cannot be captured again. The teacher or a student crosses the colored number out with an *x* once it is captured by a team.

4. Scoring points is done as follows: For each captured square, the team gets one point. If the captured square is adjacent to a previously captured square, the team gets one point for each of those adjacent squares. If the square has a blue background, the team multiplies its total score by three. If the square has a yellow background, the team adds three points. If the square has a lavender background, the team multiplies its total score by five. If the square has a green background, the team adds five points. This is summarized in the chart below.

Scoring

Square Captured	1 pt
Each square already captured around the captured square	1 pt each
Square captured has a blue background	**Multiply total score by 3**
Square captured has a yellow background	+3 pts
Square captured has a lavender background	**Multiply total score by 5**
Square captured has a green background	+5 pts

5. The activity ends when all squares have been taken or time runs out. Highest final score wins. The teams start each round with new random numbers.

Research Base

Cole (1995)

Elliot & Thurlow (2005)

What to Watch for With ELL/CLD Students

i. Newcomers will need to have the fifty grid steps modeled and explained in their most proficient language before they can proceed independently.

ii. Students can be paired with partners who are slightly more bilingual than themselves to facilitate their learning this process.

FIST—READING STRATEGY

Purpose of the Strategy

   i. Build academic transfer skills

   ii. Build foundation for learning

   iii. Build awareness of learning process

   iv. Assist students to learn information through paraphrasing

   v. Increase time on task

   vi. Develop cognitive academic language

   vii. Develop cognitive learning strategies

   viii. Develop content knowledge foundation

   ix. Develop extended time on task

   x. Develop field independent skills

   xi. Encourage questioning and exploration of new learning

   xii. Enhance ability of students to focus on learning

   xiii. Expand and elaborate on learning

   xiv. Expand comprehension

   xv. Retention of content

   xvi. Strengthen language development

   xvii. Strengthen learning to learn skills

   xviii. Strengthen retention and application abilities

   xix. Develop analytical skills

   xx. Build metacognition skills

   xxi. Facilitate language development

   xxii. Improve reading comprehension

How to Do It

   i. This strategy is done within the general education classroom with mixed groups of students. The FIST analysis strategy framework provides a structure for understanding reading and building reading comprehension.

   ii. The FIST strategy assists students to actively pursue responses to questions related directly to materials being read.

   iii. Students follow the steps in the FIST strategy while reading paragraphs in assigned readings.

iv. The teacher posts the steps for F, I, S, T on a chart and gives each student papers in the form of checklists with FIST down the side. Using an example paragraph, she goes step by step through FIST: reading the first sentence in the paragraph, indicating a question based on that first sentence, searching for the answer to those questions within the paragraph, and tying question and answer together. Then the students put the question and answers together in their own words, comparing it to the original example written paragraph.

v. The following are the steps in FIST:

1. First sentence is read

2. Indicate a question based on first sentence

3. Search for the answer to the question

4. Tie question and answer together through paraphrasing

vi. The teacher can remind students before each reading activity to use the FIST strategy and the FIST checklist as they gather information from a paragraph for their assignment.

Research Base

Allington & Cunningham (2002)

Cole (1995)

Dang, Dang, & Ruiter (2005)

Derwinger, Stigsdotter Neely, & Baeckman (2005)

Ellis & Lenz (1987)

Moore, Alvermann, & Hinchman (2000)

Odean (1987)

What to Watch for With ELL/CLD Students

i. Newcomers will need to have the FIST steps modeled and explained in their most proficient language before they can proceed independently.

ii. Students can be paired with partners who are slightly more bilingual than themselves to facilitate their learning this process.

FIST Element	What am I to do at this step?	What did I do about it?	Notes
First sentence is read			
Indicate a question based on first sentence			
Search for the answer to the question			
Tie question and answer together through paraphrasing			

ABCDEF**G**HIJKLMOPQRSTUVW

GRAPHIC ORGANIZERS

Purpose of the Strategy

i. Access prior knowledge

ii. Build awareness of learning

iii. Build awareness of appropriate cognitive academic language

iv. Build foundation for learning

v. Build transfer skills

vi. Develop field sensitive skills

vii. Expand and elaborate on learning

viii. Expand comprehension

ix. Facilitate access of prior knowledge

x. Facilitate acquisition of content knowledge

xi. Facilitate analogy strategies

xii. Improve retention of content

xiii. Improve students' ability to organize and prioritize information

xiv. Reduce low-persistence behaviors

xv. Reduce misperceptions

xvi.   Strengthen language development

xvii.   Strengthen learning to learn skills

xviii.   Strengthen retention and application abilities

xix.   Develop analytical skills

xx.   Develop categorization skills

xxi.   Develop cognitive academic language

xxii.   Expand and elaborate on learning foundation

xxiii.   Build first language to English transfer skills

xxiv.   Build awareness of the appropriate content language

xxv.   Develop thinking and planning skills

xxvi.   Reduce response fatigue

xxvii.   Improve mnemonic retrieval

xxviii.   Increase students generating a correct response

How to Do It

i.   The teacher or assistant previews lesson content in the first language when possible, using graphic diagrams, shapes, or images related to the content. He or she uses these to outline and detail key issues, rehearsing vocabulary, and reviewing related prior knowledge. Examples of graphic organizers are shown below. Advanced fluency students help less advanced students understand how to organize their reading and writing materials.

ii.   This strategy may be done with small groups. The teacher has the target students preview lessons for less advanced students, using graphs, diagrams, shapes with words outlining key issues, rehearsing vocabulary, and reviewing related prior knowledge. Advanced fluency students help less advanced students understand how to organize their reading and writing materials.

iii.   The teacher may use the analogy strategy described below to teach one or more of the advanced organizer tools: KWL+, W-Star, graphic organizer, or mind map. Students implement strategies with specific tasks or lessons.

Examples

i.   KWL+ is done by asking the students to discuss the following questions before beginning the lesson: What do you already know about this content? What do you want to know about this content? What will we learn about this? Why should we learn this? And how will we learn this content? This may be done on a chart and student answers posted on the chart.

ii. W-Star is done by asking the students to brainstorm before beginning a reading: Who do you think this story/event is about? Where do you think the story/event is located? When do you think the story/event occurs? How do you think the story/event turns out? The answers are written on the points of a star diagram, each point of which represents one of the "w" questions.

iii. Mind mapping has various forms, but the basic idea is to put the central concept or vocabulary word related to what will be in the lesson in a circle on the board or on a piece of paper. Students then generate other words or concepts related to that main idea and connect them to the center like spokes on a wheel. For each of these ideas or words, another set of connections may be made and so on and so on outward from the center concept.

Example With a Read-Aloud

i. When applying the advanced organizer strategy, students work through problems or tasks using a sequence of ordering, sequencing, and connecting techniques. Suppose you want your students to write a short personal reflection about the story, Everyone Cooks Rice by Norah Dooley, that the class has just finished reading together.

ii. (Step 1) Start by having your students work in small groups of similar ability level. You would show a copy of a graphic organizer form outline on the overhead projector/document camera or drawn on the whiteboard.

Figure G.1 Example of Venn Diagram Graphic Organizer

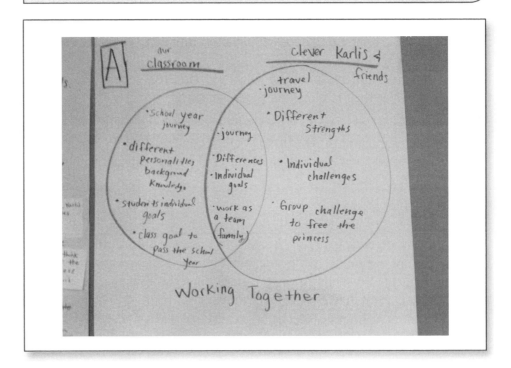

iii. (Step 2) Assign two or three of the boxes in the graphic organizer to each group. For example, you might assign the most challenged group to fill in the box about title, author, location, and country. Another group would be responsible for the main and supporting characters. Another group would be responsible for identifying the sequence of events in the story and a summary statement about these. Another group could be assigned to identify the main problem faced by the main character.

iv. (Step 3) After reading the story through the first time, the groups complete their tasks, and you or they write down their answers on the large or projected graphic organizer.

v. (Step 4) Next, as a group you ask about how this main problem was resolved, what the barriers to resolution were, and how things in the story helped solve the problem.

vi. (Step 5) The students can now discuss the final resolution and what the moral of the story might be in their perspective.

vii. You can expand this activity by comparing and contrasting the story with others like it or with happenings in the students' own lives.

viii. You might now step back from the lesson and discuss the metacognitive learning that you have provided students, the learning to learn lesson that is represented by the strategy you had them use.

Figure G.2 Example of Flowchart Graphic Organizer

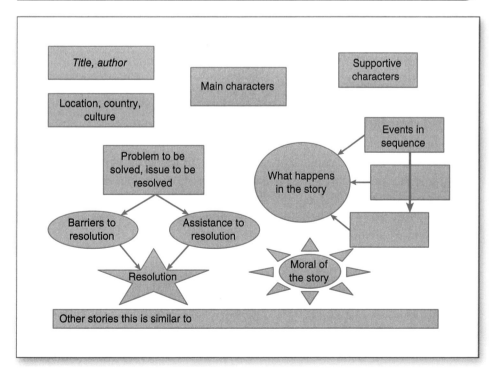

Figure G.3 Example of Plot Graphic Organizer

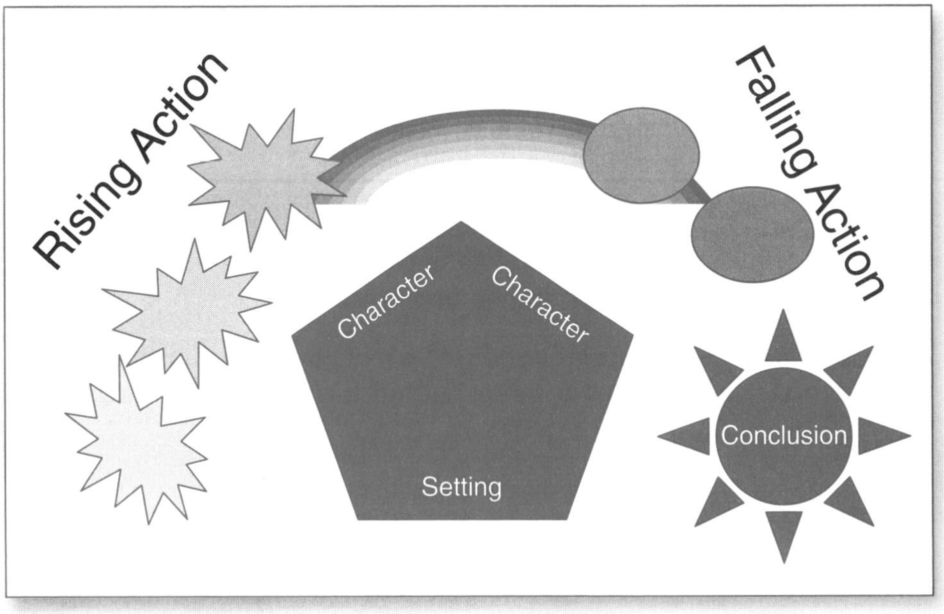

Teaching Graphic Organizers

Steps for Teaching Advanced Organizers

1. *Inform* the students what advanced organizers are, how they operate, when to use them, and why they are useful. Begin by saying that advanced organizers are a way to help them (the students) plan and remember. They work by previewing or putting information concerning the lesson or assignment they are working on into graphic form. Once they learn how to use advanced organizers, they can use them anytime and with any content or lesson you give them to do.

2. *Use cues*, metaphors, analogies, or other means of elaborating on a description of advanced organizers combined with visual cues. One way to do this is to have the group look at a blueprint of a house or other building they are familiar with. Have them see how the architect had to plan for everything ahead of time and create a preview or graphic image of what everyone was going to have to do to complete the construction. Explain that almost anyone could help construct the house or building by reading the blueprint, and the ability to read and understand these is a special and critical skill that will be useful to them later in life.

3. *Lead group discussions* about the use of advanced organizers. Have students start with talking about a lesson they have just successfully completed. They can go back through the lesson or book using different advanced organizer tools to see how they work and what is required. Encourage them to ask you anything about the learning process they want clarified.

Figure G.4 Example of Personal Timeline

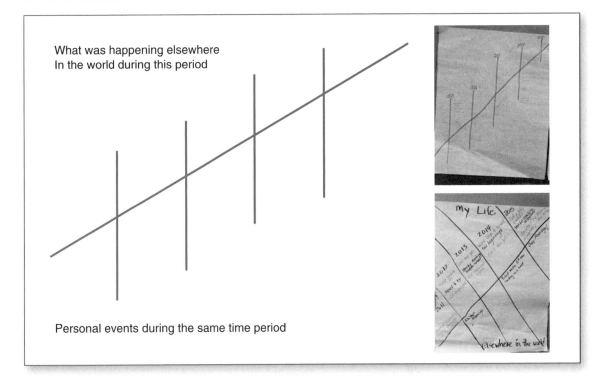

4. *Provide guided practice* in applying advanced organizers to particular tasks. Work directly with student groups demonstrating and modeling how to identify elements. Have more skilled students demonstrate for the class.

5. *Provide feedback* on monitoring use and success of advanced organizers. While students use advanced organizers in small groups, you should move around the room listening and supplying encouragement for consistent use of the tools. As students get more comfortable using these tools, you can have them monitor one another in the use of the strategy.

Research Base

Collier (2002)

Harwell (2001)

Heacox (2002)

Moore, Alvermann, & Hinchman (2000)

Opitz (1998)

What to Watch for With ELL/CLD Students

i. There are cultural differences in cognitive/learning style, and some English language learner (ELL) / culturally and linguistically diverse (CLD) students may not respond to the brainstorming construct behind most advanced organizers.

ii. By keeping the graphic design of the advanced organizer as close as possible to the illustrations in the text or some aspect of the lesson, the teacher can more tightly connect the concepts being studied with the what/who/where questioning that precedes the lesson.

iii. This is another activity that works best with preparation in the students' most proficient language and relevance to their culture before proceeding.

GUIDED LECTURE PROCEDURE

Purpose of the Strategy

i. Adapt content to meet individual or unique student needs

ii. Adapts mode of response required of students

iii. Build awareness of academic expectations

iv. Build foundation for learning

v. Build awareness of appropriate academic behaviors

vi. Build awareness of appropriate behaviors for school language and rules

vii. Build awareness of appropriate cognitive academic language

viii. Build awareness of appropriate communication behaviors for school language and rules

ix. Build awareness of appropriate social and academic language

x. Build awareness of learning process

xi. Develop cognitive learning strategies

xii. Develop confidence in academic interactions

xiii. Develop confidence in school culture interactions

xiv. Enhance ability of student to focus on learning

xv. Enhance ability of students to learn new things

xvi. Facilitate school adaptation process

xvii. Facilitate students assuming responsibility for learning

xviii. Reduce fears associated with assignments

xix. Reinforce content lessons

xx. Strengthen awareness of learning process

xxi. Sustain engagement

xxii. Strengthen learning to learn skills

xxiii. Increase time on task

xxiv. Reduce distractibility

xxv. Build vocabulary

xxvi. Facilitate acquisition of content knowledge

xxvii. Develop content knowledge foundation

xxviii. Enhance ability of student to focus on learning

How to Do It

i. The teacher uses step-by-step frames, icons, or illustrations to high-light each part of the content within lecture or oral presentations to the class. He or she provides students with a structure for taking notes during oral presentations and openly discusses the importance of note taking with illustrations.

ii. The teacher or assistant points to the frames or icons while making the presentation, pausing periodically to allow groups to compare notes and fill in missing information.

iii. Group activity is involved to facilitate effective note taking. Students listen to teacher or student presentations, take notes during the presentation, and share their notes afterward. The teacher leads discussion about how to use notes for recall during application activities.

Research Base

Kelly & Holmes (1979)

Kirschner, Sweller, & Clark (2006)

Toole (2000)

What to Watch for With ELL/CLD Students

i. This strategy is especially useful with upper elementary and secondary students. The teacher may need to physically model how to listen and take notes appropriately.

ii. Not all students will have prior educational experiences where they have listened to someone present and are then responsible for taking notes or developing commentary about what was said.

iii. This can be paired with general guided practice in test preparation and test taking.

GUIDED MEMORIES—PERSONAL TIMELINES

Purpose of the Strategy

i. Build transfer skills

ii. Access prior knowledge

iii. Build appreciation that everyone belongs and is needed

iv. Build appreciation that everyone has a contribution to make

v. Build first language to English transfer skills

vi. Build foundation for learning

vii. Develop self-esteem

viii. Develop thinking and planning skills

ix. Enhance student interaction with family during transition

x. Expand and elaborate on learning

xi. Expand and improve comprehension

xii. Facilitate access of prior knowledge

xiii. Facilitate analogy strategies

xiv. Facilitate connections between known and new

xv. Build vocabulary

xvi. Develop categorization skills

xvii. Improve access to prior knowledge

xviii. Improve confidence and self-esteem

xix. Improve school/parent partnership

xx. Improve sequencing skills

xxi. Sustain engagement

xxii. Build upon family culture

xxiii. Develop association skills

xxiv. Reduce culture shock and its side effects

xxv. Develop awareness of cause and effect

xxvi. Develop time on task

xxvii. Facilitate discussion about new learning

xxviii. Strengthen school/parent partnerships

How to Do It

i. The teacher selects the events or length of time to cover, for example, two years, five years, or such as appropriate to the age and developmental level of the students. The teacher gives the students an event in time or a length of time as a framework. The students research and then tell about their personal or family history during this event or length of time. Students may create booklets about their memories, their families, and so on.

ii. Students tell about their homeland or family history and create booklets about their memories. Their family or personal memories for a period of time can be juxtaposed against a national or historical event during the same time period and compared with what was happening to other students during that same time period.

Research Base

Carrigan (2001)

What to Watch for With ELL/CLD Students

i. Students may be reluctant to describe or discuss what happened to their family during this time period or specific event. Very difficult or painful things may have occurred for this student or family.

ii. The teacher must be prepared to deal with sensitive information should it arise and also to know when not to push further for information. Only elicit information that the student is comfortable sharing at that particular point in time.

iii. Students may share more as they become more comfortable in the classroom or more trusting that the information will not be used against them or their family.

GUIDED PRACTICE AND PLANNED INTERACTIONS

Purpose of the Strategy

i. Build academic transfer skills

ii. Build foundation for learning

iii. Clarify responsibilities, assignments, and rewards

iv. Develop confidence in academic interactions

v. Develop confidence in school language and school culture interactions

vi. Eliminate inappropriate behavior

vii. Enhance awareness of the school adaptation process

viii. Ensure students are familiar with specific academic and behavioral expectations

ix. Ensure that students are aware of and responsible for their own actions

x. Expand and elaborate on learning

xi. Expand comprehension

xii. Facilitate students' comfort with the learning environment

xiii. Facilitate acquisition of content knowledge

xiv. Increase time on task

xv. Lower anxiety levels

xvi. Minimize ambiguity in the classroom

xvii. Reduce distractibility

xviii. Reduce misperceptions

xix. Reduce stress for new students

xx. Reinforce content lessons

xxi. Strengthen and facilitate language development

xxii. Strengthen learning to learn skills

xxiii. Develop higher persistence

xxiv. Build awareness of appropriate school language and rules for communication behaviors

xxv. Build awareness of school culture expectations

xxvi. Develop confidence in school language and rules for academic and social interactions

xxvii. Develop cognitive academic language

xxviii. Develop personal control of situations

xxix. Reduce anxiety in social/academic interactions

xxx. Reduce response fatigue

How to Do It

i. This can be paired with role-play of school interactions.

ii. Primary grades: Intermediate student, peer, or specialist demonstrates how to act in a given school or school culture situation. The situation is explained, in home and community language when possible, and each stage is modeled. Students then practice each stage of the interaction with familiar participants until comfortable and successful in appropriate behaviors.

iii. Student, peer, or specialist demonstrates how to act in a given school or school culture situation. The situation is explained, in home and community language when possible, and each stage is modeled. Students then practice each stage of the interaction with familiar participants until comfortable and successful in appropriate behaviors.

iv. This strategy facilitates the transition of ELL/CLD students from their primary language base to bilingualism and helps with their interaction with all students in the general education classroom.

v. Peer or specialist demonstrates how to act or speak in a given school culture situation. The situation is explained in the home and community language when possible, and each part of the situation is modeled.

vi. Representatives of the mainstream school language and rules who are familiar to the learners come into the classroom and act out the situation with the instructor. Students then practice each part of the interaction with these familiar participants until comfortable with the interaction. To expand upon this strategy, students can select new interactions they wish to learn.

vii. Peer or specialist demonstrates conflict resolution techniques in a given school culture situation. The situation is explained in home and community language when possible, and each step is modeled. Students then practice each step of the resolution with familiar participants until comfortable and successful in appropriate behaviors.

Research Base

Aram & Shlak (2008)

Davis (2005)

Fitzell (1997)

Hafernik, Messerschmitt, & Vandrick (2002)

Haneda (2008)

Nelson, Martella, & Galand (1998)

Reggy-Mamo (2008)

Rubenstein (2006)

What to Watch for With ELL/CLD Students

i. It is important to have the example speakers be people with whom the students are familiar and comfortable.

ii. Particular social groups and cultures have different expectations of adults and children when it comes to being accountable for task completion. This is a learned difference between cultures. The teacher needs to be aware that the expectations in an American school may need to be taught directly to CLD students and not just assumed to be understood.

iii. One way to introduce the idea of behavior and strategies specific to your classroom is to ask students about how their parents have them behave at home or learn by playing games. This can then be expanded to the idea of acting appropriately in a classroom.

iv. Demonstrate all of the desired behaviors and strategies. Some role-play may be helpful. Examples of bad behaviors may be used with caution.

v. Learning to survive and thrive in a new environment is challenging for anyone. This can be especially difficult for ELL and CLD learners and their families as they learn to interact in a new language and with new social rules and expectations.

vi. Bring in people from the community with whom the participants are comfortable first. Gradually expand the interaction circle as folks become more confident.

vii. Small social support groups within school and within the community can provide a safe group within which to ask questions and learn ways to succeed at tasks or in solving problems.

viii. Particular social groups and cultures have different expectations of adult and children when it comes to conflict resolution. This is a learned difference between cultures. The teacher needs to be aware that the expectations in an American school may need to be taught directly to CLD students and not just assumed to be understood.

ix. One way to introduce the idea of conflict resolution behavior and strategies specific to your classroom is to ask students about how their parents have them behave at home when they disagree with their siblings. This can then be expanded to the idea of acting appropriately in a classroom.

x. Demonstrate all of the desired behaviors and strategies. Some role-play may be helpful. Examples of bad behaviors may be used with caution.

GUIDED READING AND WRITING IN HOME AND COMMUNITY LANGUAGE

Purpose of the Strategy

i. Use and access prior knowledge

ii. Ensure that students are familiar with specific academic and behavioral expectations

iii. Increase frequency of appropriate behaviors

iv. Build awareness of the learning process

v. Build awareness of the school culture expectations

vi. Build first language to English transfer skills

vii. Build a foundation for learning

viii. Build home and community language to English transfer skills

ix. Build transfer skills

x. Build upon existing language skills of students

xi. Build upon existing language strengths of student

xii.   Build upon family language and culture

xiii.   Build upon the diverse language foundations of students and parents

xiv.   Build vocabulary

xv.   Develop content knowledge foundation

xvi.   Encourage pride in home language and culture

xvii.   Enhance student interaction with family during transition

xviii. Expand and elaborate on learning

xix.   Expand comprehension

xx.   Facilitate access of prior knowledge

xxi.   Facilitate acquisition of content knowledge

xxii.   Facilitate writing process

xxiii. Improve reading comprehension

xxiv.   Improve retention of content

xxv.   Improve school/parent partnership

xxvi.   Reduce fears associated with assignments

xxvii. Reduce frustration

xxviii. Reduce frustration in students due to unclear expectations

xxix.   Improve motivation

xxx.   Minimize behavior problems

xxxi.   Build academic transfer skills

xxxii. Build awareness of appropriate social and academic language

xxxiii. Develop confidence in school language and rules for academic and social interactions

xxxiv. Reduce code switching

xxxv.   Develop cognitive academic language

How to Do It

i. This strategy facilitates the transition of ELL/CLD students from their primary language base to bilingualism and helps with their interaction with all students in the general education classroom.

ii. For literate non-English or nonstandard English speaking students, the teacher or assistant and a small group of students all have the same book or text in the same non-English language or diverse dialect of English to read or write. The teacher projects a copy of the text or target writing topics on an overhead screen so all can see and follow along. The teacher reads sentences or paragraphs and has students read, alternately pointing out the words or phrases on the overhead projection. The teacher can then stop and have students discuss the content at key points or to discuss spelling or phonics issues. Another way to do this is to have the teacher walk around and select different students to read or write portions of the reading

iii. Another way to do this is for an advanced-fluency student to lead a guided reading or writing activity in the home and community language. Students can reread parts of a story in pairs after the directed reading activity rather than have one student read while the others all listen. Students then write their own summaries of what they have read. Writing can be either in home and community language or English. During this time, the students have a chance to help each other. Advanced-fluency students can dramatize and create dialogue to illustrate the action.

iv. To expand this strategy, students can create dialogue and dramatize to illustrate the action of the story or passage.

Research Base

Cole (1995)

Haneda (2008)

Reggy-Mamo (2008)

Strickland, Ganske, & Monroe (2002)

What to Watch for With ELL/CLD Students

i. Not all ELL/CLD students are literate in their home or community language.

ii. Picture dictionaries with bilingual words and definitions are usually the most practical reference to use with younger, less educated students.

HOME ACTIVITIES

Purpose of the Strategy

    i. Access prior knowledge

   ii. Build awareness of learning

  iii. Build appreciation that everyone has a contribution to make

  iv. Build awareness of academic expectations

   v. Build awareness of adaptation process

  vi. Build awareness of appropriate academic behaviors

 vii. Build upon existing language skills of students

viii. Build upon existing language strengths of students

  ix. Encourage pride in home language and culture

   x. Enhance student interaction with family during transition

  xi. Expand and elaborate on learning

 xii. Expand comprehension

xiii. Facilitate access of prior knowledge

xiv. Facilitate acquisition of content knowledge

 xv. Facilitate school adaptation process

xvi.   Build upon family language and culture

xvii.   Facilitate student assuming responsibility for learning

xviii.   Improve access to prior knowledge

xix.   Improve comprehension

xx.   Improve confidence and self-esteem

xxi.   Improve students' ability to organize and prioritize information

xxii.   Reinforce content lessons

xxiii.   Reinforce school/parent partnership

xxiv.   Retention of content

xxv.   Strengthen awareness of learning process

xxvi.   Strengthen home/school relationship

xxvii.   Strengthen knowledge of academic content

xxviii.   Strengthen language development

xxix.   Strengthen learning to learn skills

xxx.   Strengthen retention and application abilities

xxxi.   Strengthen school/parent partnerships

xxxii.   Build upon diverse language foundations of students and parents

xxxiii.   Improve retention

xxxiv.   Develop cognitive academic language

xxxv.   Build academic transfer skills

xxxvi.   Improve school/parent partnership

xxxvii.   Develop content knowledge foundation

How to Do It

i.   There are many ways a teacher can use this strategy. Teacher sends home specific content support activities for parents and students to do together. Parents are asked to read and work through the activities in both home and community language and English with their students.

Example: Activity Calendars

Teachers and staff meet together and come up with ideas for parents or caregivers to engage with their children every day. These are short 15 to 30 minute activities that support academic content and roughly match what is being taught in the school during the same period of time. The activities are put into a calendar of the school year. The calendar shows all important events and dates for the school year as well as the recommended home activities.

At parent/teacher meetings and gatherings at the beginning and throughout the year, the calendar is brought out and discussed with parents. Once familiar with the process, parents can volunteer ideas to add to the calendars. Calendars can be printed in any language most helpful to the parents and community.

Example: "Bilingual Brain" Extensions

The teacher prepares simple worksheets that reflect what was learned that day or that week and sends them home with the students. The students go over the materials with their parents/caregivers in their home languages. The worksheets can be in English and reflect what was learned in English, but the students are asked to explain the content in their home languages and go through the worksheet items in their home languages. The parents/caregivers sign off on the worksheet, and the students bring them back to school the next day or week. This activity assists the students in transitioning back and forth in cognitive academic language and strengthens both content and language skills.

Example: Libros Sin Fronteras

In one district, *"Libros Sin Fronteras"* was established as an evening and weekend activity for Spanish speaking families. Parents and their children were invited to attend sessions where they received a copy of a bilingual or Spanish book and met the author of the book, for example, Alma Flor Ada. She presented a discussion about her book, read sections aloud, and answered questions from parents in Spanish. School staff members gave lessons on how to use books at home, the importance of reading to children, and demonstrating how to read to and discuss books in a comfortable family situation. *Libros Sin Fronteras* was held every other weekend, and families ended up with several books to keep and read at home.

Research Base

Cole (1995)

Garcia, Hasson, Hoffman, Paneque, & Pelaez (1996)

Sink, Jr., Parkhill, Marshall, Norwood, & Parkhill (2005)

What to Watch for With ELL/CLD Students

i. Not all parents will be literate in their home language, so you cannot just send materials home. Someone must explain what is intended and what will be sent to the home.

ii. Parents will need to have the process explained and what is expected explained in the home language.

iii. Some programs provide training to parents about how to read to their children and provide books in the home language to facilitate this process.

ABCDEFGH**I**JKLMOPQRSTUVW

INDIVIDUALIZING

Purpose of the Strategy

    i. Adapt content to meet individual or unique student needs

    ii. Adapt the mode of response required of students

    iii. Build appreciation that everyone has a contribution to make

    iv. Build foundation for learning

    v. Build metacognition skills

    vi. Build transfer skills

    vii. Build upon existing language skills of students

    viii. Build upon existing language strengths of students

    ix. Develop cognitive learning strategies

    x. Develop confidence in academic interactions

    xi. Develop confidence in school culture interactions

    xii. Develop higher persistence

    xiii. Develop independence in learning situations

    xiv. Enhance ability of students to learn new things

    xv. Expand and elaborate on learning

xvi. Expand comprehension

xvii. Facilitate access of prior knowledge

xviii. Facilitates acquisition of content knowledge

xix. Improve retention of content

xx. Increase students' probability of generating a correct response

xxi. Increase students' time on task

xxii. Increase the frequency of appropriate responses or behaviors

xxiii. Reinforce content lessons

xxiv. Retention of content

xxv. Strengthen ability to discuss what is happening

xxvi. Strengthen awareness of learning process

xxvii. Strengthen knowledge of academic content

xxviii. Enhance ability of student to focus on learning

xxix. Facilitate individualization

xxx. Improve motivation

xxxi. Reduce fears associated with assignments

How to Do It

i. Design instruction so individual needs and abilities are addressed. Learners are motivated and complete tasks appropriate to their needs, interests, and abilities.

ii. Begin where students are.

iii. Build upon learners' differences.

iv. Engage students through different learning styles.

v. Use varied rates of instruction.

vi. Ensure student competes against himself or herself rather than others.

vii. Provide specific ways for each student to learn.

viii. Establish learner-responsive, teacher-facilitated classrooms based on essential skills.

Research Base

Ferris & Hedgcock (2005)

Herrera & Murry (2004)

Krumenaker, Many, & Wang (2008)

Murrey (2008)

Tomlinson (1999)

What to Watch for With ELL/CLD Students

i. A basic premise of differentiation is that one type of instruction does not necessarily work for all students, that is, one size does not fit all. Teachers are advised to begin where their students are with their learning differences and their learning strengths.

ii. For ELL and CLD students, instructional personnel are to build upon learners' cultural and linguistic differences and strengths by developing instructional activities based on essential topics and concepts, significant processes and skills, and multiple ways to display learning while providing flexible approaches to content, instruction, and outcomes.

INFORMATION ORGANIZATION—EASY

Purpose of the Strategy

i. Develop analytic skills

ii. Build confidence in independent work

iii. Build academic transfer skills

iv. Build awareness of academic expectations

v. Develop extended time on task

vi. Develop field independent skills

vii. Develop cognitive learning strategies

viii. Develop thinking and planning skills

ix. Enhance ability of students to focus on learning

x. Enhance ability of students to learn new things

xi. Improve comprehension

xii. Improve confidence and self-esteem

xiii. Build awareness of learning

xiv. Develop higher persistence

xv. Develop self-monitoring skills

xvi. Improve sequencing skills

xvii. Improve test-taking skills

xviii. Increase focus on reading

xix. Increase students' probability of generating a correct response

xx. Increase students' time on task

xxi. Improve student's ability to organize and prioritize information

xxii. Reduce confusion in locus of control

xxiii. Strengthen awareness of the learning process

xxiv. Strengthen learning to learn skills

xxv. Sustain engagement

xxvi. Sustain engagement with reading and writing

xxvii. Facilitate student self-concept as a successful person

xxviii. Facilitate students' comfort with the learning environment

xxix. Facilitate students' ownership in their education

How to Do It

i. This strategy helps students organize and prioritize information within their reading by focusing on questions designed to identify important content.

ii. The teacher introduces EASY by pointing to the steps on a large poster or projection. It is best to have graphics that serve as cues for what each step in EASY stands for. As he or she points to the step, the teacher says the phrase and explains the meaning of each step. The teacher provides examples of the action to take at each step of EASY using a current reading selection as an illustration.

iii. Posters with the EASY framework are posted around the room for easy reference during reading activities.

iv. The teacher reviews this strategy several times before students are to read articles or passages in a content lesson.

v. Students can create cue cards to remember each step. Students follow steps while reading passages or thematic elements. The following are the steps in EASY:

a. Elicit questions (who, what, where, when, why, and how)

b. Ask self which information is least difficult

c. Study easy content initially, followed by difficult

d. Yes! Provide self-reinforcement through rewards or points for self

Research Base

Lapp, Flood, Brock, & Fisher (2007)

Moore, Alvermann, & Hinchman (2000)

What to Watch for With ELL/CLD Students

i. Much like the other mnemonics provided in these strategy lists, English language learner (ELL)/ culturally and linguistically diverse (CLD) students need bilingual explanations of the teacher's expectations and guided practice in implementing the steps in the strategy.

ii. Newcomers will need to have the EASY steps modeled and explained in their most proficient language before they can proceed independently.

iii. Students can be paired with partners who are slightly more bilingual than themselves to facilitate their learning this process.

EASY Element	What am I to do at this step?	What did I do about it?	Notes
Elicit questions (who, what, where, when, why, and how)			
Ask self which information is least difficult			
Study easy content initially, followed by difficult			
Yes! Provide self-reinforcement			

INQUIRY CHARTS

Purpose of the Strategy

    i. Build awareness of the learning process

    ii. Develop cognitive learning strategies

    iii. Encourage questioning and exploration of new learning

    iv. Build awareness of academic expectations

    v. Build learners' confidence in their control of the learning process

    vi. Build metacognition skills

    vii. Develop categorization skills

    viii. Develop cognitive academic language

    ix. Develop higher tolerance

    x. Develop independence in learning situations

    xi. Expand and elaborate on learning

    xii. Expand comprehension

    xiii. Facilitate access of prior knowledge

    xiv. Develop student understanding of prediction

    xv. Facilitate student ownership of education

    xvi. Organize and prioritize information

    xvii. Strengthen student ability to discuss what is happening

    xviii. Reduce frustration in students due to unclear expectations

    xix. Reduce impulsivity

    xx. Strengthen language development

    xxi. Strengthen learning to learn skills

    xxii. Build upon existing language skills and strengths

    xxiii. Build awareness of appropriate cognitive academic language

    xxiv. Develop problem-solving skills

    xxv. Access background knowledge

    xxvi. Reduce misconceptions

How to Do It

    i. This strategy can be used to model how to develop reading and writing skills and also teach revision and leaning as a continuous process. The key vocabulary words to teach and reinforce here are think, predict, and hypothesize.

ii. The teacher posts the frame "what do I know" and "what do I want to know" about whatever the focal topic is for the lesson. He or she then records students' comments using their words. In the primary level, the teacher can record students' names after their comments, or comments can be color coded to show changes over the course of the lesson.

iii. The teacher returns to the inquiry chart often, continuing to add student comments. The teacher can use a different color marker each time. When revisiting, the teacher should ask students to cite the source of their new information.

Research Base

Brechtel (2001)

What to Watch for With ELL/CLD Students

i. This strategy will need to be demonstrated to ELL/CLD students. For very limited English proficient students, choices should be provided either in printed words, phrases, or pictures.

ii. Models of completed inquiry charts can be posted to illustrate the process, and the teacher can lead discussions with more advanced students to show the relationship between what is known, what is desired, and what becomes known as learning about the subject continues to develop.

What I know about xyz	What I want to know about xyz

INQUIRY TECHNIQUE

Purpose of the Strategy

i. Build transfer skills

ii. Build appreciation that everyone has a contribution to make

iii. Access prior knowledge

iv. Build awareness of the learning process

v. Build awareness of relation between cause and effect

vi. Build confidence in independent work

vii. Develop awareness of cause and effect

viii. Develop content knowledge foundation

ix. Develop extended time on task

x. Develop field independent skills

xi. Encourage questioning and exploration of new learning

xii. Enhance ability of students to focus on learning

xiii. Facilitate connections between known and new

xiv. Facilitate discussion about new learning

xv. Retention of content

xvi. Strengthen ability to discuss what is happening

xvii. Strengthen awareness of learning process

xviii. Develop cognitive academic language

xix. Build foundation for learning

xx. Develop cognitive learning strategies

xxi. Reduce misperceptions

xxii. Develops student understanding of prediction and confirmation

xxiii. Facilitate acquisition of content knowledge

xxiv. Builds learner confidence in their control of the learning process

xxv. Facilitate student self-evaluation skills

How to Do It

i. The teacher actively engages students in constructing mathematical or scientific knowledge through the use of activities that encourage them to explore and investigate content principles or ideas. For example, students visit a garden and observe, count, and measure the different petals that are attached to different species of flowers. Students could also explore the different configurations in which leaves grow on each stem.

ii. The National Science Education Standards call for students to do inquiry and to know about inquiry. When students do inquiry, they use the same ideas as scientists do when they are conducting research. Students become miniscientists.

iii. Inquiry, or open learning, has many benefits. It means students do not simply perform experiments in a routine-like fashion but actually think about the results they collect and what they mean. With traditional nonopen lessons there is a tendency for students to say that the experiment "went wrong" when they collect results contrary to what they are told to expect. In open lessons, there are no wrong results, and students have to evaluate the strengths and weaknesses of the results they collect themselves and decide their value. Because the path taken to a desired learning target is uncertain, open lessons are more dynamic and less predictable than traditional lessons

Research Base

Banchi and Bell (2008)

Bruner (1961)

Cole (1995)

Olson & Loucks-Horsley (2000)

What to Watch for With ELL/CLD Students

i. This strategy is not appropriate for newcomer or very limited English proficient students. Introduce it to ELL/CLD students only after they have spent some time in American classrooms and are comfortable with the expectations and processes used regularly in the science or math class.

ii. Many CLD students from other countries have been in educational systems that do not allow or encourage open exploration, inquiry, or free thinking about content material. These school systems teach students through routines and correct answers and often expect rote memorization and recitation by students to demonstrate their understanding of the lesson.

iii. CLD students may be very hesitant and uncomfortable about stepping outside of books and other information sources and may not initiate an open inquiry or discovery lesson.

INTERDISCIPLINARY UNIT/THEMATIC INSTRUCTION

Purpose of the Strategy

i. Build vocabulary

ii. Build transfer skills

iii. Use and access prior knowledge

iv.   Adapt to meet individual or unique student needs

v.   Adapt the mode of response required of students

vi.   Build awareness of the learning process

vii.   Develop association skills

viii.   Expand and elaborate on learning

ix.   Expand comprehension

x.   Facilitate access of prior knowledge

xi.   Facilitate acquisition of content knowledge

xii.   Improve vocabulary

xiii.   Strengthen learning to learn skills

xiv.   Strengthen retention and application abilities

xv.   Sustain engagement

xvi.   Develop content area skills

xvii.   Establish and elaborate on learning

xviii.   Improve comprehension

xix.   Reinforce content lessons

xx.   Develop thinking and planning skills

xxi.   Facilitate connections between known and new

xxii.   Improve access to prior knowledge

xxiii.   Strengthen language development

How to Do It

i.   This strategy is a way of organizing curricular elements that cuts across subject-matter lines to focus upon comprehensive life problems or broad areas of study that bring together the various segments of the curriculum into meaningful association.

ii.   The teacher uses thematic, interdisciplinary teaching to help students connect what they learn from one subject to another, to discover relationships.

iii.   Primary: Students plan a trip to the grocery store. They set up schedule, timing, measuring, counting, reading, identifying, describing, comparing, assessing, and budgeting activities in relation to their trip.

iv.   Intermediate: Same trip to grocery store, but add spatial orientation, nutrition, and considerations of the quality of life.

v.   Secondary: Students study the social impact of a given scientific or technological development at the same time that they are becoming acquainted with the science or technology itself.

vi. Bondi (1988) recommends the following steps in designing interdisciplinary units:

1. *Select a theme together.* Brainstorm together possible themes. Look for themes that relate to district/school goals and that interest students. Expand or narrow your theme as appropriate to reflect the teaching situation in which you are involved. Appoint a team leader for the duration of the development of the unit.

2. *Work independently.* Identify topics, objectives, and skills from within your subject area that could be developed within this unit.

3. *Meet together to define objectives for the unit.* Share all topics, objectives, and skills, and combine them into a manageable package.

4. *Meet together or select activities.* Match these activities to your goals in individual subjects. Stretch a little, if need be. Look for activities that provide student options and exploratory activities.

5. *Brainstorm resources.* Consider here both material resources and people resources.

6. *Develop your activities (individually and collectively).* Divide up the responsibility among the team to order, collect, and contact.

7. *Schedule your unit.* This includes setting the dates for when to teach it but also scheduling the use of rooms, speakers, and so on.

8. *Advertise your unit.* Do whatever you can to excite student and parent interest in the unit. Advertise in the school newsletter. Put up a "Coming Attractions" bulletin board. Wear slogans on your lapel.

9. *Implement your unit.* Have fun and don't expect everything to be perfect.

Research Base

Bondi (1988)

Cole (1995)

What to Watch for With ELL/CLD Students

i. This is an excellent strategy for making content relevant to the lives of diverse learners. Be sure to include real activities related to the specific communities that your students come from.

ii. For newcomers and beginning level ELL students, the teacher should assign a bilingual peer helper or partner as the unit is explained.

INVERTED PYRAMID—WRITING STRATEGY

Purpose of the Strategy

i. Build vocabulary

ii. Assist learners to defend a particular position in a written assignment

iii. Assist students to learn information through paraphrasing

iv. Build academic transfer skills

v. Develop cognitive academic language

vi. Develop extended time on task

vii. Develop thinking and planning skills

viii. Expand and elaborate on learning

ix. Expand comprehension

x. Facilitate access of prior knowledge

xi. Facilitates acquisition of content knowledge

xii. Facilitate writing process

xiii. Facilitate language development

xiv. Improve retention of content

xv. Improve sequencing skills

xvi. Strengthen knowledge of academic content

xvii. Strengthen language development

xviii. Strengthen learning to learn skills

xix. Strengthen retention and application abilities

xx. Build transfer skills

xxi. Develop content area skills

xxii. Establish and elaborate on learning

xxiii. Improve comprehension

How to Do It

i. One of the skills of a good writer is being able to tell a story clearly, concisely, and in a way that grabs the reader's attention right from the start. This is especially true of those working in journalism; a quick flick through any newspaper will reveal many examples of how to tell a story in as few words as possible.

ii. The teacher introduces the inverted pyramid by reminding students that they will have many situations in school and in the workplace where they will have to write quickly and succinctly. The teacher demonstrates how to summarize and how to identify what is most important to focus on. She models how to avoid over long communications.

iii. The teacher demonstrates how to create simple and effective content in student writing by using the inverted pyramid. He or she shows how to take the elements of writing, such as introductions, descriptions, conclusions, and explanations, and put them into order according to their importance.

Figure I.1 Example of Inverted Pyramid

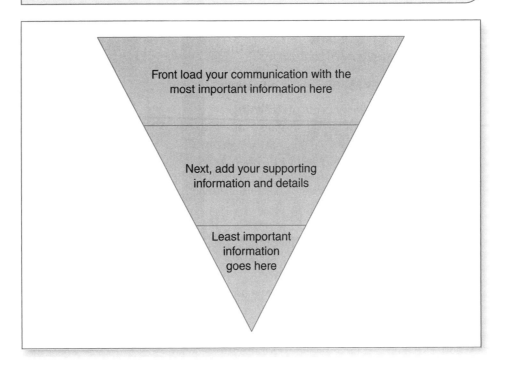

iv. In the inverted pyramid model (see Figure I.1), the most important information goes first. This is called front loading. This opening section should summarize your entire message in a few sentences. Subsequent paragraphs then present less critical information, in order of diminishing importance.

v. The following are four simple steps for using the inverted pyramid.

1. Choose the most important information: Pinpoint the most important part of your message, and work out the least amount of information you need to give people to get it across. Decide which details are less and least important, and plan a running order for your piece.

2. Front load your communication with a short, strong summary: Set a maximum of thirty words for your crucial opening section or as many as will fit on a screen before you have to scroll down. Limit it to a few short paragraphs or sentences that summarize the key details, and lead with your most important point. Covering the "five Ws and one H" of a story (what, who, where, when, why, and how) here can be too much. Make your priority the what and the who. The where and when can follow next and then the why and how. Remember to keep things simple; use everyday language, and avoid jargon.

3. Add your supporting information and detail: This is where you include the bulk of your information, expand on your argument,

describe the issues, or supply contextual material. Illustrations, quotes, and statistics can also go here. Such details will help the reader but aren't essential for understanding your message. Keep this section clear and concise. Your communication might have more room to breathe here than in your introduction, but you don't want to lose your readers by overwhelming them with detail. Split your points into separate paragraphs, and front load them by making your point and then elaborating on it.

4. Close your piece with background or bonus information: You can end your communication with information that may not be directly related to its main subject but which might help someone to understand it. This could include background or historical detail.

vi. Avoiding potential pitfalls

1. The inverted pyramid is a multipurpose writing tool, but it isn't a universal one. It doesn't group similar information together or present it in chronological order. So, if you don't shuffle your information with great care, you risk confusing your reader.

2. You also risk losing your readers after your summary. They will have the key points, but if that's all they read, they will miss out on the supporting information and other important but not necessarily attention-grabbing, detail.

3. It's not appropriate for every writing situation, either. You often need to hook people with a good opening, but you may not always want to say everything straight away. For example, sometimes, you'll want to build a compelling, step-by-step argument or follow a prescribed template for a report. Or, you may be writing for people with lots of time on their hands or who are looking for a more predictable storytelling approach, with a beginning, a middle, and an end.

Research Base

Peregoy & Boyle (2005)

What to Watch for With ELL/CLD Students

i. This strategy is for intermediate to fluent speakers, who are literate in their own or the target language. It will not be effective for newcomers, beginning level, or less proficient speakers or those who are not literate.

ii. However, it can be used in simplified form as students become more comfortable with reading and writing and could be introduced by showing existing examples of the inverted pyramid in reading for comprehension.

JIGSAW—COMPREHENSION STRATEGY

Purpose of the Strategy

i. Access prior knowledge

ii. Adapt to meet individual or unique student needs

iii. Build academic transfer skills

iv. Build appreciation that everyone belongs and is needed

v. Build appreciation that everyone has a contribution to make

vi. Build awareness of academic expectations

vii. Build awareness of appropriate academic behaviors

viii. Build awareness of appropriate cognitive academic language

ix. Build awareness of learning process

x. Build awareness of the appropriate content language in English culture/language

xi. Build foundation for learning

xii. Build metacognition skills

xiii. Build transfer skills

xiv. Build upon family language and culture

xv. Clarify responsibilities, assignments, and rewards

xvi. Develop academic language

xvii. Develop analytical skills

xviii. Develop association skills

xix. Develop basic interpersonal communication

xx. Develop categorization skills

xxi. Develop cognitive academic language

xxii. Develop cognitive learning strategies

xxiii. Develop confidence in academic interactions

xxiv. Develop content knowledge foundation

xxv. Develop extended time on task

xxvi. Develop higher persistence

xxvii. Develop higher tolerance

xxviii. Develop positive peer relationships

xxix. Develop problem-solving skills

xxx. Develop self esteem

xxxi. Develop thinking and planning skills

xxxii. Encourage questioning and exploration of new learning

xxxiii. Enhance ability of students to focus on learning

xxxiv. Enhance ability of students to learn new things

xxxv. Expand comprehension

xxxvi. Facilitate access of prior knowledge

xxxvii. Facilitate acquisition of content knowledge

xxxviii. Facilitate connections between known and new

xxxix. Facilitate discussion about new learning

xl. Facilitate language development

xli. Facilitate students' comfort with learning environment

xlii. Facilitate acquisition of content knowledge

xliii. Improve access to prior knowledge

xliv. Improve comprehension

xlv. Improve reading comprehension

xlvi. Improve retention of content

xlvii. Improve vocabulary

xlviii. Increase focus on reading

xlix. Increase students' time on task

l. Increase time on task

li. Improve students' ability to organize and prioritize information

lii. Recognize the importance of working together

liii. Reinforce content lessons

liv. Retention of content

lv. Strengthen ability to discuss what is happening

lvi. Strengthen awareness of learning process

lvii. Strengthen knowledge of academic content

lviii. Strengthen language development

lix. Strengthen learning to learn skills

lx. Strengthen retention and application abilities

lxi. Sustain engagement

lxii. Sustain engagement with reading and writing

lxiii. Use prior knowledge

How to Do It

i. The teacher uses flexible grouping arrangements to facilitate learning among diverse group of learners. For example, the teacher uses the large group setting for introducing the general unit, then breaks the students into smaller groups for research activities or pairs for sharing information and ideas about the topic, then returns to the large group where individual teams can share their information with the whole class.

ii. The following are the steps for doing jigsaw:

1. Divide the class into the same number of sections to be read in the text (pages or paragraphs—no more than three or four).

2. Assign each group a section to become experts on and to teach to the class.

3. Each group will read with a specific goal in mind (e.g., Choose four key words and ideas to share).

4. Try to incorporate collaboration and self-selection (e.g., Select three facts as a group and one you personally consider important).

5. Allow time after reading the text for groups to discuss and complete the form together.

6. Students teach their text to the class, either one-on-one or as a group.

7. The teacher can then post all the information into one document for the students or assist them in creating a combined document with all their information.

Research Base

Collier (2012b)

Heacox (2002)

What to Watch for With ELL/CLD Students

i. Many cultures have guidelines about who children may associate with and how they are to interact with others. Familiarize yourself with these beliefs and values enough to prepare for specific difficulties that might arise, for example, boys may not be allowed to sit next to girls, or two members of old political enemies should not sit next to each other (one may know that the other's parents slaughtered their grandmother).

ii. This is not to say you cannot mix and match groups in your classroom, but by preparing ahead you can be sensible about what works most effectively for different activities.

iii. Build in numerous variations so students become familiar with your expectation that group work will occur in many different configurations and that their work partners will be quite varied.

iv. Start with easy, comfortable groupings and work gradually to the more complex ones.

JUMPING TO CONCLUSIONS— COMPREHENSION STRATEGY

Purpose of the Strategy

i. Access prior knowledge

ii. Build academic transfer skills

iii. Build appreciation that everyone belongs and is needed

iv. Build appreciation that everyone has a contribution to make

v. Build awareness of learning process

vi. Build awareness of the appropriate content language in English culture/language

vii. Build foundation for learning

viii. Build metacognition skills

ix. Build transfer skills

x. Develop academic language

xi. Develop analytical skills

xii. Develop association skills

xiii.   Develop basic interpersonal communication

xiv.   Develop cognitive academic language

xv.   Develop cognitive learning strategies

xvi.   Develop confidence in academic interactions

xvii.   Develop content knowledge foundation

xviii.   Develop extended time on task

xix.   Develop problem-solving skills

xx.   Develop self-esteem

xxi.   Develop thinking and planning skills

xxii.   Encourage questioning and exploration of new learning

xxiii.   Enhance ability of students to focus on learning

xxiv.   Enhance ability of students to learn new things

xxv.   Expand comprehension

xxvi.   Facilitate access of prior knowledge

xxvii.   Facilitate acquisition of content knowledge

xxviii.   Facilitate connections between known and new

xxix.   Facilitate discussion about new learning

xxx.   Facilitate language development

xxxi.   Facilitate acquisition of content knowledge

xxxii.   Improve access to prior knowledge

xxxiii.   Improve comprehension

xxxiv.   Improve reading comprehension

xxxv.   Improve retention of content

xxxvi.   Improve vocabulary

xxxvii.   Increase focus on reading

xxxviii.   Increase students' time on task

xxxix.   Increase time on task

xl.   Improve students' ability to organize and prioritize information

xli.   Recognize the importance of working together

xlii.   Reinforce content lessons

xliii.   Retention of content

xliv.   Strengthen ability to discuss what is happening

xlv.   Strengthen awareness of learning process

xlvi.   Strengthen knowledge of academic content

xlvii.   Strengthen language development

xlviii.   Strengthen learning to learn skills

xlix.   Strengthen retention and application abilities

l.   Sustain engagement

li.   Sustain engagement with reading and writing

lii.   Use prior knowledge

How to Do It

i.   The teacher assigns a portion of text to be read. He or she writes the text in the left top corner of a large chart with three columns. The headings are conclusion, proof, and picture.

ii.   Students work in pairs or small groups to decide on the big picture or overall conclusion of the text to write in the "conclusion" box.

iii.   As a group, the students return to the text to find up to three support sentences or phrases to prove the conclusion, which they write in their "proof" box.

Text being read by the student groups is written here on the chart.	Conclusions reached by each group based on the text are written here on the chart.	Support sentences used by each group used to prove the conclusion are written here on the chart.	Each group draws a picture illustrating the conclusion and posts it here on the chart.
Group 1			
Group 2			
Group 3			

iv.   If there is enough time, the group or individuals within the group complete a "quick draw" to help embed information for visual learners and put their illustration in the "picture" box.

Research Base

Collier (2012b)

Davey (1983)

Heacox (2002)

Wood & Algozzine (1994)

What to Watch for With ELL/CLD Students

i. It will help introduce this strategy to students with limited English proficiency to group them with varied ability speakers of the same language or at least with a bilingual peer.

ii. The teacher or aide can model the process by taking a paragraph and demonstrating what to do with it on a large chart or on the board.

ABCDEFGHIJ**K**LMOPQRSTUVW

KRYPTO—MATH STRATEGY

Purpose of the Strategy

   i. Build academic transfer skills

   ii. Access and use prior knowledge

   iii. Develop analytical skills

   iv. Develop association skills

   v. Develop awareness of cause and effect

   vi. Develop content area skills

   vii. Develop content knowledge foundation

   viii. Develop extended time on task

   ix. Develop field independent skills

   x. Develop thinking and planning skills

   xi. Enhance ability of students to focus on learning

   xii. Expand and elaborate on learning

   xiii. Facilitate access of prior knowledge

   xiv. Facilitate acquisition of content knowledge

   xv. Facilitate analogy strategies

xvi.   Improve motivation

xvii.   Improve problem solving of math word problems

xviii.   Increase students' time on task

xix.   Recognize the importance of working together

xx.   Sustain engagement

xxi.   Strengthen knowledge of academic content

xxii.   Build metacognitive skills

xxiii.   Strengthen learning to learn skills

xxiv.   Build foundation for learning

xxv.   Develop independence in learning

xxvi.   Facilitate student ownership in education

xxvii.   Develop problem-solving skills

xxviii.   Reduce impulsivity

xxix.   Build confidence in the learning process

xxx.   Strengthen retention and application abilities

How to Do It

i.   This strategy may be used in versatile ways to supplement mathematics lessons at any grade level. It is best used as a review, reinforcement, or assessment tool. This set of cards, Krypto, is one of a series of content and language development card decks designed for use in dual language, bilingual education, or English as a second language (ESL) programs. Each deck of cards is designed to reinforce or assess specific content and language learning concepts.

ii.   There are 84 cards in Krypto, consisting of 20 sets of four cards illustrating the numbers from one to ten, and one set of four zero cards.

iii.   The strategy of Krypto is primarily a game to reinforce the four basic math operations, adding, subtracting, multiplying, and dividing. Krypto can also be played to reinforce receptive and expressive language, visual and auditory memory, or math literacy. It can be played periodically during the school year to provide a review of foundational concepts when making a transition to a new topic or subject matter. The cards may also be used individually as flashcards to review numbers and math operations vocabulary words.

iv.   Krypto may be used as an alternate assessment process. By watching the students play Krypto, especially when a lot of expressive and receptive language is required, the teacher is able to observe the extent to which individual students have acquired the number names, basic mathematics operations, or how well they have retained previously presented information.

v.   Krypto can be played to reinforce receptive and expressive language, visual and auditory memory, or content literacy. If students are non-verbal, Krypto can be played through cognitive visual matching. If students do not speak English or are limited English proficient, Krypto can be played in their native language or bilingually. They can play using as much English as they have acquired or wholly in English.

vi.   There should be at least two and not more than six players in each group playing.

vii.   The objective of Krypto is to make a math sentence using five numbers that solve an equation.

viii.   The following are the steps in Krypto:

1.   Deal: Each group gets enough cards for each player to receive five cards plus have several left over. For example, two players would need at least ten random cards. Four players would need at least 20 random cards. Cards are drawn from the group's set one at a time. Each player receives five cards face up. The remainder are placed face down in the center of the table.

2.   Verify the set of five: Each player in the group looks at their set of five and determines if they have the appropriate mix of cards. Each individual player is to make sure they have a mix of odd and even cards. If they have all odd or all even cards, they must trade a card with their partner or a member of their group so each player has a mix of odd and even cards. One odd and four even is okay. Each player is also to determine if they have any doubles or two of a kind in their set of five. If a player has two of a kind, they must trade one of the doubles with another player to make sure they have five cards that are all different from one another.

3.   Play: Have the students choose the first player by names alphabetically, ages, or some other method. The first player draws a card randomly from the remainder pile in the center of the table and turns it face up. This becomes the target number for the group. Zero cannot be used as a target number, so if a zero card is drawn as the target it must be replaced and another card drawn. Each player first tries to solve his or her own set of five for the target. Each player must use all of his or her cards to solve the equation and can only use each card one time in the equation.

Example

i.   One player has 4, 5, 8, 2, and 6. If his or her target card is 3, he or she must use all five of these numbers to make an equation that equals 3. Such as $4+2-6+8-5 = 3$, that is, $4+2 = 6$, $6-6 = 0$, $0+8 = 8$,

8−5 = 3. Another player may have 1, 3, 9, 7, and 10. Their solution might be 1+9 = 10, 10−10 = 0, 0x7 = 0, 0+3 = 3. Another solution might be 1×10= 10, 10−9 = 1, 7−1 = 6, 6−3 = 3. Many solutions are possible. All players are to tell their partners what their solutions re and how they arrived at them. Players are to assist one another when difficulties arise. After all players have solved their problems or have declared to their partner(s) that they are stumped, the other players in their group work to solve the unresolved problems, speaking out loud while solving the problem.

ii. Krypto can also be played with four cards each, but this will require substantially more use of multiplication and division. Another way to play Krypto within a classroom is for the teacher to draw one target number for the whole class. All groups of students will then use their cards to solve for the same target number. In this situation, each group can come up to an over-head projector and share their solution to the whole class. They should tell the class how they solved the problem and tell why their solution worked for their group.

iii. When using Krypto with students who need to review and reinforce the process of self-monitoring, the teacher can have the students use the following guidelines as they go through Krypto: (1) I will know I've completed the problem when I have a correct answer and have used all five numbers to equal the remaining sixth number; (2) the elements of the task are to use all the numbers, to add, subtract, divide, or multiply the five numbers; (3) my criteria are no frustration, making progress, and getting closer to remainder; (4) I will get feedback by checking my answers with my partners; and (5) I can generalize to other number combinations.

Research Base

Collier (2003a)

Sperling (2016)

What to Watch for With ELL/CLD Students

i. I have personally used this with students from very diverse back-grounds, including those with very limited English. but only after they have had basic arithmetic and are able to do simple addition, subtraction, multiplication, and division problems, either in English or their home language. Students from second or third grade and up can usually solve for five cards without a problem, while it usually takes higher skills to solve for four cards at a time. High school students have enjoyed using Krypto with algebra approaches.

1	0
8	4
2	7
3	5
6	9
10	1

KWL+

Purpose of the Strategy

    i. Access and use prior knowledge

    ii. Build awareness of academic expectations

    iii. Develop problem-solving skills

    iv. Expand and elaborate on learning

    v. Facilitate access of prior knowledge

    vi. Improve access to prior knowledge

    vii. Improve mnemonic retrieval

    viii. Improve sequencing skills

    ix. Improve students' ability to organize and prioritize information

    x. Reduce resistance to change

    xi. Reduce stress for new students

    xii. Reinforce content lessons

    xiii. Strengthen awareness of learning process

    xiv. Build first language to English transfer skills

    xv. Build upon the diverse language foundations of students and parents

    xvi. Build awareness of the appropriate cognitive academic language

    xvii. Build transfer skills

    xviii. Minimize ambiguity

    xix. Reduce misperceptions

    xx. Strengthen learning to learn skills

    xxi. Develop categorization skills

    xxii. Expand and improve comprehension

    xxiii. Facilitate connections between known and new

    xxiv. Develop confidence in academic interactions

How to Do It

    i. The teacher or assistant previews the lesson content in the home language, when possible, or in sheltered English outlining key issues, rehearsing vocabulary, and reviewing related prior knowledge.

    ii. Advanced fluency students could help less advanced students understand how to organize their reading and writing materials.

iii. KWL+ is done by asking the students to discuss the following questions before beginning the lesson:

    1. What do you already KNOW about this content?

    2. What do you WANT to know about this content?

    3. What will we LEARN about this?

    4. WHY should we learn this?

    5. And HOW will we learn this content?

iv. The teacher uses a graph or chart with K—What do we already KNOW about the topic, W—What do we WANT to learn about the topic, and L—What will we LEARN about this topic, WHY should we learn about this topic, and HOW will we learn this topic, as a preview/view/review structure for all lesson content, outlining key issues, rehearsing vocabulary, and reviewing related prior knowledge.

v. The teacher leads the students through the KWL+ structure step by step. Use review or retention techniques to spiral back to and reinforce the use of KWL+ during lesson.

vi. After a lesson or unit is completed, the teacher leads the students back through the KWL+ chart as a review:

    1. What did you KNOW?

    2. Did you learn what you WANTED to?

    3. What did you LEARN?

    4. WHY did we learn this?

    5. HOW did we learn this?

Example

i. When applying the KWL+ strategy, students work through problems or tasks using a sequence of ordering, sequencing, and connecting techniques. Suppose you want your students to write a short personal reflection about the story, Everyone Cooks Rice by Norah Dooley, that the class has just finished reading together. You would start by having your students work in small groups of similar ability level. You would show a copy of a graphic organizer form outline on the overhead projector or drawn on the whiteboard. Each group would be assigned two or three of the boxes in the graphic organizer. For example, you might assign the most challenged group to fill in the boxes about title, author, location, and country. Another group would be responsible for the main and supporting characters. Another group would be responsible for identifying the sequence of events in the story and a summary statement about them. Another group could be assigned to identify the main problem faced by the main character. After reading the story through the first time, the groups complete their tasks, and you or they write down their answers on the large or projected graphic organizer. Then, as a group, you would discuss how this main problem was resolved, the barriers to resolution that were faced, and things in the story that helped solve the problem. The students can then discuss the final resolution and what the moral of the story might be from their perspectives. You can expand this activity by comparing and contrasting the story with others like it or with happenings in the students' own lives.

ii. You might now step back from the lesson and discuss the metacognitive learning that you have provided students, the learning to learn lesson that is represented by the strategy you had them use.

iii. The following are the steps for teaching KWL+

1. *Inform* the students what KWL+ is, how it operates, when to use it, and why it is useful. Begin by saying that KWL+ is a way to help them (the students) plan and remember. It works by previewing or putting information concerning the lesson or assignment they are working on into graphic form. Once they learn how to use KWL+, they can use it anytime and with any content or lesson you give them to do.

2. *Use cues*, metaphors, analogies, or other means of elaborating on a description of KWL+ combined with visual cues. One way to do this is to have the group look at a blueprint of a house or other building they are familiar with. Have them see how the architect had to plan for everything ahead of time and create a preview or graphic image of what everyone was going to have to do to complete the construction. Explain that almost anyone could help construct the house or building by reading the blueprint, and the ability to read and understand it is a special and critical skill that will be useful to them later in life.

3. *Lead group discussions* about the use of KWL+. Have students start with talking about a lesson they have just successfully completed. They can go back through the lesson or book using different tools to see how they work and what is required. Encourage them to ask you anything about the learning process they want clarified.

4. *Provide guided practice* in applying KWL+ to particular tasks. Work directly with student groups demonstrating and modeling how to identify elements. Have more-skilled students demonstrate for the class.

5. *Provide feedback* on monitoring use and success of KWL+. While students use KWL+ in small groups, you should move around the room listening and supplying encouragement for consistent use of the tools. As students get more comfortable using these tools you can have them monitor one another in the use of the strategy.

Research Base

Collier (2002)

Harwell (2001)

Heacox (2002)

Moore, Alvermann, & Hinchman (2000)

Opitz (1998)

What to Watch for With ELL/CLD Students

i.   There are cultural differences in cognitive/learning style and some English language learner (ELL)/culturally and linguistically diverse (CLD) students may not respond to the brainstorming construct behind most advanced organizers.

ii. By keeping the graphic design of the advanced organizer as close as possible to the illustrations in the text or some aspect of the lesson the teacher can more tightly connect the concepts being studied with the Know/Want/Learn/Why/How questioning that precedes the lesson.

iii. This is another activity that works best with preparation in the students' most proficient language and relevance to their culture before proceeding.

WHAT DO WE **KNOW** ABOUT THIS ALREADY?

HOW WILL WE LEARN THIS?

WHAT WILL WE **LEARN** ABOUT THIS?

WHAT DO WE **WANT** TO KNOW ABOUT THIS?

WHY WILL WE LEARN THIS?

ABCDEFGHIJK**L**MOPQRSTUVW

LANGUAGE GAMES

Purpose of the Strategy

i. Access and use prior knowledge

ii. Build and develop appropriate cognitive academic language

iii. Develop academic and cognitive academic language

iv. Develop analytical skills

v. Develop confidence in academic interactions

vi. Develop problem-solving skills

vii. Expand and elaborate on learning

viii. Expand and improve comprehension

ix. Facilitate access of prior knowledge

x. Facilitate acquisition of content knowledge

xi. Improve vocabulary

xii. Reinforce content lessons

xiii. Strengthen and facilitate language development

xiv. Build awareness of learning process

xv. Build home language to English transfer skills

xvi.   Build transfer skills

xvii.   Build upon existing language skills of students

xviii.   Build upon existing language strengths of student

xix.   Build upon family language and culture

xx.   Build upon the diverse language foundations of students and parents

xxi.   Build vocabulary

xxii.   Develop basic interpersonal communication

xxiii.   Develop content knowledge foundation

xxiv.   Develop thinking and planning

xxv.   Reduce code switching

How to Do It

i. Students may play in groups with culture and language peers at first and then mixed groups of diverse students as they become comfortable with the games activities.

ii. Students play language games that reinforce specific content. The games are structured to reinforce and elaborate on content knowledge while developing home and community language and English language skills including turn taking, asking questions, giving appropriate responses, giving directions, and other game, communication, and interaction skills.

iii. Examples of game structures are memory games like Concentration, rummy games such as Go Fish, and matching games such as Old Maid.

iv. The content topics of the games can be chosen and developed to match a specific topic or lesson in the classroom and to reinforce the vocabulary words of that lesson. Some examples might be terms from the rainforest, historical events, types of animals, mathematical equations, visits to community locations, workers in the community, and so on.

v. These are also useful in illustrating second language learning strategies. All of the three basic games, SETS, PAIRS, and MEMORY, can be played to reinforce receptive and expressive language, visual and auditory memory, or content literacy.

vi. The games can be played periodically during the school year to provide a review of foundation concepts when making a transition to a new topic or subject matter. The cards may also be used individually as flashcards to review the vocabulary words and language content.

vii. The games may be used as an alternate assessment process. By watching the students play the card games, especially when a lot of expressive and receptive language is required, the teacher will be able to observe the extent to which individual students have acquired the learning concepts and content or how well they have retained previously presented information.

viii. All of the games can be played to reinforce receptive and expressive language, visual and auditory memory, or content literacy. If students are nonverbal, the games can be played through cognitive visual matching. If students do not speak English or are limited English proficient, the games can be played in their native language or bilingually. They can play using as much English as they have acquired or wholly in English.

Example Game

i. The WEATHER game may be used in versatile ways to supplement content lessons at any grade level. It is best used as a review, reinforcement, or assessment tool. There are three basic games that can be played with these cards: sets, pairs, and memory. Each of the three basic games can be varied according to specific lesson objectives. The cards in WEATHER consist of seven sets of four cards per set illustrating common weather conditions in English. These are the weather words most often used in calendar activities in the classroom.

1. Players: Two to six in each group playing.

2. Object: To collect the most sets of four of a kind.

3. Deal: Cards are dealt one at a time. Each player receives five cards. The rest of the pack is placed face down in the center of the table to form the draw pile.

4. Play: Have the students choose the first player by names alphabetically, ages, or other method. Starting with the first player, each player calls another by name and requests cards of a specific type, such as, "David, do you have any sunny days?" The player asking must hold at least one of the types of card requested. The player asked must give up the card requested, saying, "Yes, Kala, I have a sunny day." Another variation of this is to have the player ask for a category first. If Kala successfully identifies the picture, "cloudy day," then she gets the card. The player asked does not have to say she has more of the set of cards if she has more than one of the same set of cards. The player requesting has to ask for each individual card: e.g. "David, do you have another cloudy day?"

5. If the player asked does not have any cards of the type requested, then she says "Draw," and the asker draws the top card from the draw pile. A player's turn to ask continues as long as he or she

is successful in getting the cards requested. If the player is told to draw and happens to draw a card of the type requested, the player may show this card, name it, and continue the turn. As soon as any player gets a set of all four cards of one type, he or she must show them and give the names of the cards out loud, placing them on the table in front of him or her. If played competitively, the player who collects the most sets by the end of the game wins.

Research Base

Ajibade & Ndububa (2008)

Law & Eckes (2000)

Padak & Rasinski (2008)

Wright, Betteridge, & Buckby (2006)

What to Watch for With ELL/CLD Students

i. Be sure to establish consistent game playing rules and phrases that all students are to use when playing the game. At first, these can be as simple as "Do you have an xxx?" "Is this an xxx?" "Here are xxx."

ii. The phrases can become more complex and more natural as students become more comfortable playing the games.

Figure L.1   Example of Language Game About Weather Words

(Continued)

Figure L.1 (Continued)

Images from http://www.clipart.com/. Sunny Image: 3805836, Windy Image: 3805619, Rainy Image: 3805840, Snowy Image: 3805830, Cloudy Image: 3805626, Foggy Image: 3707703, Cold Image: 3805764.

LEARNING CENTERS OR STATIONS

Purpose of the Strategy

    i. Build confidence in independent work

    ii. Adapt to meet individual or unique student needs

    iii. Adapt the mode of response required of students

    iv. Develop content area skills

    v. Develop content knowledge foundation

    vi. Develop extended time on task

    vii. Develop independence in learning situations

    viii. Improve retention of content

    ix. Develop problem-solving skills

    x. Develop thinking and planning skills

    xi. Increase time on task

    xii. Improve students' ability to organize and prioritize information

    xiii. Reinforce content lessons

    xiv. Strengthen knowledge of academic content

    xv. Strengthen language development

    xvi. Strengthen learning to learn skills

    xvii. Strengthen retention and application abilities

    xviii. Expand and elaborate on learning

    xix. Facilitate acquisition of content knowledge

    xx. Facilitates student self-evaluation skills

    xxi. Improve access to prior knowledge

    xxii. Adapt the mode of response required of students

    xxiii. Develop confidence in academic interactions

    xxiv. Sustain engagement

    xxv. Enhance ability of student to focus on learning

    xxvi. Reinforce content lessons

    xxvii. Expand and improve comprehension and retention

    xxviii. Facilitate individualization

How to Do It

i. The teacher creates areas or locations in the classroom where students work on various tasks simultaneously.

ii. This strategy is worked into the layout of the classroom with use of furniture and other means of demarking specific learning areas. Learning centers or areas can also be designated by hanging charts or putting up activities on different walls of the room.

iii. These areas can be formal or informal and can be distinguished by signs, symbols, or colors. Centers differ from stations in that centers are distinct content locations while stations work in concert with one another. For example, there may be a science center, math center, writing center, and reading center in the classroom; each with its special furniture, equipment, materials, and so on. Stations might all be related to an assignment about World War II where one station is about the countries involved, one is about the chronology of principal events, another about the Holocaust, and other stations related to major aspects. The students move through the stations and then reconvene to discuss the whole experience.

iv. Assignments or tasks specific to each center or station activity are either handed out ahead of time or available at each location. For example, create a literacy center where different activities exist for practicing commonly used sight words, reading vocabulary words, and spelling words.

Example

Designate a learning center where materials and activities are available for individual or group use about a geography unit. Different activities could include a map of the United States with tracing paper and colored pencils, as well a puzzle, and, if possible, a computer game that supports the content (such as *Oregon Trail*). Students should be given the choice of working alone or in a small group.

Research Base

Ashworth & Wakefield (2004)

Movitz & Holmes (2007)

Tomlinson (1999)

What to Watch for With ELL/CLD Students

i. English language learner (ELL)/culturally and linguistically diverse (CLD) students should not go to separate learning centers for primary instruction in a content lesson or task. They need direct instruction in the content or task including key vocabulary and guided practice in what is expected of them at each learning center.

ii. After the ELL/CLD students have been prepared for the learning centers and shown how to use the materials or equipment at each center, they can join in the activities at each center just as the rest of the class does.

iii. Learning centers are a good way to reinforce content knowledge and allow students to become engaged in applications of this new knowledge.

LEARNING STYLES (ENTRY POINTS)

Purpose of the Strategy

i. Build awareness of learning process

ii. Adapt to meet individual or unique student needs

iii. Adapt the mode of response required of students

iv. Build awareness of academic expectations

v. Build awareness of adaptation process

vi. Build confidence in independent work

vii. Build foundation for learning

viii. Develop self-esteem

ix. Enhance ability of students to focus on learning

x. Enhance ability of students to learn new things

xi. Expand and elaborate on learning

xii. Expand comprehension

xiii. Facilitate students assuming responsibility for learning

xiv. Facilitate student self-concept as a successful person

xv. Facilitate students' comfort with learning environment

xvi. Facilitate students' ownership in their education

xvii. Improve confidence and self-esteem

xviii. Improve confidence in academic interactions

xix. Improve motivation

xx. Improve retention of content

xxi. Increase students' probability of generating a correct response

xxii. Increase students' time on task

xxiii. Increase the frequency of appropriate responses or behaviors

xxiv. Reduce fears associated with assignments

xxv. Reduce frustration

xxvi. Reduce frustration in students due to unclear expectations

xxvii. Reduce anxiety and stress and responses

xxviii. Reduce anxiety in social/academic interactions

xxix. Retention of content

xxx. Strengthen ability to discuss what is happening

xxxi. Strengthen awareness of learning process

xxxii. Build appreciation that all can contribute

xxxiii. Build transfer skills

xxxiv. Develop independence in learning situations

xxxv. Develop extended time on task

xxxvi. Develop personal control of situations

How to Do It

i. The teacher ensures that students with different abilities work with the same essential ideas and use the same key content but provides different points of entry for a variety of skills and abilities. For example, a student having difficulty with reading still needs to make sense of the basic concepts and ideas of a story. Simultaneously, a student who is advanced in the same subject needs to find genuine challenge in working with these same concepts and ideas. Providing different entry points to the content of the lesson facilitates students' focus on essential understandings and skills but at different levels of complexity, abstractness, and open endedness. This is done by keeping the focus of the activity the same but providing routes of access at varying degrees of difficulty.

ii. This is also related to the idea of multiple intelligences developed by Howard Gardner wherein the teacher adapts lessons to students' varied intelligence preferences or strengths. For example, a student who is strong spatially may take in information, solve problems, and express learning differently than a student whose strength is verbal-linguistic. Teachers can facilitate the learning process by considering these differences when planning and carrying out instructions.

Research Base

Heacox (2002)

Gardner (1993a)

Tomlinson (1999)

What to Watch for With ELL/CLD Students

i. A basic premise of differentiation is that one type of instruction does not necessarily work for all students, that is, one size does not fit all. Teachers are advised to begin where their students are with their learning differences and their learning strengths.

ii. For ELL and CLD students, instructional personnel are to build upon learners' cultural and linguistic differences and strengths by developing instructional activities based on essential topics and concepts, significant processes and skills, and multiple ways to display learning while providing flexible approaches to content, instruction, and outcomes.

LEVELED ACTIVITIES

Purpose of the Strategy

i. Build awareness of learning process

ii. Develop confidence in school culture interactions

iii. Adapt content to meet individual or unique student needs

iv. Adapt the mode of response required of students

v. Build academic transfer skills

vi. Build foundation for learning

vii. Develop academic language

viii. Encourage questioning and exploration of new learning

ix. Enhance ability of students to focus on learning

x. Enhance ability of students to learn new things

xi. Facilitate individualization

xii. Expand and elaborate on learning

xiii. Facilitate acquisition of content knowledge

xiv. Improve access to prior knowledge

xv. Improve comprehension

xvi. Lower and reduce anxiety and stress levels

xvii. Reduce anxiety and stress and responses

xviii. Reduce anxiety in social/academic interactions

xix. Strengthen learning to learn skills

xx. Strengthen and improve retention and application abilities

xxi. Sustain engagement

xxii. Increase student time on task

xxiii. Reduce frustration

xxiv. Develop extended time on task

xxv. Develop personal control of situations

xxvi. Build awareness of learning process

xxvii. Build awareness of appropriate cognitive academic language

xxviii. Develop higher tolerance

How to Do It

i. This strategy is an application of universal design, which is a set of principles for curriculum development that gives all individuals equal opportunities to learn. These strategies provide a blueprint for creating instructional goals, methods, materials, and assessments that work for everyone—not a single, one-size-fits-all solution but rather flexible approaches that can be customized and adjusted for individual needs.

ii. The teacher ensures that students with different learning needs work with the same essential ideas and the same key skills as all other students. For example, a student having difficulty with reading still needs to make sense of the basic concepts and ideas of a story. Simultaneously, a student who is advanced in the same subject needs to find genuine challenge in working with these same concepts and ideas.

iii. Leveled activities are used so all students focus on essential understandings and skills but at different degrees of complexity, abstractness, and open endedness. This is done by keeping the focus of the activity the same but providing routes of access at varying degrees of difficulty.

Research Base

Heacox (2002)

Tomlinson (1999)

What to Watch for With ELL/CLD Students

i. The key to integrating instruction in mixed-skill classrooms is the creation of or access to leveled reading, writing, or content materials. Several publishers have excellent leveled materials that can be used as models.

ii. An example is books about the ecosystem within a pond. All illustrations are the same, and all content is the same, but the reading level of the content in the booklets varies for the ability level of the students, for example, Level 1, Level 2, Level 3, and so on, depending upon the classroom needs.

iii. For example, National Geographic publishes magazines that are coded in the upper left corner of the cover for beginner, middle, and advanced readers. They also have topic-specific books coded on the back of the cover for levels with one spot, two spots, three spots, or four spots.

LISTENING COMPREHENSION—TQLR

Purpose of the Strategy

    i. Access and use prior knowledge

    ii. Expand and elaborate on learning

    iii. Expand comprehension

    iv. Facilitate acquisition of content knowledge

    v. Improve retention of content

    vi. Improve mnemonic retrieval

    vii. Improve comprehension

    viii. Increase time on task

    ix. Reduce distractibility

    x. Reduce off-task behaviors

    xi. Retention of content

    xii. Sustain engagement

    xiii. Build awareness of appropriate academic behaviors

    xiv. Clarify responsibilities, assignments

    xv. Build awareness of learning

    xvi. Encourage questioning and exploration of new learning

    xvii. Enhance ability of students to focus on learning

    xiii. Develop personal control of situations

    xix. Build awareness of academic expectations

    xx. Build academic transfer skills

    xxi. Improve access to prior knowledge

    xxii. Strengthen language development

How to Do It

    i. This strategy assists with listening comprehension. Students generate questions and listen for specific statements related to those questions.

    ii. The teacher hands out sheets of paper or uses other individualized ways for students to follow and use the TQLR frame. She demonstrates how to use the TQLR frame to take notes while listening to an oral or video presentation. The teacher guides students through thinking about TQLR by asking them to consider what they are to do when (1) tuning in, (2) questioning, (3) listening, and (4) reviewing. The teacher then has the students consider what they did and how many times they did these active listening actions.

iii. The teacher creates posters or projections showing the TQLR steps and points them out step by step at the beginning of each new discussion and lesson until he or she is sure students know how to use this active listening strategy.

iv. After this detailed introduction, with demonstration and modeling if necessary, the teacher or assistant can then refer to the poster to remind students to use the strategy while listening to someone present information.

v. The following are the steps in TQLR:

1. Tuning in

2. Questioning

3. Listening

4. Reviewing

Research Base

Artis (2008)

Fisher & Frey (2004)

Irvin & Rose (1995)

Law & Eckes (2000)

Popp (1997)

Robinson (1946)

Sakta (1999)

What to Watch for With ELL/CLD Students

i. Newcomers will need to have the TQLR steps modeled and explained in their most proficient language before they can proceed independently.

ii. Students can be paired with partners who are slightly more bilingual than themselves to facilitate their learning this process.

Steps in the TQLR Process	What am I to do at this step?	What did I do about it?	How many times did I do this?
Tuning In			
Questioning			
Listening			
Reviewing			

ABCDEFGHIJKL**M**OPQRSTUVW

MAGIC BAG—SORTING

Purpose of the Strategy

    i. Access prior knowledge

    ii. Build awareness of appropriate academic behaviors

    iii. Build academic transfer skills

    iv. Build appreciation that everyone belongs and is needed

    v. Build appreciation that everyone has a contribution to make

    vi. Build foundation for learning

    vii. Build metacognition skills

    viii. Develop cognitive academic language

    ix. Develop cognitive learning strategies

    x. Develop problem-solving skills

    xi. Encourage questioning and exploration of new learning

    xii. Enhance ability of student to focus on learning and learn new things

    xiii. Expand and elaborate on learning

    xiv. Expand comprehension

    xv. Facilitate access of prior knowledge

    xvi. Facilitate discussion about new learning

    xvii. Facilitate language development

xviii. Improve students' ability to organize and prioritize information

xix. Reinforce content lessons

xx. Retention of content

xxi. Strengthen ability to discuss what is happening

xxii. Strengthen awareness of learning process

xxiii. Strengthen knowledge of academic content

xxiv. Strengthen language development

xxv. Strengthen learning to learn skills

xxvi. Strengthen retention and application abilities

xxvii. Sustain engagement

xxviii. Use prior knowledge

xxix. Develop analytical skills

xxx. Build awareness of learning process

xxxi. Develop association skills

xxxii. Develop categorization skills

xxxiii. Develop field independent skills

xxxiv. Improve mnemonic retrieval

How to Do It

i. In essence, the teacher gives each group a bag of items related to some topic of discussion or recent unit of instruction. These can be models of objects or the actual items themselves such as colored balls, square blocks, toy animals, plastic fruit, coins, items from a place just visited, or items related to a specific topic. The students are divided into small groups and given a bag full of random items. They are instructed to group or sort the items into groups or sets according to categories selected by the teacher or by the nature of the lesson. The following are the steps for students to follow in implementing this strategy:

1. What items go together and why?

2. What attribute of these am I using to group them?

3. What do we call each set of items?

4. How are the groups similar to one another?

5. How are the groups different from one another?

6. How can we generalize this information?

ii. The teacher may assign students of similar language and ability to either heterogeneous or homogeneous groups depending upon his or her specific goals. Rather than preparing a bag of items, the teacher could also direct students to empty out their backpacks and work in small groups. Each small group goes through their steps, sorting all the items in their piles together. They make lists of their groups of items to share with the class.

iii. When applying the magic bag strategy, students work through problems or tasks using the above sequence of self-monitoring questions. For example, you are going to have a new unit about rocks and minerals, that is, igneous, sedimentary, conglomerate, and so on. Many of your students are unfamiliar with these ways of grouping natural materials that they consider generically as rocks. One group of students comes from a culture where rocks are grouped by hard versus soft and another from a culture that groups rocks by whether they can be used to produce something in the home. You might introduce your class to the lesson by having actual examples of the rocks to handle or take the class on a field trip to the museum or a local mine or industrial area to observe them. You could also show pictures or videos of chemists interacting with the materials. Have the students look for patterns in appearance, use, environment, chemical reactions, and so on. They could chart the attributes and characteristics of the rocks and minerals on a graph or in Venn diagrams (Step 1 of magic bag, "What items go together and why?"). Now they should look for distinctive patterns of commonality between rocks and minerals that shows whether or not they go together (Step 2 of magic bag, "What attribute of these am I using to group them?"). Ask the students what they would name the group of rocks and minerals based upon the major attributes. Now introduce them to the common English name of the group (Step 3 of magic bag, "What do we call each set of items?"). Discuss how the materials within each group share certain common characteristics, and then discuss the characteristics that all rocks and minerals share in common as rocks and minerals (Step 4 of magic bag, "How are the groups similar to one another?"). Discuss how the rocks within each group might differ from each other, how each group of rocks and minerals differs from the other groups, and how rocks differ from nonrocks (Step 5 of magic bag, "How are the groups different from one another?"). Finish the unit with a discussion of how to find patterns in anything you are studying (Step 6 of sorting, "How can we generalize this information?").

iv. You might now step back from the lesson and discuss the enhanced cognitive learning that you have provided students, the learning to learn lesson that is represented by the strategy you had them use. At this point, you would discuss how everything in the world is composed of various elements that need to be identified in order to understand the whole thing being studied (field independence) and that when all the parts are put together, the meaning of the whole thing results (field sensitive).

Research Base

Ferris & Hedgcock (2005)

Iachini, Borghi, & Senese (2008)

What to Watch for With ELL/CLD Students

i. The strategy preparation can be done in the native language or dialect of the students to assure their understanding of your expectations and their task prior to carrying the assignment out in English or other communication mode.

ii. Understand that all cultures have different ways of thinking of common attributes of a group of similar objects. What constitutes the criteria to pay attention to will vary based upon cultural values and learning practices. While it seems obvious to one group that the predominant surface color of a set of objects is what links them together as a set of objects, to another group it might be that surface texture or size is more important as an attribute for sorting out similarity and difference.

Participant	Weight	Where Object Found	Name of Thing	Color	Function or Use	Size	What Made Of	Shape
1								
2								
3								
4								
5								
Other sorting categories								

Participant	Taste or Smell	Color	Function or Use	Size	What Made Of	Shape	Texture	Weight
1								
2								
3								
4								
5								
Other sorting categories								

MANIPULATIVES

Purpose of the Strategy

    i.   Adapt content to meet individual or unique student needs

    ii.   Adapt the mode of response required of students

    iii.   Build awareness of learning process

    iv.   Build confidence in independent work

    v.   Develop categorization skills

    vi.   Develop cognitive academic language

    vii.   Develop cognitive learning strategies

    viii.   Develop field sensitive skills

    ix.   Develop higher persistence

    x.   Enhance ability of student to focus on learning and learn new things

    xi.   Encourage questioning and exploration of new learning

    xii.   Facilitate analogy strategies

    xiii.   Expand comprehension

    xiv.   Facilitate connections between known and new

    xv.   Facilitate discussion about new learning

    xvi.   Minimize ambiguity in classroom

    xvii.   Reduce confusion in locus of control

    xviii.   Reduce low-persistence behaviors

    xix.   Reduce misperceptions

    xx.   Reduce off-task behaviors

    xxi.   Reduce stress for new students

    xxii.   Strengthen learning to learn skills

    xxiii.   Strengthen retention and application abilities

    xxiv.   Build foundation for learning

    xxv.   Develop association skills

    xxvi.   Develop extended time on task

    xxvii.   Expand and increase comprehension

    xxviii.   Reduce distractibility

    xxix.   Reinforce content lessons

    xxx.   Improve retention

How to Do It

   i. The teacher uses multiple representations, materials, and other hands-on resources to illustrate content vocabulary and processes.

Figure M.1   Example of the Magic Bag Sorting Activity

Example

   i. For mathematics, the teacher or assistant uses cans, cubes, rods, coins, bottle caps, or so on for counting and sorting into fractions.

Research Base

Cole (1995)

Collier (2012a)

Krashen (2003)

What to Watch for With ELL/CLD Students

   i. The strategy preparation can be done in the native language or dialect of the students to assure their understanding of your expectations and their task prior to carrying the assignment out in English or other communication mode.

   ii. Understand that all cultures have different ways of thinking of objects, how to handle them, and whether or not it is appropriate to handle them.

MARKING TEXT

Purpose of the Strategy

    i. Build academic transfer skills

    ii. Build awareness of appropriate cognitive academic language

    iii. Enhance ability of student to focus on learning

    iv. Expand and elaborate on learning

    v. Facilitate reading process

    vi. Increase focus on reading

    vii. Increase time on task

    viii. Reduce distractibility

    ix. Reduce low-persistence behaviors

    x. Reduce misperceptions

    xi. Strengthen knowledge of academic content

    xii. Strengthen language development

    xiii. Strengthen learning to learn skills

    xiv. Strengthen retention and application abilities

    xv. Build awareness of learning process

    xvi. Build vocabulary

    xvii. Develop analytical skills

    xviii. Develop cognitive learning strategies

    xix. Develop higher persistence

    xx. Develop thinking and planning

    xxi. Expand comprehension

    xxii. Improve reading comprehension

    xxiii. Increase focus on reading

    xxiv. Increase time on task

    xxv. Retention of content

    xxvi. Sustain engagement with reading

How to Do It

    i. This strategy is sometimes called coding text. In the marking text strategy, students mark their text as a way to stay engaged in their reading. They may use special symbols or may just keep track of where they are or to indicate beginning and end of main ideas.

ii. The teacher introduces this strategy by projecting a copy of text, for example, a paragraph from a current unit, on a chart and marking key elements with the code or marks he or she wants students to use while reading the text.

iii. The teacher and students may use codes to indicate the type of thinking they are to use with particular passages. For example, if you want the students to make connections between their lives and the text, they might mark those passages with "REM" for "remember when." They can use underline or "MI" to indicate the "main idea," and "SI" for "supporting information," and so on. Students can also put "?" marks where they have questions about the text.

Research Base

Davey (1983)

Tovani (2000)

What to Watch for With ELL/CLD Students

i. This is an easy strategy to assist students who are beginning to do more reading to organize and think about what they are reading.

ii. This can be done in any language in which the students are literate.

MATH STRATEGY—FIFTY GRID

Purpose of the Strategy

i. Access prior knowledge

ii. Build academic transfer skills

iii. Build awareness of learning process

iv. Develop field independent skills

v. Develop academic language in math

vi. Develop extended time on task

vii. Develop problem-solving skills

viii. Improve retention of content

ix. Develop independence in learning math

x. Reinforce content lessons

xi. Strengthen awareness of learning process

How to Do It

i. This strategy has been used with students from third grade and up and works every time. For less prepared groups, use less random numbers. Calculators could be provided for individuals.

ii.   You need this 10x5 grid. You can print it on paper or on an acetate transparency sheet for use with an overhead projector. The students will need to be able to mark off the numbers on the grid so it should be projected onto a whiteboard.

1	2	**3**	4	**5**	6	7	8	9	10
11	12	**13**	14	15	16	17	**18**	19	**20**
21	**22**	23	24	25	**26**	27	28	29	30
31	32	33	34	**35**	36	37	**38**	39	40
41	42	43	44	45	46	47	48	**49**	50

1.   The numbered squares on the grid need to be randomly colored either white, blue, yellow, lavender, or green. There should be ten squares of each of the five colors in the grid.

2.   The pupils are divided into five teams. Each team is given five random numbers generated by rolling a variety of dice. This is best recorded in a table on a flipchart or on the board:

Team	Dice-Generated Numbers					Score
1	8	7	11	12	10	
2	3	7	2	1	6	
3	10	6	1	4	3	
4	10	2	5	14	4	
5	6	8	7	2	13	

3.   The teams take turns using their random numbers to make a number from one to fifty using any mathematical operation. The object is to capture one of the cells on the colored board by making the number inside it. Once a cell has been captured it cannot be captured again. The teacher or a student crosses the colored number out with an *x* once it is captured by a team.

4.   Scoring points is done as follows: For each captured square, the team gets one point. If the captured square is adjacent to a previously captured square, the team gets one point for each of those adjacent squares. If the square has a blue background, the team multiplies its total score by three. If the square has a yellow background, the team adds three points. If the square has a lavender background, the team multiplies its total score by five. If the square has a green background, the team adds five points. This is summarized in the chart below.

Scoring

Square captured	1 pt
Each square already captured around the captured square	1 pt each
Captured square has a blue background	Multiply total score by 3
Captured square has a yellow background	+3 pts
Captured square has a lavender background	Multiply total score by 5
Captured square has a green background	+5 pts

5. The activity ends when all squares have been taken or time runs out. The highest final score wins. The teams start each round with new random numbers.

Research Base

Cole (1995)

Elliot & Thurlow (2005)

What to Watch for With ELL/CLD Students

i. Newcomers will need to have the fifty grid steps modeled and explained in their most proficient language before they can proceed independently.

ii. Students can be paired with partners who are slightly more bilingual than themselves to facilitate their learning this process.

MATH STRATEGY—KRYPTO

Purpose of the Strategy

i. Build academic transfer skills

ii. Access and use prior knowledge

iii. Develop analytical skills

iv. Develop association skills

v. Develop awareness of cause and effect

vi. Develop content area skills

vii. Develop content knowledge foundation

viii. Develop extended time on task

ix. Develop field independent skills

x. Develop thinking and planning skills

xi. Enhance ability of students to focus on learning

xii. Expand and elaborate on learning

xiii. Facilitate access of prior knowledge

xiv. Facilitate acquisition of content knowledge

xv. Facilitate analogy strategies

xvi. Improve motivation

xvii. Improve problem solving of math word problems

xviii. Increase students' time on task

xix. Recognize the importance of working together

xx. Sustain engagement

xxi. Strengthen knowledge of academic content

xxii. Develop content area skills

xxiii. Build metacognitive skills

xxiv. Strengthen learning to learn skills

xxv. Build foundation for learning

xxvi. Develop independence in learning

xxvii. Facilitate student ownership in education

xxviii. Develop problem-solving skills

xxix. Reduce impulsivity

xxx. Build confidence in the learning process

xxxi. Strengthen retention and application abilities

How to Do It

i. This strategy may be used in versatile ways to supplement mathematics lessons at any grade level. It is best used as a review, reinforcement, or assessment tool. This set of cards, Krypto, is one of a series of content and language development card decks designed for use in dual language, bilingual education, or English as a second language (ESL) programs. Each deck of cards is designed to reinforce or assess specific content and language learning concepts.

ii. There are 84 cards in Krypto consisting of 20 sets of four cards per set illustrating the numbers from one to ten and one set of four zero cards.

iii. The strategy of Krypto is primarily a game to reinforce the four basic math operations, adding, subtracting, multiplying, and dividing. Krypto can also be played to reinforce receptive and expressive language, visual and auditory memory, or math literacy. It can be played periodically during the school year to provide a review of foundation concepts when making a transition to a new topic or subject matter.

The cards may also be used individually as flashcards to review numbers and math operations vocabulary words.

iv. Krypto may be used as an alternate assessment process. By watching the students play Krypto, especially when a lot of expressive and receptive language is required, the teacher will be able to observe the extent to which individual students have acquired the number names, basic mathematics operations, or how well they have retained previously presented information.

v. Krypto can be played to reinforce receptive and expressive language, visual and auditory memory, or content literacy. If students are nonverbal, Krypto can be played through cognitive visual matching. If students do not speak English or are limited English proficient, Krypto can be played in their native language or bilingually. They can play using as much English as they have acquired or wholly in English.

vi. There should be at least two and not more than six players in each group playing.

vii. The object of Krypto is to make a math sentence using five numbers that solve an equation.

viii. The following are the steps in Krypto:

1. Deal: Each group gets enough cards for each player to receive five cards plus have several left over. For example, two players would need at least ten random cards. Four players would need at least twenty random cards. Cards are drawn from the group's set one at a time. Each player receives five cards face up. The remainder are placed face down in the center of their table.

2. Verifying the set of five: All players in the group look at their sets of five and determine if they have the appropriate mix of cards. All players are to make sure they have a mix of odd and even cards. If they have all odd or all even cards, they must trade a card with their partner or a member of their group so each player has a mix of odd and even cards. One odd and four even is okay. Each player is also to determine if they have any doubles or two of a kind in their set of five. If a player has two of a kind, he or she must trade one of the doubles with another player to make sure he or she has five cards that are all different from one another.

3. Play: Have the students choose the first player by names alphabetically, ages, or other device. The first player draws a card randomly from the remainder pile in the center of the table and turns it face up. This becomes the target number for the group. Zero cannot be used as a target number, so if a zero card is drawn as the target it must be replaced and another card drawn. Each player first tries to solve his or her own set of five for the target. Each player must use all of his or her cards to solve the equation and can only use each card one time in the equation.

Example

i. One player has 4, 5, 8, 2, and 6. If their target card is 3, they must use all five of these numbers to make an equation that equals 3. Such as 4+2–6+8–5=3, that is, 4+2=6, 6–6=0, 0+8=8, 8–5=3. Another player may have 1, 3, 9, 7, and 10. Their solution might be 1+ 9=10, 10–10=0, 0x7=0, 0+3=3. Another solution might be 1x10=10, 10–9=1, 7–1=6, 6–3=3. Many solutions are possible. Player are to tell their partners what their solutions are and how they arrived at them. Players are to assist one another where difficulties arise. After all players have solved their problems or have declared to their partner(s) that they are stumped, the other players in their group work to solve the unresolved problems, speaking out loud while solving the problem.

ii. Krypto can also be played with four cards each, but this will require substantially more use of multiplication and division. Another way to play Krypto within a classroom is for the teacher to draw one target number for the whole class. All groups of students will then use their cards to solve for the same target number. In this situation, each group can come up to an overhead projector and share their solution with the whole class. They should tell the class how they solved the problem and tell why their solution worked for their group

iii. When using Krypto with students who need to review and reinforce the process of self-monitoring, the facilitator can have the student use the following guidelines as they go through Krypto: (1) I will know I've completed the problem when I have a correct answer and have used all five numbers to equal the remaining sixth number; (2) the elements of the task are to use all the numbers, to add, subtract, divide, or multiply the five numbers; (3) my criteria are no frustration, making progress, and getting closer to remainder; (4) I will get feedback by checking my answers with my partners; and (5) I can generalize to other number combinations.

Research Base

Collier (2003a)

Robertson (2009)

Sperling (2016)

What to Watch for With ELL/CLD Students

i. I have personally used this with students from very diverse backgrounds including those with very limited English, but only after they have had basic arithmetic and are able to do simple addition, subtraction, multiplication, and division problems, either in English or their home language. Students from second or third grade up can usually solve for five cards without a problem while it usually takes higher skills to solve for four cards at a time. High school students have enjoyed using Krypto with algebra approaches.

1	0
8	4
2	7
3	5
6	9
10	1

1	0
8	4
2	7
3	5
6	9
10	1

MATH STRATEGY—SQRQCQ

Purpose of the Strategy

    i. Build awareness of academic expectations

    ii. Build learners' confidence in their control of the learning process

    iii. Build awareness of appropriate academic behaviors

    iv. Build awareness of appropriate behaviors for school language and rules

    v. Build awareness of appropriate cognitive academic language

    vi. Develop cognitive academic language

    vii. Develop cognitive learning strategies

    viii. Develop field independent skills

    ix. Develop higher persistence

    x. Develop thinking and planning skills

    xi. Expand and elaborate on learning

    xii. Expand comprehension

    xiii. Facilitate students assuming responsibility for learning

    xiv. Improve comprehension

    xv. Improve mnemonic retrieval

    xvi. Increase students' probability of generating a correct response

    xvii. Increase students' time on task

    xviii. Increase the frequency of appropriate responses or behaviors

    xix. Increase time on task

    xx. Improve students' ability to organize and prioritize information

    xxi. Retention of content

    xxii. Strengthen ability to discuss what is happening

    xxiii. Strengthen awareness of learning process

    xxiv. Sustain engagement

    xxv. Strengthen retention and application abilities

    xxvi. Develop analytical skills

    xxvii. Improve comprehension

    xxviii. Develop problem-solving skills

    xxix. Facilitate language development

    xxx. Improve retention of information

    xxxi. Improve problem solving of math word problems

    xxxii. Strengthen language development

How to Do It

i. This strategy provides a systematic structure for identifying the question being asked in a math word problem, computing the response, and ensuring that the question in the problem was answered.

ii. The teacher projects the SQRQCQ frame upon a chart and goes through it step by step while students look at copies of the pattern at their desks. The teacher presents a math word problem and shows how using the SQRQCQ frame helps understand the word problem and the steps to solve the word problem: (1) What am I to do at this step, (2) what did I do about it, and (3) any notes to themselves about what worked or didn't work to solve the problem.

iii. The following are the steps in SQRQCQ:

1. Survey word problems
2. Question asked is identified
3. Read more carefully
4. Question process required to solve problem
5. Compute the answer
6. Question self to ensure that the answer solves the problem

Research Base

Cole (1995)

Elliot & Thurlow (2005)

What to Watch for With ELL/CLD Students

i. Newcomers will need to have the SQRQCQ steps modeled and explained in their most proficient language before they can proceed independently.

ii. Students can be paired with partners who are slightly more bilingual than themselves to facilitate their learning this process.

SQRQCQ Element	What am I to do at this step?	What did I do about it?	Notes
Survey word problems			
Question asked is identified			

SQRQCQ Element	What am I to do at this step?	What did I do about it?	Notes
Read more carefully			
Question process required to solve problem			
Compute the answer			
Question self to ensure that the answer solves the problem			

MEDIATED STIMULI IN CLASSROOM

Purpose of the Strategy

   i. Adapt content to meet individual or unique student needs

   ii. Adapt the mode of response required of students

   iii. Build awareness of academic expectations

   iv. Build awareness of adaptation process

   v. Develop association skills

   vi. Develop confidence in school culture interactions

   vii. Enhance ability of students to learn new things

   viii. Expand comprehension

   ix. Improve retention of content

   x. Reduce frustration

   xi. Reduce stress for new students

   xii. Build foundation for learning

   xiii. Reduce anxiety

   xiv. Encourage questioning and exploration of new learning

xv. Improve comprehension

xvi. Reduce culture shock

xvii. Reduce distractibility

xviii. Enhance ability of students to focus on learning

xix. Facilitate discussion about new learning

xx. Reduce distractibility

xxi. Reduce resistance to change

How to Do It

i. This strategy is particularly helpful with new students, students with sensory issues, and those with self-control issues but is also a good way to start the school year with a new class of students.

ii. The teacher may start the year with very little up on the walls or hanging from the ceiling of the room. The goal is fewer distractions and less visual noise and auditory noise, that is, sights and sounds that may be meaningless to students who are unfamiliar with them.

iii. As topics and materials are introduced to the students and become part of their academic world, they can become part of the visual and auditory environment in the classroom. Put up items only after you have introduced them to the students or the students have had a chance to examine them or make them.

iv. The teacher previews new content, new materials, new sounds, and any new activity with the students. Peers provide home and community language explanations.

Research Base

Echevarria, Vogt, & Short (2007)

Feuerstein (1986)

Feuerstein & Hoffman (1982)

Gibbons (2002)

What to Watch for With ELL/CLD Students

i. Newcomers may become overly stimulated by lots of bright, new, unfamiliar, or strange objects, signs, sounds, and miscellany within their new classroom. They do not know what is important to attend to and what is not important. It is all new and exciting.

ii. This also impacts students with undiagnosed neurological conditions that they have not yet learned to accommodate.

iii. It is better to start out with less and add as students become comfortable and familiar with what is in the classroom

MET EXPECTATIONS

Purpose of the Strategy

    i. Alleviate power struggles between teacher and student

    ii. Build appreciation that everyone belongs, is needed

    iii. Build appreciation that everyone has a contribution to make

    iv. Build awareness of academic expectations

    v. Build awareness of school culture expectations

    vi. Clarify responsibilities

    vii. Develop independence in learning situation

    viii. Enhance ability of students to focus on learning

    ix. Improve confidence in school interactions

    x. Reduce anxiety

    xi. Reduce confrontations over minor misbehaving

    xii. Reduce conflicts

How to Do It

    i. This strategy is designed to create a culture in the classroom that is inclusive of all students and allows student to feel comfortable, a sense of belonging, and safe by understanding what is expected of them.

    ii. Before each assignment or independent work time, the teacher explains the expectations and reminds the class of MET on a chart so that everyone has a clear understanding. Pictures can be used for younger classrooms.

MET

    i. **Movement**—what movement is allowed (e.g., can they go to the bathroom, find a different spot, etc.)

    ii. **Expectation**—what students are to accomplish during this period of time

    iii. **Talk Level**—what level the students are supposed to be at (e.g., silent, whisper, etc.)

Research Base

Sousa & Tomlinson (2011)

What to Watch for With ELL/CLD Students

    i. Don't assume students from diverse backgrounds understand how your school or classroom works or what the rules for movement, talk, and expectation are. Each of these need to be explained in language the students understand and can be demonstrated by the teacher or older students.

ii. Students could share stories of how things were done in other schools or other places where there were specific expectations for movement, talk, and task performance.

MIND MAPPING

Purpose of the Strategy

i. Access prior knowledge

ii. Build academic transfer skills

iii. Build first language to English transfer skills

iv. Build upon existing language strengths of student

v. Build upon family language and culture

vi. Build upon the diverse language foundations of students and parents

vii. Build vocabulary

viii. Build awareness of the appropriate content language

ix. Develop analytical skills

x. Facilitate analogy strategies

xi. Develop field sensitive skills

xii. Develop thinking and planning

xiii. Expand and elaborate on learning

xiv. Expand and improve comprehension

xv. Improve retention of content

xvi. Improve writing strategies

xvii. Reinforce content

xviii. Sustain engagement

How to Do It

i. The mind mapping strategy has various forms, but the basic idea is to put the central concept or vocabulary word related to what will be in the lesson in a circle on the board or on a piece of paper. Students then generate other words or concepts related to that main idea and connect them to the center like spokes on a wheel. For each of these ideas or words, another set of connections may be made and so on and so on outward from the center concept.

ii. When applying the mind mapping strategy, students work through problems or tasks using a sequence of ordering, sequencing, and connecting techniques. Suppose you want your students to write a short personal reflection about the story, *Everyone Cooks Rice* by

Norah Dooley, that the class has just finished reading together. You would start by having your students work in small groups of similar ability level.

iii. You would show a copy of a graphic organizer form on the overhead projector or drawn on the whiteboard. Each group would be assigned two or three of the boxes in the graphic organizer. For example, you might assign the most challenged group to fill in the boxes about title, author, location, and country. Another group would be responsible for the main and supporting characters. Another group would be responsible for identifying the sequence of events in the story and a summary statement about these. Another group could be assigned to identify the main problem faced by the main character. After reading the story through the first time, the groups complete their tasks, and you or they write down their answers on the large or projected graphic organizer. Now as a group you ask about how the main problem was resolved, the barriers to resolution, and things in the story that helped solve the problem. The students can discuss the final resolution and what the moral of the story might be from their perspectives. You can expand this activity by comparing and contrasting the story with others like it or with happenings in the students' lives.

iv. You might now step back from the lesson and discuss the metacognitive learning that you have provided students, the learning to learn lesson that is represented by the strategy you had them use.

v. The following are the steps for teaching mind mapping:

1. *Inform* the students what mind mapping is, how it operates, when to use it, and why it is useful. Begin by saying that mind mapping is a way to help them (the students) plan and remember. It works by previewing or putting information concerning the lesson or assignment they are working on into graphic form. Once they learn how to use mind mapping, they can use it anytime and with any content or lesson you give them to do.

2. *Use cues,* metaphors, analogies, or other means of elaborating on a description of mind mapping combined with visual cues. One way to do this is to have the group members look at a blueprint of a house or other building they are familiar with. Have them see how the architect had to plan for everything ahead of time and create a preview or graphic image of what everyone was going to have to do to complete the construction. Explain that almost anyone could help construct the house or building by reading the blueprints, and the ability to read and understand these is a special and critical skill that will be useful to them later in life.

3. *Lead group discussions* about the use of mind mapping. Have students start with talking about a lesson they have just successfully completed. They can go back through the lesson or book using

different mind mapping tools to see how they work and what is required. Encourage them to ask you anything about the learning process they want clarified.

4. *Provide guided practice* in applying mind mapping to particular tasks. Work directly with student groups demonstrating and modeling how to identify elements. Have more skilled students demonstrate for the class.

5. *Provide feedback* on monitoring use and success of mind mapping. While students use mind mapping in small groups, the teacher should move around the room listening and supplying encouragement for consistent use of the tools. As students get more comfortable using these tools, the teacher can have them monitor one another in the use of the strategy.

Research Base

Collier (2002)

Harwell (2001)

Heacox (2002)

Moore, Alvermann, & Hinchman (2000)

Opitz (1998)

What to Watch for With ELL/CLD Students

i. There are cultural differences in cognitive/learning style, and some English language learner (ELL)/culturally and linguistically diverse (CLD) students may not respond to the brainstorming construct behind most mind mapping.

ii. By keeping the graphic design of the mind map as close as possible to the illustrations in the text or some aspect of the lesson, the teacher can more tightly connect the concepts being studied with the questioning that precedes the lesson.

iii. This is another activity that works best with preparation in the students' most proficient language and relevance to their culture before proceeding.

MODELING

Purpose of the Strategy

i. Adapt content to meet individual or unique student needs

ii. Build transfer skills

iii. Sustain engagement

iv. Build awareness of adaptation process

Figure M.2   Example of Mind Mapping

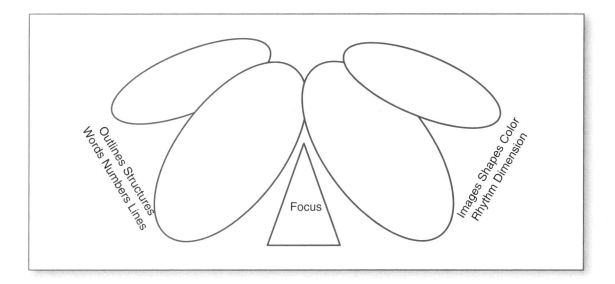

v.   Build awareness of learning process

vi.   Reduce code switching

vii.   Develop cognitive academic language

viii.   Develop independence in learning

ix.   Facilitate connections between known and new

x.   Facilitate acquisition of content

xi.   Improve comprehension and retention

xii.   Minimize ambiguity

xiii.   Reduce anxiety

xiv.   Build transfer skills

xv.   Reduce misperceptions

xvi.   Develop content knowledge foundation

How to Do It

i.   The teacher or assistant uses gestures and diagrams to demonstrate and act out what is expected of the students. The modeling of what to do and what is expected should be done in a realistic context or setting so the students clearly understand what is expected of them when and in what manner.

ii.   The teacher models academic responses and expectations. The situation is explained in home and community language when possible, and each response and expectation is modeled. Students then practice each response and interaction until comfortable and successful.

Research Base

Cole (1995)

Collier (2010a)

Tovani (2000)

What to Watch for With ELL/CLD Students

i.   Remember that some ELL and CLD students have had very little experience with school or with being with people outside of their own family or culture. They may not know what action you are modeling if it is something they have never experienced or seen.

ii. The desired action and response need to be explained in the students' most proficient language.

ABCDEFGHIJKLM**O**PQRSTUVW

OBSERVATION CHARTS

Purpose of the Strategy

   i. Use prior knowledge

  ii. Expand and elaborate on learning

 iii. Facilitate language development

  iv. Reduce off-task behaviors

   v. Expand comprehension

  vi. Build awareness of the learning process

 vii. Facilitate discussion about new learning

viii. Build upon existing language skills of students

  ix. Develop time on task

   x. Develop higher persistence

  xi. Develop thinking and planning skills

 xii. Build academic transfer skills

How to Do It

i. This strategy is very helpful to stimulate students' curiosity about a lesson or upcoming topic. It is a type of inquiry chart that can build up background information for the students while providing the teacher with a diagnostic tool or what students already know or don't know about a topic.

ii. The teacher puts up photographs or illustrations on large pieces of paper, that is, the picture above with space below for writing. Or, the pictures go up in a sequence around the wall of the room with pieces of blank white paper next to each one. This can also be done on a whiteboard or tablets.

iii. The teacher has students work in pairs or small groups in front of each picture. The students are to look at and discuss each picture and then write down their thoughts. Each team is only allowed one pencil so they have to share their ideas and choose which member of the group is going to write down their ideas. They are told to write the following:

- An observation about the picture
- A question about the picture
- A comment about the picture

iv. After everyone has done this, all of the pictures and written remarks are shared with the whole class. The teacher uses this as a way to introduce new content and also as a way to see what students know. He or she can go back and revisit the charts as a way to monitor growth.

Research Case

Brechtel (2001)

What to Watch for With ELL/CLD Students

i. This will work with limited English speaking students if they are paired with students who are fluent bilinguals.

ii. The students will need to have lots of modeling and demonstration to understand what is required of them for each picture and writing.

ORAL DISCUSSIONS

Purpose of the Strategy

i. Build appreciation that everyone has a contribution to make

ii. Build awareness of appropriate cognitive academic language

iii. Reduce code switching

iv. Develop cognitive academic language

v. Improve use of discourse techniques

    vi. Build upon existing language skills and strengths of students

   vii. Reduce distractibility

  viii. Strengthen ability to discuss what is happening

    ix. Encourage questioning and exploration of new learning

    x. Facilitate discussion about new learning

   xi. Develop basic interpersonal communication

   xii. Build transfer skills

  xiii. Develop confidence in school language and rules for academic and social interactions

How to Do It

i. Some teachers may do this so regularly that they do not see it as a separate strategy, but this is not universally the case, and some teachers are not as comfortable with open and wide-ranging discussions in their classrooms.

ii. This strategy is very good for improving language development in all students within an academic content area.

iii. The teacher sets up a routine in the classroom such that students are given multiple opportunities to discuss all aspects of content lessons and to prepare for assessment situations. They are encouraged to hold discussions in both home and community language and English whenever they need to clarify content or directions.

iv. Specific homogeneous and heterogeneous discussion groups may be established and used alternately in varied content-focused activities.

Research Base

Collier (2003a)

Flowerdew & Peacock (2001)

Law & Eckes (2000)

Youb (2008)

What to Watch for With ELL/CLD Students

i. Some teachers are threatened or concerned about students speaking to each other when the teachers do not understand what they are saying. To assure teachers that the students are indeed on task, the teacher can always have these oral discussions focus upon specific tasks, with worksheets or other task production involved so that they can see what is being attended to.

ii. The teacher can also have bilingual student monitors report on what was discussed after these activities.

ORGANIZATION—SORTING

Purpose of the Strategy

i. Access prior knowledge

ii. Build awareness of appropriate academic behaviors

iii. Build academic transfer skills

iv. Build appreciation that everyone belongs and is needed

v. Build appreciation that everyone has a contribution to make

vi. Build foundation for learning

vii. Build metacognition skills

viii. Develop cognitive academic language

ix. Develop cognitive learning strategies

x. Develop problem-solving skills

xi. Encourage questioning and exploration of new learning

xii. Enhance ability of students to focus on learning

xiii. Enhance ability of students to learn new things

xiv. Expand and elaborate on learning

xv. Expand comprehension

xvi. Facilitate access of prior knowledge

xvii. Facilitate discussion about new learning

xviii. Facilitate language development

xix. Improve students' ability to organize and prioritize information

xx. Reinforce content lessons

xxi. Retention of content

xxii. Strengthen ability to discuss what is happening

xxiii. Strengthen awareness of learning process

xxiv. Strengthen knowledge of academic content

xxv. Strengthen language development

xxvi. Strengthen learning to learn skills

xxvii. Strengthen retention and application abilities

xxviii. Sustain engagement

xxix. Use prior knowledge

xxx. Develop analytical skills

xxxi. Build awareness of learning process

xxxii.   Develop association skills

xxxiii.   Develop categorization skills

xxxiv.   Develop field independent skills

xxxv.   Improve mnemonic retrieval

How to Do It

i.   In essence, the teacher gives each group a bag of items related to some topic of discussion or recent unit of instruction. These can be models of objects or the actual items themselves such as colored balls, square blocks, toy animals, plastic fruit, coins, items from a place just visited, or items related to a specific topic. The students are divided into small groups and given a bag full of random items. They are instructed to group or sort the items into groups or sets according to categories selected by the teacher or by the nature of the lesson. The following are the steps for students to follow in implementing this strategy:

1.   What items go together, and why?

2.   What attribute of these am I using to group them?

3.   What do we call each set of items?

4.   How are the groups similar to one another?

5.   How are the groups different from one another?

6.   How can we generalize this information?

ii.   The teacher may assign students of similar language and ability to either heterogeneous or homogeneous groups depending upon his or her specific goals. Rather than preparing a bag of items, the teacher could also direct students to empty out their back packs and work in small groups. Each small group goes through their steps, sorting all the items in their piles together. They make lists of their groups of items to share with the class.

iii.   When applying the organization-sorting strategy, students work through problems or tasks using the above sequence of self-monitoring questions. For example, imagine you are going to have a new unit about rocks and minerals, that is, igneous, sedimentary, conglomerate, and so on. Many of your students are unfamiliar with these ways of grouping natural materials that they consider generically as rocks. One group of students comes from a culture where rocks are grouped by hard versus soft and another from a culture that groups rocks by whether they can be used to produce something in the home. You might introduce your class to the lesson by having actual examples of the rocks to be studied present to handle or take the class on a field trip to the museum or a local mine or industrial area to observe them. You could also show pictures or videos of chemists interacting with the materials. Have the students look for patterns in appearance, use, environment, chemical reactions, and so on. They could chart the attributes and characteristics of the rocks and minerals on a graph or in Venn diagrams (Step 1 of sorting, "What elements go together?"). Now they should look for distinctive patterns of commonality between rocks and minerals that show whether or not they go together (Step 2 of sorting, "What attribute of these am I using to group them?"). Ask the students what they would name the group of rocks and minerals based upon the major attributes. Now introduce them to the common English name of the group (Step 3 of sorting, "What do we call each group?"). Discuss how the materials within each group share certain common characteristics, and then discuss the characteristics that all rocks and minerals share in common as rocks and minerals (Step 4 of sorting, "How are the groups similar to one another?"). Discuss how the rocks within each group might differ from each other, how each group of rocks and minerals differs from the other groups, and how rocks differ from nonrocks (Step 5 of sorting, "How are the groups different from one another?"). Finish the unit with a discussion of how to find patterns in anything you are studying (Step 6 of sorting, "What generalizable patterns do I see?").

iv. You might now step back from the lesson and discuss the enhanced cognitive learning that you have provided students, the learning to learn lesson that is represented by the strategy you had them use. At this point, you would discuss how everything in the world is composed of various elements that need to be identified in order to understand the whole thing being studied (field independence) and that when all the parts are put together the meaning of the whole thing results (field sensitive).

Research Base

Ferris & Hedgcock (2005)

Iachini, Borghi, & Senese (2008)

What to Watch for With ELL/CLD Students

i. The strategy preparation can be done in the native language or dialect of the students to assure their understanding of your expectations and their task prior to carrying the assignment out in English or other communication mode.

ii. Understand that all cultures have different ways of thinking of common attributes of a group of similar objects. What constitutes the criteria to pay attention to will vary based upon cultural values and learning practices. While it seems obvious to one group that the predominant surface color of a set of objects is what links them together as a set of objects, to another group it might be that surface texture or size is more important as an attribute for sorting out similarity and difference.

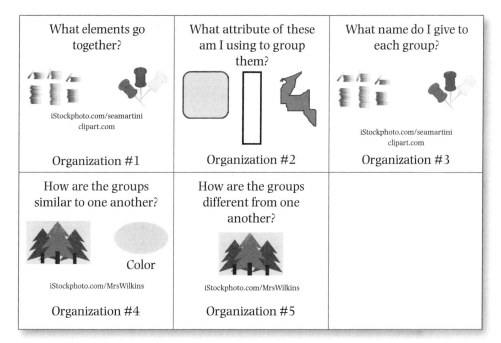

What elements go together?	What attribute of these am I using to group them?	What name do I give to each group?
iStockphoto.com/seamartini clipart.com		iStockphoto.com/seamartini clipart.com
Organization #1	Organization #2	Organization #3
How are the groups similar to one another?	How are the groups different from one another?	
Color		
iStockphoto.com/MrsWilkins	iStockphoto.com/MrsWilkins	
Organization #4	Organization #5	

Source: Collier (2008).

ABCDEFGHIJKLMNOPQRSTUVW

PARAPHRASING—RAP

Purpose of the Strategy

  i. Build academic transfer skills

  ii. Build awareness of appropriate cognitive academic language

  iii. Assist students to learn information through paraphrasing

  iv. Facilitate language development

  v. Improve comprehension

  vi. Improve reading comprehension

  vii. Improve retention of content

  viii. Build foundation for learning

  ix. Build vocabulary

  x. Develop academic language

  xi. Develop thinking and planning

  xii. Enhance ability of students to focus on learning

xiii. Expand comprehension

xiv. Facilitate reading process

xv. Improve retention of content

xvi. Improve writing strategies

xvii. Improve students' ability to organize and prioritize information

xviii. Strengthen knowledge of academic content

xix. Strengthen language development

xx. Strengthen learning to learn skills

xxi. Strengthen retention and application abilities

How to Do It

i. This strategy is a way to assist students to learn information through paraphrasing and is one of several reading comprehension techniques for improved retention of information.

ii. The teacher creates a chart or poster with RAP and reminders with pictures or symbols for what each letter stands for: Read the paragraph, ask about the main idea and two supporting details, and put main idea and details into own words.

iii. The teacher demonstrates what this means and how to do it with different writing excerpts from books the students are familiar with. He or she asks different students to put these familiar excerpts into their own words and puts all the examples up on the chart.

iv. The following are the steps in RAP:

1. Read paragraph

2. Ask self the main idea and two supporting details

3. Put main idea and details into own words

Research Base

Cole (1995)

Dang, Dang, & Ruiter (2005)

Ellis & Lenz (1987)

Odean (1987)

	Check this box when you have completed the step	What do you think about what you read, asked, or did?
Read paragraph		
Ask self the main idea and two supporting details		
Put main idea and details into own words		

What to Watch for With ELL/CLD Students

    i. Newcomers will need to have the RAP steps modeled and explained in their most proficient language before they can proceed independently.

    ii. Students can be paired with partners who are slightly more bilingual than themselves to facilitate their learning this process.

PARS—RETENTION STRATEGY

Purpose of the Strategy

    i. Build academic transfer skills

    ii. Develop cognitive learning strategies

    iii. Access prior knowledge

    iv. Build awareness of school culture expectations

    v. Develop thinking and planning skills

    vi. Improve retention of content

    vii. Increase students' time on task

    viii. Increase the frequency of appropriate responses or behaviors

    ix. Increase time on task

    x.   Strengthen knowledge of academic content

    xi.   Strengthen language development

    xii.   Strengthen learning to learn skills

    xiii.   Sustain engagement

    xiv.   Expand and elaborate on learning

    xv.   Facilitate reading process

    xvi.   Expand and improve comprehension

    xvii.   Build awareness of learning process

    xviii.   Develop academic language

    xix.   Improve mnemonic retrieval

    xx.   Reduce confusion in locus of control

    xxi.   Retention of content

    xxii.   Develop extended time on task

How to Do It

    i.   The PARS retention strategy framework provides a structure for understanding what is being learned and retaining the information for later application.

    ii.   The teacher or assistant introduces students to PARS with charts and diagrams going through each step before giving students their own PARS chart or sheet with the PARS frame upon it.

    iii.   The teacher models each PARS element with a lesson with which the students are familiar, showing students what is meant by previewing the content, then asking questions about the content going on, reading the materials completely, and finally summarizing what has been read in your own words.

    iv.   PARS is recommended for use with students who have limited experiences with study strategies. Students can create cue cards or use posters to remind themselves of the steps.

    v.   The following are the steps in PARS:

        1. Preview

        2. Ask questions

        3. Read

        4. Summarize

PARS Element	What am I to do at this step?	What did I do about it?	Notes
Preview			
Ask questions			
Read			
Summarize			

Research Base

Derwinger, Stigsdotter Neely, & Baeckman (2005)

Lee (2005)

Smith (2000)

What to Watch for With ELL/CLD Students

i. Newcomers will need to have the PARS steps modeled and explained in their most proficient language before they can proceed independently.

ii. Students can be paired with partners who are slightly more bilingual than themselves to facilitate their learning this process.

PARTICIPANT COLLAGE

Purpose of the Strategy

i.   Build appreciation that everyone belongs and is needed

ii. Build appreciation that everyone has a contribution to make

iii. Build awareness of adaptation process

iv. Build awareness of appropriate academic behaviors

v.   Develop confidence in school culture interactions

vi. Develop positive peer relationships

vii. Encourage pride in students' personal history

viii. Facilitate school adaptation

ix. Facilitate student self-concept

x.   Improve confidence and self-esteem

xi. Lower anxiety levels

How to Do It

i.   his strategy is used to facilitate a culture in the classroom that is inclusive of all students and to allow for the students to feel comfortable, a sense of belonging, and safe

ii. The teacher creates a collage representing the whole class with images for each student.

iii. The collage is a visual representation of each student. It can be done with magazine pictures or item brought from home. The collage is to represent them and should be displayed in the classroom so that each student has a piece of work displayed. For older students it can be a quilt or timeline.

iv. The teacher and any specialist should also partake, as well as any volunteers. This allows for everyone in the classroom to be represented.

v.   Teachers can present theirs and offer students to present as well.

vi. The collage should be allowed to be added onto as a student grows.

Research Base

Herrera (2010)

Sousa & Tomlinson (2011)

What to Watch for With ELL/CLD Students

i.   Newcomers or individuals from certain cultures may struggle with the concept of a piece of work representing themselves. The work can represent their family or culture.

PARTNERS—READING STRATEGY

Purpose of the Strategy

   i.   Adapt content to meet individual or unique student needs

  ii.   Build academic transfer skills

 iii.   Build awareness of learning process

  iv.   Build foundation for learning

   v.   Ensure that each student is familiar with specific academic and behavioral expectations

  vi.   Build upon students' existing language skills

 vii.   Develop basic interpersonal communication

viii.   Develop, reinforce, strengthen content knowledge foundation

  ix.   Extend, develop time on task

   x.   Facilitate discussion about new learning

  xi.   Recognize importance of working together

 xii.   Reduce misperceptions

xiii.   Facilitate students' comfort with learning environment

 xiv.   Develop constructive peer relationships

  xv.   Improve motivation

 xvi.   Minimize behavior problems

How to Do It

   i.   This strategy is a reading/listening technique that can be used in any content area. Students read aloud to one another from the textbook.

  ii.   The teacher matches up students with a stronger reader partnered with a student who needs more practice. The reading/listening pairs can be switched out as often as needed to give everyone a chance.

 iii.   With partners, each student participates either as an interested listener or as reader, while the teacher moves from pair to pair listening. Reading can be varied by changing partners. Children can reread parts of a story in pairs after the directed reading activity rather than have one student read while the others all listen. During this time, the students have a chance to help each other.

  iv.   With science and math lessons, different partners may be used, matching a successful learner with one just slightly less successful and so on down the line. Problem solution can be revisited by changing partners and redoing the problem and solution.

Research Base

Kamps (2007)

Koskinen & Blum (1984)

Wood & Algozzine (1994)

Wood & Harmon (2001)

Zutell & Rasinski (1991)

What to Watch for With ELL/CLD Students

i. Partners must be selected carefully with specific objectives in mind. If competence and understanding of the content is the goal, then similar language skills are necessary.

ii. If expansion and transition of learning is the goal, then paring a less proficient student with a more proficient bilingual partner will help.

iii. If challenging application is the goal, then paring very differently skilled students may work.

PEARL

Figure P.1 Example of the PEARL Stragegy

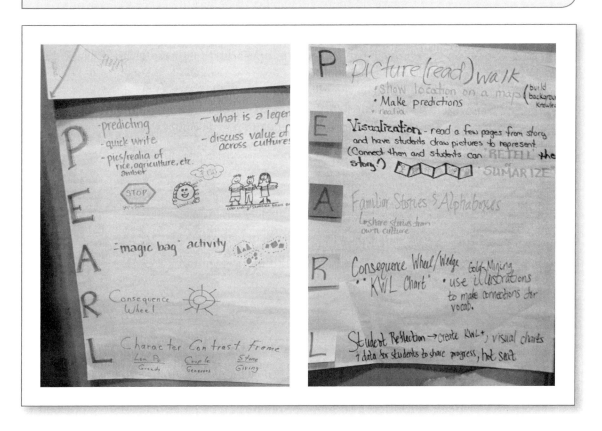

Purpose of the Strategy

    i. Access prior knowledge

    ii. Build academic transfer skills

    iii. Build awareness of academic expectations

    iv. Build awareness of appropriate academic behaviors

    v. Build awareness of appropriate social and academic language

    vi. Build awareness of learning process

    vii. Build foundation for learning

    viii. Build awareness of school culture expectations

    ix. Build upon existing language skills of students

    x. Develop content knowledge foundation

    xi. Develop problem-solving skills

    xii. Develop self-monitoring skills

    xiii. Develop thinking and planning skills

    xiv. Enhance awareness of school adaptation process

    xv. Facilitate acquisition of content knowledge

    xvi. Improve retention of content

    xvii. Increase students' probability of generating a correct response

    xiii. Increase students' time on task

    xx. Increase the frequency of appropriate responses or behaviors

    xxi. Increase time on task

    xxii. Reduce fears associated with assignments

    xxiii. Reduce resistance to change

    xxiv. Strengthen knowledge of academic content

    xxv. Develop cognitive academic language

    xxvi. Develop cognitive learning strategies

    xxvii. Enhance ability of students to focus on learning

    xxviii. Facilitate discussion about new learning

    xxix. Improve and expand comprehension

    xxx. Strengthen learning to learn skills

    xxxi. Strengthen retention and application abilities

How to Do It

    i. PEARL is a strategy for organizing every instructional interaction or intervention to maximize cognitive learning for all students regardless of background or language ability. It consists of five key action focus points for teacher and students to take together at every instructional interaction.

ii. These 5 focal points are preparing, embedding, attaching, ratcheting, and looking back. Students discuss each step and why they are to do it.

1. PREPARE and preview everything using comprehensible input strategies. Use prediction, preparation, preview, and general overview of what is to come in the lesson or activity. This may involve questioning, imagining, or anticipating what is to come or a full-fledged brainstorming activity.

2. EMBED all instruction in context rich activities. Embed instruction in concrete, explicit structure or models, making sure that concrete context is used. This may involve using real objects, models, and demonstrations or the use of specific cues and guide structures.

3. ATTACH to what has already been learned at home and in previous schooling. Always connect learning to prior lessons and knowledge. Make connections between the new content or activity and things that are familiar to the learner, making meaningful attachments through analogies and illustrations between the known and the unknown. This may involve lessons highlighting similarities and differences between the new and the known or compare and contrast activities.

4. RATCHET up learning. Extend and build upon what is learned like cogs in a gear mechanism Enrich and expand upon learning. Use skills in Lesson 1 to strengthen Lesson 2 learning, use skills in Lesson 2 to strengthen Lesson 1, and so on. This may involve teaching specific generalization techniques or using transfer and application strategies.

5. LOOK BACK at what was learned and how learning occurred. Review content as well as the strategies used to learn. Have students reflect upon what they have learned and how they will use this information. Have students discuss why the lesson was taught the way it was and what strategies facilitated their learning. This may involve teaching specific strategies for summarizing and reflecting upon the lessons.

Research Base

Collier (2012b)

Collins Block & Mangieri (2003)

Gardner (1993b)

Roessingh, Kover, & Watt (2005)

Strickland, Ganske, & Monroe (2002)

Walter (2004)

What to Watch for With ELL/CLD Students

i. Particular social groups and cultures have different expectations for learning and teaching. This is a learned difference between cultures. The teacher needs to be aware that the expectations in an American school and assumptions about how learning occurs may need to be taught directly to culturally and linguistically diverse (CLD) students and not just assumed to be understood.

ii. One way to introduce the idea of learning to learn strategies specific to your classroom is to ask students about how their parents have them learn things, actions, or tasks at home. This can then be expanded to the idea of learning to learn in your classroom.

iii. Demonstrate all of the desired behaviors and strategies. Some role-play may be helpful. Examples of good learning strategies are helpful. Examples of ineffective or poor learning behaviors may be used with caution.

Student's Name	Teacher	
Date of intervention	Lesson	
P	Plan	
PREVIEW	Observation	
E	Plan	
EMBED	Observation	
A	Plan	
ATTACH	Observation	

R	Plan
RATCHET	Observation
L	Plan
LOOK BACK	Observation

PEER/SCHOOL ADAPTATION PROCESS SUPPORT

Purpose of the Strategy

   i. Adapt to meet individual or unique student needs

   ii. Adapt the mode of response required of students

   iii. Build academic transfer skills

   iv. Build awareness of academic expectations

   v. Build awareness of appropriate academic behaviors

   vi. Build awareness of appropriate behaviors for school language and rules

   vii. Build awareness of appropriate communication behaviors for school language and rules

   viii. Build awareness of adaptation process

   ix. Build foundation for learning

   x. Develop basic interpersonal communication

   xi. Develop confidence in school culture interactions

   xii. Reduce culture shock

   xiii. Build retention

   xiv. Strengthen knowledge of academic content

   xv. Strengthen ability to discuss what is happening

   xvi. Reduce anxiety and stress

How to Do It

i. This strategy is most effective where there are more than a few diverse learners at each grade level and where some of these students have been in the school for more than a year or two.

ii. Primary level: Successful older students in the upper grades assist younger students around the school building and during lunch and play times. This can be used in conjunction with and as a supplement to a peer buddy system within individual classrooms.

iii. Intermediate level: This strategy works well with facilitating adaptation and communication. A peer support group is established and given time to meet regularly. The support group discusses their experiences with school adaptation and how they are dealing with culture shock. Successful students from the secondary level may assist as peer support models.

iv. Secondary level: This strategy works well with facilitating adaptation and communication and also may assist as students prepare to transition out of school into the work environment. A peer support group is established and given time to meet regularly. The peer support group discusses their experiences with school adaptation and how they are dealing with culture shock and specific language and learning transition issues. This may be paired with a college mentor program.

Research Base

Carrigan (2001)

What to Watch for With ELL/CLD Students

i. Students may wish to discuss their struggles only in the home language and with peers from similar backgrounds. With first generation refugee and immigrant groups, the teacher must be careful about pairing students of similar language background without also considering cultural and class differences that may exist.

ii. The teacher must be prepared to deal with prejudice between populations where language is the same but culture, class, or racial issues may impede comfort and communication. American all togetherness may come in time, but the teacher must proceed slowly and not push.

iii. Students may interact more as they become more comfortable in the classroom or more trusting that they are accepted and valued.

PENS—WRITING STRATEGY

Purpose of the Strategy

i. Facilitate access of prior knowledge

ii. Build academic transfer skills

  iii. Build foundation for learning

  iv. Build awareness of appropriate social and academic language

  v. Build awareness of learning process

  vi. Develop thinking and planning skills

  vii. Facilitate language development

  viii. Facilitate writing process

  ix. Improve vocabulary

  x. Improve writing strategies

  xi. Increase focus on reading

  xii. Reduce distractibility

  xiii. Reduce impulsivity

  xiv. Reinforce content lessons

  xv. Strengthen language development

  xvi. Strengthen learning to learn skills

  xvii. Sustain engagement with reading and writing

  xviii. Build and improve vocabulary

  xix. Develop academic language

  xx. Develop analytical skills

  xxi. Develop basic sentence structure

  xxii. Develop extended time on task

  xxiii. Develop problem-solving skills

  xxiv. Expand and improve comprehension

  xxv. Improve reading and writing strategies

How to Do It

  i. PENS is a strategy for writing and composition skills to expand language arts capabilities and developing basic sentence structure.

  ii. The teacher introduces PENS with charts and individual worksheets that students can use while working on a writing assignment. He or she gives the students several formulas for sentence construction using cloze techniques or other graphic frames and models. The teacher also provides word subject action object lists to choose from in completing the sentences.

  iii. PENS assists students to write different types of sentences following formulas for sentence construction. The following are the steps in PENS:

  1. Pick a formula

  2. Explore different words that fit the formula

3. Note the words selected

4. Subject and verb selections follow

Research Base

Derwinger, Stigsdotter Neely, & Baeckman (2005)

Eskritt & McLeod (2008)

What to Watch for With ELL/CLD Students

i. Newcomers will need to have the PENS steps modeled and explained in their most proficient language before they can proceed independently.

ii. Students can be paired with partners who are slightly more bilingual than themselves to facilitate their learning this process.

PENS Process Steps	What am I to do at this step?	What did I do about it?	Example of What I Used
Pick a formula			
Explore different words that fit the formula			
Note the words selected			
Subject and verb selections follow			

PERSONAL TIMELINES

Purpose of the Strategy

i. Build transfer skills

ii. Access prior knowledge

iii. Build appreciation that everyone belongs and is needed

iv. Build appreciation that everyone has a contribution to make

    v.   Build first language to English transfer skills

   vi.   Build foundation for learning

  vii.   Develop self-esteem

 viii.   Develop thinking and planning skills

   ix.   Enhance student interaction with family during transition

    x.   Expand and elaborate on learning

   xi.   Expand comprehension

  xii.   Facilitate access of prior knowledge

 xiii.   Facilitate analogy strategies

 xiv.   Facilitate connections between known and new

  xv.   Build vocabulary

 xvi.   Develop categorization skills

 xvii.   Improve access to prior knowledge

xviii.   Improve comprehension

 xix.   Improve confidence and self-esteem

  xx.   Improve school/parent partnership

 xxi.   Improve sequencing skills

 xxii.   Sustain engagement

xxiii.   Build upon family culture

xxiv.   Develop association skills

 xxv.   Reduce culture shock

xxvi.   Develop awareness of cause and effect

xxvii.   Develop time on task

xxiii.   Facilitate discussion about new learning

xxiv.   Strengthen school/parent partnerships

How to Do It

   i.   The teacher selects the events or length of time to cover, for example, two years, five years, or such as appropriate to the age and developmental level of the students. The teacher gives the students an event in time or a length of time as a framework. The students research and then tell about their personal or family history during this event or length of time. Students may create booklets about their memories, their families, and so on.

ii. Students tell about their homeland or family history and create booklets about their memories. Their family or personal memories for a period of time can be juxtaposed against a national or historical event during the same time period and compared with what was happening to other students during that same time period.

Research Base

Carrigan (2001)

What to Watch for With ELL/CLD Students

i. Students may be reluctant to describe or discuss what happened to their family during this time period or specific event. Very difficult or painful things may have occurred for this student or family.

ii. The teacher must be prepared to deal with sensitive information should it arise and also to know when not to push further for information. Only elicit information that the student is comfortable sharing at that particular point in time.

iii. Students may share more as they become more comfortable in the classroom or more trusting that the information will not be used against them or their family.

Figure P.2   Example of Personal Timeline

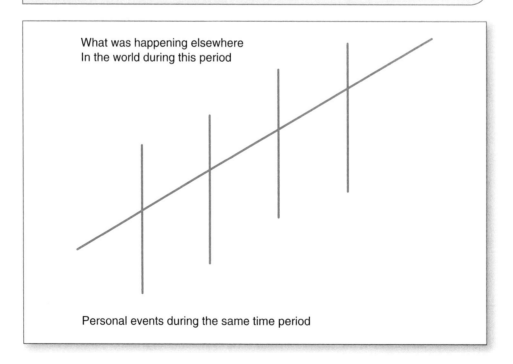

What was happening elsewhere
In the world during this period

Personal events during the same time period

Beginning = 1   Developing = 2   Proficient = 3   Advanced = 4

Data Collection for Monitoring: __Timeline activity____

Participant	Following directions	Provided personal items	Able to come up with world events	Able to compare own to others	Able to describe similarities	Able to explain process
1						
2						
3						
4						
5						

PICTURE THIS!

Purpose of the Strategy

i. Build transfer skills

ii. Adapt content to meet individual or unique student needs

iii. Adapt the mode of response required of students

iv. Improve retention of information

v. Build foundation for learning

vi. Facilitate comprehension

vii. Strengthen retention and application abilities

viii. Sustain engagement

ix. Reduce misperceptions

x. Reinforce content

xi. Organize information

xii. Develop vocabulary

How to Do It

i. Teachers can use this strategy to illustrate unit vocabulary and concepts when introducing a new unit of instruction. It provides graphic cues about content that will help struggling learners and reinforce the learning of more able learners.

ii. Ahead of time, the teacher creates a faint line drawing of the concept you will be discussing using an opaque, overhead, or document camera. The teacher enlarges the picture and traces it on butcher paper in light pencil, including vocabulary words and notes. It should be very light as the teacher will be the only one seeing these guidelines and will be marking over them in darker ink.

iii. When using this to teach, the teacher will hang it up on the wall where students can see you. He or she will give the while tracing over the images with markers, providing verbal input, and adding vocabulary words on the image.

iv. The teacher can make smaller versions of the image for students to use and color later and write in vocabulary words as pertinent.

v. Revisit to add word cards and review the information.

vi. Make smaller versions of the image for students to use and color in later.

Research Base

Brechtel (2001)

What to Watch for With ELL/CLD Students

i. Make sure the image you use for this is very clear. You want to be sure the students can recognize and follow what you are speaking about.

ii. Some cultures have taboos on graphic representations of certain people, objects, actions, or symbols. Be sure to double check this before proceeding.

PIRATES—TEST TAKING STRATEGY

Purpose of the Strategy

i. Build academic transfer skills

ii. Build awareness of learning process

iii. Build awareness of school culture expectations

iv. Clarify responsibilities, assignments, and rewards

v. Develop confidence in academic interactions

vi. Develop extended time on task

vii. Develop thinking and planning skills

viii. Improve confidence and self-esteem

ix. Improve mnemonic retrieval

x. Improve test-taking skills

xi. Increase students' probability of generating a correct response

   xii. Increase students' time on task

   xiii. Reduce anxiety and stress

   xiv. Reduce distractibility

   xv. Sustain engagement

   xvi. Enhance and improve time on task

   xvii. Develop problem-solving skills

   xviii. Expand and elaborate on learning

   xix. Improve student ability to organize and prioritize information

   xx. Build awareness of learning process

   xxi. Improve test-taking skills for typical achievement tests

How to Do It

i. PIRATES may assist learners to complete tests more carefully and successfully. Students can create cue cards of the mnemonic and use them to work through each test and individual test item. The following are the steps in PIRATES:

1. Prepare to succeed
2. Inspect instructions carefully
3. Read entire question, remember strategies, and reduce choices
4. Answer question or leave until later
5. Turn back to the abandoned items
6. Estimate unknown answers by avoiding absolutes and eliminating similar choices
7. Survey to ensure that all items have a response

Research Base

DeVries Guth & Stephens Pettengill (2005)

Hughes, Deshler, Ruhl, & Schumaker (1993)

Lebzelter & Nowacek (1999)

What to Watch for With ELL/CLD Students

i. Newcomers will need to have the PIRATES steps modeled and explained in their most proficient language before they can proceed independently.

ii. Students can be paired with partners who are slightly more bilingual than themselves to facilitate their learning this process.

PIRATES Step	PIRATES Test Taking Outcomes
P Prepare to succeed	
I Inspect instructions carefully	
R Read entire question, remember strategies, and reduce choices	
A Answer question or leave until later	
T Turn back to the abandoned items	
E Estimate unknown answers by avoiding absolutes and eliminating similar choices	
S Survey to ensure that all items have a response	

PLANNED IGNORING

Purpose of the Strategy

i. Build awareness of appropriate behaviors

ii. Build self-awareness of behavior

iii. Adapt to meet individual or unique student needs

iv. Adapt the mode of response required of students

v. Reduce inappropriate behaviors

vi. Reduce off-task behaviors

vii. Facilitate nondirective guidance about student misbehavior

viii. Facilitate student regaining control over self

ix. Prevent minor inappropriate behaviors from escalating

x. Reduce confrontations over minor misbehaving

xi. Eliminate inappropriate behavior after a few moments

How to Do It

i. The teacher purposely ignores certain behaviors exhibited by students.

ii. For example, the teacher elects to ignore some whispering between two students during independent work time.

iii. This can also be accompanied by commenting on or recognizing another student's appropriate behavior without saying anything about the student who is misbehaving.

Research Base

Grossman (2003)

Hall & Hall (1998)

Rafferty (2007)

What to Watch for With ELL/CLD Students

i. Some English language learner (ELL) and culturally and linguistically diverse (CLD) students may have limited experience with attending schools and not know what the rules are within classrooms.

ii. In some cultures, a student who understands some task is expected to assist his or her relative or friend who may not be doing so well with a task, so some quiet helping should be allowed as long as it appears to be on task.

PLANNED MOVEMENT

Purpose of the Strategy

i. Build awareness of appropriate behaviors

ii. Build self-awareness of behavior

iii. Facilitate nondirective guidance about student misbehavior

iv. Facilitate student regaining control over self

v. Prevent minor inappropriate behaviors from escalating

vi. Reduce confrontations over minor misbehaving

vii. Eliminate inappropriate behavior after a few moments

viii. Prevent inappropriate moving around the room

ix. Minimize behavior problems in the classroom

How to Do It

i. The teacher establishes specific times and under what specific circumstances students are allowed to move about the classroom.

ii. Periodically provide students opportunities to move about the classroom for appropriate reasons.

iii. For example, the teacher allows students to move to a learning center or study booth for part of their independent work time instead of remaining seated at their desks for the entire period.

Research Base

Evertson & Neal (2006)

Evertson & Weinstein (2006)

Kaufman (2001)

Williams (2008)

What to Watch for With ELL/CLD Students

i. Differences in mobility and movement by children are learned differences among cultures and social groups. In some families, children are expected to get up and move around whenever they want to, in others, children are expected to remain seated or in one place unless and until they are given permission to move elsewhere.

ii. Some children may have undiagnosed conditions that inhibit their sitting or standing in one place without moving occasionally. Using planned movement and making accommodations for opportunities for students to move facilitates learning for all students.

POSITIVE REINFORCEMENT

Purpose of the Strategy

i. Alleviate power struggles between teacher and student

ii. Build appreciation that everyone has a contribution to make

iii. Build awareness of academic expectations

iv. Build student self-awareness of behavior

v. Clarify responsibilities, assignments, and rewards

vi. Build awareness of relation between cause and effect

vii. Build awareness of school culture expectations

viii. Develop association skills

ix. Develop extended time on task

x. Ensure student is familiar with specific academic and behavioral expectations

xi. Ensure that students are aware of and responsible for their own actions

xii. Improve confidence in school interactions

xiii. Lower anxiety levels

xiv. Develop awareness of cause and effect

xv. Develop higher persistence

xvi. Develop self-esteem

xvii. Facilitate student self-concept as a successful person

xviii. Facilitate students' comfort with learning environment

xix. Improve confidence and motivation

xx. Increase the frequency of appropriate responses or behaviors

xxi. Minimize behavior problems

xxii. Reduce confusion of locus of control

xxiii. Reduce low persistence behaviors

xxiv. Sustain engagement

How to Do It

i. The teacher provides feedback or rewards for completing appropriate tasks or behaving in appropriate ways.

ii. For example, the teacher provides a student extra free time when his or her math or reading assignment has been completed.

Research Base

Cole (1995)

Harwell (2001)

Opitz (1998)

What to Watch for With ELL/CLD Students

i. What is rewarding to one person is not necessarily rewarding to another. This is another learned preference.

ii. The teacher should use a variety of affirmatives, words, and phrases to denote reinforcement.

iii. When using physical rewards, always do some research to identify culturally, developmentally, and gender appropriate items.

iv. When using extra time or a special activity as a reward, vary these depending upon the students' interests.

Affirmatives This is really complete.	Good thinking.	You really out did yourself today.
You haven't missed a thing.	Sensational!	I really appreciate _____ (be specific).
That's a very good observation.	Thank you.	Where did you get so much information on that topic?
That's the way to do it!	Super!	I'm proud of the way you worked today.
I appreciate your help.	Excellent!	You're working like you're getting paid.
That's coming along really well.	Great!	That's an interesting way of looking at it.
You are really going to town.	Perfect. That's it.	That kind of behavior makes me happy.
I appreciate your insight.	Exactly right.	That really shows effort on your part.
That kind of work makes my day!	Good for you.	I can see that you are really concerned.
Now you have it.	Marvelous!	Thanks, gang! Let's share what we have.
Thank you for your contribution.	Wow!	I appreciate the way you're working.
I appreciate your spirit.	Good!	It is a pleasure to help when you work like this.
Can you expand on that idea for me?	Beautiful.	I'm very proud of the way you participated today.
Thanks for the effort.	That's really nice.	Thank you for _____ (be specific).
You really care, don't you?	Absolutely!	That looks like it's going to be a great report.
I appreciate your concern.	That's great!	You're on the right track now.
Keep up the good work.	This is a good job.	That is a good point.
That's quite an improvement.	Much better.	Thank you for raising your hand, Joe. What is it?
I can really tell you're thinking.	Very creative.	That is an interesting point of view.
Thanks for doing this project for us.	Excellent work.	Now you've figured it out.
You like that, don't you?	Good point.	I appreciate your sincerity.
That's a powerful thought.	Fantastic.	Very interesting.
Thank you very much.	Good going!	Incredible!

PQ4R—READING COMPREHENSION

Purpose of the Strategy

     i. Build awareness of learning process

    ii. Access prior knowledge

    iii. Build academic transfer skills

    iv. Build confidence in independent work

    v. Build foundation for learning

    vi. Build learners' confidence in their control of the learning process

    vii. Build students' self-awareness of behavior

    viii. Enhance ability of students to focus on learning

    ix. Expand and elaborate on learning

    x. Expand comprehension

    xi. Facilitate access of prior knowledge

    xii. Facilitate reading process

    xiii. Increase focus on reading

    xiv. Increase students' probability of generating a correct response

    xv. Increase students' time on task

    xvi. Improve student's ability to organize and prioritize information

    xvii. Reduce off-task behaviors

    xviii. Strengthen awareness of learning process

    xix. Develop analytical skills

    xx. Develop confidence in independent learning

    xxi. Increase focus on reading

    xxii. Increase and expand time on task

    xxiii. Improve ability to organize and prioritize information

    xxiv. Encourage questioning and exploration of new learning

    xxv. Develop problem solving

    xxvi. Develop thinking and planning

    xxvii. Improve and expand reading comprehension

    xxviii. Improve access to prior knowledge

    xxix. Expand and elaborate on learning foundation

    xxx. Build transfer skills

How to Do It

i. PQ4R may assist students to become more discriminating readers and retain more of what they are reading.

ii. The teacher creates a poster or chart of PQ4R with the words preview, question, read, reflect, recite, and review down the side. He or she reviews each word and what it means in the context of reading a book or text about something. The teacher demonstrates how to do each of these active reading techniques.

iii. The teacher gives each student his or her own worksheet with PQ4R on it and has students consider what they are to do at each step while reading a particular passage in their textbook or story. They write down what they are to do on their worksheets. As they read, they make notes that correspond to the steps. After they are done reading, they go back over their worksheet and write down what they did for each step.

iv. The following are the steps in PQ4R:

1. Preview
2. Question
3. Read
4. Reflect
5. Recite
6. Review

Research Base

Anderson (2000)

Hamachek (1994)

Pelow & Colvin (1983)

Sanacore (1982)

What to Watch for With ELL/CLD Students

i. Newcomers will need to have the PQ4R steps modeled and explained in their most proficient language before they can proceed independently.

ii. Students can be paired with partners who are slightly more bilingual than themselves to facilitate their learning this process.

PROMPTING

Purpose of the Strategy

i. Adapt the mode of response required of students

ii. Adapt content to meet individual or unique student needs

PQ4R Element	What am I to do at this step?	What did I do about it?	Notes
Preview			
Question			
Read			
Reflect			
Recite			
Review			

iii. Build academic transfer skills

iv. Build awareness of school culture expectations

v. Build confidence in independent work

vi. Build students' self-awareness of behavior

vii. Clarify responsibilities, assignments, and rewards

viii. Develop confidence in academic interactions

ix. Develop association skills

x. Develop extended time on task

xi. Enhance awareness of school adaptation process

xii. Expand and elaborate on learning

xiii.   Expand comprehension

xiv.   Facilitate individualization

xv.   Facilitate school adaptation process

xvi.   Facilitate student self-evaluation skills

xvii.   Improve motivation

xviii.   Increase students' time on task

xix.   Minimize behavior problems

xx.   Reduce culture shock

xxi.   Reduce distractibility

xxii.   Build awareness of academic expectations

xxiii.   Build upon existing skills of students

xxiv.   Enhance ability to focus on learning

xxv.   Develop higher tolerance

xxvi.   Expand and elaborate on comprehension and learning

xxvii.   Build transfer skills

xxviii.   Sustain engagement

xxix.   Develop personal control of situations

xxx.   Increase students' probability of generating a correct response.

xxxi.   Use prior knowledge

How to Do It

i.   The teacher provides reminders through cues or prompts to students about the task or activity they are working on. He or she observes students working on an assignment, goes to a student who is struggling, and offers a clue or hint about what to do next.

ii.   Sometimes prompts are offered about classroom behavior. These can be light taps on a shoulder or pointing at a poster illustrating the appropriate behavior. I have used sound cues to prompt shifts between activities or as a reminder about when it is almost time to stop a task.

iii.   For example, the teacher could underline one letter of a pair of letters that a student is studying. Focus attention on characteristics of both letters to reduce confusion.

Research Base

Ferris & Hedgcock (2005)

Houghton & Bain (1993)

What to Watch for With ELL/CLD Students

   i. All cultures have guidelines about how you should give help to a child or another person. Prompting is a kind of helping.

   ii. These guidelines are mostly unspoken and learned through being raised in the culture and community.

   iii. Find someone in the cultural community who can brief you about what is acceptable or expected regarding supporting and helping learners. It may well be that you are expected to help a great deal more than you think is appropriate. This will be your own cue that your students will need a lot of guidance in how to use prompts appropriately.

PROOF READING—COPS

Purpose of the Strategy

   i. Build awareness of learning

   ii. Build awareness of adaptation process

   iii. Facilitate and access prior knowledge

   iv. Build transfer skills

   v. Build vocabulary

   vi. Develop academic language

   vii. Develop analytical skills

   viii. Develop cognitive academic language

   ix. Develop cognitive learning strategies

   x. Develop extended time on task

   xi. Develop field independent skills

   xii. Facilitate student writing

   xiii. Facilitate student self-evaluation skills

   xiv. Improve access to prior knowledge

   xv. Facilitate language development

   xvi. Sustain engagement with reading and writing

   xvii. Use prior knowledge

   xviii. Strengthen learning to learn skills

   xix. Strengthen retention and application abilities

   xx. Improve mnemonic retrieval

   xxi. Improve test taking

xxii. Reduce impulsivity

xxiii. Improve writing strategies.

How to Do It

i. This strategy provides a structure for proofreading written work prior to submitting it to the teacher.

ii. The teacher introduces COPS by writing the steps on the board next to a passage from a hypothetical student written paragraph or sentence depending upon the grade level of the class. The teacher then has the class walk through the steps in COPS pointing out and correcting elements in the writing sample.

iii. The teacher can provide a large COPS frame as a poster or as a projection on the screen and walk through the steps with the class.

iv. The poster can remain up on the wall as a reminder of the COPS process during any writing activity, and students should be reminded to check it periodically as they work on writing assignments.

v. Students can also be given worksheets with the COPS format on them to accompany desk work.

vi. The following are the steps in COPS:

1. Capitalization correct

2. Overall appearance

3. Punctuation correct

4. Spelling correct

Research Base

Cole (1995)

What to Watch for With ELL/CLD Students

i. Newcomers will need to have the COPS steps modeled and explained in their most proficient language before they can proceed independently.

ii. Students can be paired with partners who are slightly more bilingual than themselves to facilitate their learning this process.

PROXIMITY—PROXIMICS

Purpose of the Strategy

i. Build awareness of academic behaviors

ii. Build awareness of academic expectations

COPS Elements to Check	Correct?	Corrections Made
Capitalization		
Overall appearance		
Punctuation		
Spelling		

   iii. Build awareness of academic school culture expectations

   iv. Build awareness of learning process

   v. Build self-awareness of behavior

   vi. Develop awareness of cause and effect

   vii. Develop higher persistence

   viii. Eliminate inappropriate behavior

   ix. Enhance focus on learning

   x. Facilitate student regaining control over self

   xi. Increase students' probability of generating a correct response

   xii. Increase students' time on task

   xiii. Increase the frequency of appropriate responses or behaviors

   xiv. Minimize minor behavior problems

   xv. Prevent minor behavior problems from escalating

   xvi. Reassure frustrated students

   xvii. Reduce distractibility

   xiii. Reduce inappropriate behaviors

   xix. Reduce low-persistence behaviors

How to Do It

   i. In essence, this strategy is intentionally using touch or physical presence to manipulate or control potential misbehaviors.

   ii. Often the teacher starts by moving closer to a challenged student to get the student's attention and refocus him or her on the task. After refocusing, the teacher can stay in the student's vicinity, ready to return to his or her side, if necessary. As the student gets better at refocusing on work without the teacher's near presence, the teacher can restore focus from further and further away.

   iii. The teacher and other students are strategically positioned to provide support and to prevent or minimize misbehaviors.

   iv. For example, the teacher circulates throughout the classroom during group or independent activities, spending more time next to particular students.

Research Base

Etscheidt (1984)

Evertson & Weinstein (2006)

Gunter & Shores (1995)

Marable & Raimondi (1995)

Walters & Frei (2007)

What to Watch for With ELL/CLD Students

i. All cultures have guidelines about how close or how far away to stand or sit next to another person. These are mostly unspoken and learned through being raised in the culture and community where the proximity to another person is seen and remarked upon by those around you.

ii. These space relations are also affected by whether someone is standing over or sitting under another person. These relative positions convey power and control relationships which vary from culture to culture.

iii. The teacher must familiarize himself or herself with the proximity rules of the various cultures represented in the classroom before using proximics strategically to promote learning.

ABCDEFGHIJKLMOP**Q**RSTUVW

QUESTIONING

Purpose of the Strategy

    i. Access prior knowledge

    ii. Develop academic language

    iii. Encourage questioning and exploration of new learning

    iv. Enhance ability of students to focus on learning

    v. Adapt content to meet individual or unique student needs

    vi. Improve reading comprehension

    vii. Use discourse techniques

    viii. Build academic transfer skills

    ix. Build appreciation that everyone has a contribution to make

    x. Expand and elaborate on learning

    xi. Expand comprehension

    xii. Facilitate access of prior knowledge

    xiii. Facilitate acquisition of content knowledge

    xiv. Build awareness of academic expectations

    xv. Improve mnemonic retrieval

    xvi. Improve retention

    xvii. Develop thinking and planning skills

How to Do It

i. The teacher engages individual students in reciprocal questioning to establish appropriate question-and-answer techniques and enhance comprehension of content.

ii. Students or an assistant and student ask each other questions about a selection. Students model the teacher's questions and answers. The teacher provides feedback about the exchanges.

iii. The focus allows learners to explore the meaning of the reading material.

Research Base

Cole (1995)

Moore, Alvermann, & Hinchman (2000)

What to Watch for With ELL/CLD Students

i. Provide initial set up in the students' most proficient language.

ii. Students can practice reciprocal questioning with each other in their native language and then proceed with English proficient students.

QUICK WRITE

Purpose of the Strategy

i. Access and use prior knowledge

ii. Build academic transfer skills

iii. Build awareness of learning process

iv. Develop problem-solving skills

v. Facilitate connections between known and new

vi. Build upon existing language skills of students

vii. Strengthen retention and application abilities

viii. Build upon existing language strengths of students

ix. Improve reading comprehension

x. Use discourse techniques

xi. Sustain engagement

xii. Improve mnemonic retrieval

xiii. Improve retention

xiv. Develop thinking and planning skills

How to Do It

i. This strategy is sometimes used as an inquiry approach or a way to introduce a new unit or lesson topic.

ii. The teacher tells the students that they are going to learn about a new topic and names the topic, writing the topic and a few details on the board. He or she then directs students to get out a piece of paper and write about this topic, providing them specific suggestions. Some examples include the following:

- Math—Write about a time you have had to use multiplication in your everyday life.
- Science—Write all words related to what you know about the states of matter.
- Social Studies—Write one prediction about the next presidential election.
- Literature—Write five things you know about . . . (based on title, picture preview).

What to Watch for With ELL/CLD Students

i. Students with limited experience writing in English will need alternative ways to do a quick write. This can be done by giving them short prewritten sentences to choose from or words to select.

ii. It can also be done by giving them the option of a "quick draw" of what they already know about the topic. An example of this would be to have the students draw a picture of what they think will happen in the story, or election, or types of the object under consideration.

Beginning = 1   Developing = 2   Proficient = 3   Advanced = 4

Monitoring: __*Quick Write Activity*

Participant	Following directions	Provided information about the country	Able to come up with predictions about story	Able to say what will be learned from the story	Able to describe what will be learned from process	Able to explain process
1						
2						
3						
4						

ABCDEFGHIJKLMOPQRSTUVW

RAP—PARAPHRASING

Purpose of the Strategy

    i. Build academic transfer skills

   ii. Build awareness of appropriate cognitive academic language

  iii. Assist students to learn information through paraphrasing

  iv. Facilitate language development

   v. Improve comprehension

  vi. Improve reading comprehension

 vii. Improve retention of content

viii. Build foundation for learning

  ix. Build vocabulary

   x. Develop academic language

  xi. Develop thinking and planning

 xii. Enhance ability of students to focus on learning

xiii. Expand comprehension

xiv. Facilitate reading process

 xv. Improve retention of content

xvi. Improve writing strategies

xvii. Improve students' ability to organize and prioritize information

xviii. Strengthen knowledge of academic content

xix. Strengthen language development

xx. Strengthen learning to learn skills

xxi. Strengthen retention and application abilities

How to Do It

i. This strategy is a way to assist students to learn information through paraphrasing and is one of several reading comprehension techniques for improved retention of information

ii. The teacher creates a chart or poster with RAP and reminders with pictures or symbols for what each letter stands for: Read the paragraph, ask about the main idea and two supporting details, and put main idea and details into own words.

iii. The teacher demonstrates what this means and how to do it with different writing excerpts from books the students are familiar with. He or she asks different students to put these familiar excerpts into their own words and puts all the examples up on the chart.

iv. The following are the steps in RAP:

1. Read paragraph

2. Ask self the main idea and two supporting details

3. Put main idea and details into own words

	Check this box when you have completed the step	**What do you think about what you read, asked, or did?**
Read paragraph		
Ask self the main idea and two supporting details		
Put main idea and details into own words		

Research Base

Cole (1995)

Dang, Dang, & Ruiter (2005)

Ellis & Lenz (1987)

Odean (1987)

What to Watch for With ELL/CLD Students

i. Newcomers will need to have the RAP steps modeled and explained in their most proficient language before they can proceed independently.

ii. Students can be paired with partners who are slightly more bilingual than themselves to facilitate their learning this process.

READING COMPREHENSION—PQ4R

Purpose of the Strategy

i. Build awareness of learning process

ii. Access prior knowledge

iii. Build academic transfer skills

iv. Build confidence in independent work

v. Build foundation for learning

vi. Build learners' confidence in their control of the learning process

vii. Build students' self-awareness of behavior

viii. Enhance ability of students to focus on learning

ix. Expand and elaborate on learning

x. Expand comprehension

xi. Facilitate access of prior knowledge

xii. Facilitate reading process

xiii. Increase focus on reading

xiv. Increase students' probability of generating a correct response

xv. Increase students' time on task

xvi. Improve students' ability to organize and prioritize information

xvii. Reduce off-task behaviors

xviii. Strengthen awareness of learning process

xix. Develop analytical skills

xx. Develop confidence in independent learning

xxi. Increase focus on reading

xxii. Increase and expand time on task

xxiii. Improve ability to organize and prioritize information

xxiv. Encourage questioning and exploration of new learning

xxv. Develop problem-solving skills

xxvi. Develop thinking and planning skills

xxvii. Improve and expand reading comprehension

xxviii. Improve access to prior knowledge

xxix. Expand and elaborate on learning foundation

xxx. Build transfer skills

How to Do It

i. PQ4R may assist students to become more discriminating readers and retain more of what they are reading.

ii. The teacher creates poster or chart of PQ4R with the words preview, question, read, reflect, recite, and review down the side. He or she reviews each word and what it means in the context of reading a book or text about something. The teacher demonstrates how to do each of these active reading techniques.

iii. The teacher gives each student his or her own worksheet with PQ4R on it and has students consider what they are to do at each step while reading a particular passage in their textbook or story. They write down what they are to do on their worksheet. As they read, they make notes that correspond to the steps. After they are done reading, they go back over their worksheet and write down what they did for each step.

iv. The following are the steps in PQ4R:

1. Preview

2. Question

3. Read

4. Reflect

5. Recite

6. Review

Research Base

Anderson (2000)

Hamachek (1994)

Pelow & Colvin (1983)

Sanacore (1982)

What to Watch for With ELL/CLD Students

i. Newcomers will need to have the PQ4R steps modeled and explained in their most proficient language before they can proceed independently.

ii. Students can be paired with partners who are slightly more bilingual than themselves to facilitate their learning this process.

PQ4R Element	What am I to do at this step?	What did I do about it?	Notes
Preview			
Question			
Read			
Reflect			
Recite			
Review			

READING COMPREHENSION—SQ3R

Purpose of the Strategy

i. Develop cognitive academic language

ii. Develop and extend time on task

iii. Develop higher persistence

iv. Develop problem-solving skills

v. Facilitate discussion of new learning

vi. Facilitate reading process

vii. Access and use prior knowledge

viii. Build transfer skills

ix. Improve and strengthen retention of content

x. Expand and elaborate on learning foundations

xi. Improve access to prior knowledge

xii. Improve comprehension

xiii. Strengthen and facilitate language development

How to Do It

i. The teacher puts the steps of SQ3R up on the board with the words survey, question, read, recite, and review. He or she explains what each term means and what a student should do while reading a passage. This strategy reminds students to go through any passage or lesson carefully and thoughtfully.

ii. The teacher models how to use each step of SQ3R while reading a passage or story, making notes to remind students what they should do at each point.

iii. Students can make cue cards to remember each step. The following are the steps in SQ3R:

1. Survey

2. Question

3. Read

4. Recite

5. Review

Research Base

Allington & Cunningham (2002)

Artis (2008)

Cole (1995)

Fisher & Frey (2004)

Irvin & Rose (1995)

Law & Eckes (2000)

Moore, Alvermann, & Hinchman (2000)

Robinson (1946)

Sakta (1999)

Tovani (2000)

What to Watch for With ELL/CLD Students

   i. Newcomers will need to have the SQ3R steps modeled and explained in their most proficient language before they can proceed independently.

  ii. Students can be paired with partners who are slightly more bilingual than themselves to facilitate their learning this process.

SQ3R Element	What am I to do at this step?	What did I do about it?	Notes
Survey			
Question			
Read			
Recite			
Review			

READING STRATEGY—FIST

Purpose of the Strategy

    i. Build academic transfer skills

    ii. Build foundation for learning

    iii. Build awareness of learning process

    iv. Assist students to learn information through paraphrasing

    v. Increase time on task

    vi. Develop cognitive academic language

    vii. Develop cognitive learning strategies

    viii. Develop content knowledge foundation

    ix. Develop extended time on task

    x. Develop field independent skills

    xi. Encourage questioning and exploration of new learning

    xii. Enhance ability of student to focus on learning

    xiii. Expand and elaborate on learning

    xiv. Expand comprehension

    xv. Retention of content

    xvi. Strengthen language development

    xvii. Strengthen learning to learn skills

    xviii. Strengthen retention and application abilities

    xix. Develop analytical skills

    xx. Build metacognition skills

    xxi. Facilitate language development

    xxii. Improve reading comprehension

How to Do It

    i. This strategy is done within the general education classroom with mixed groups of students. The FIST analysis strategy framework provides a structure for understanding reading and building reading comprehension.

    ii. The FIST strategy assists students to actively pursue responses to questions related directly to materials being read.

    iii. Students follow the steps in the FIST strategy while reading paragraphs in assigned readings.

iv. The teacher posts the steps for F, I, S, T on a chart and gives each student papers in the form of checklists with FIST down the side. Using an example paragraph, he or she goes step by step through FIST: reading the first sentence in the paragraph, asking for questions based on that first sentence, and having the students search for the answer to those questions within the paragraph. Then the students put the question and answers together in their own words, comparing them to the original example written paragraph.

v. The following are the steps in FIST:

1. First sentence is read

2. Indicate a question based on first sentence

3. Search for the answer to the question

4. Tie question and answer together through paraphrasing

vi. The teacher can remind students before each reading activity to use the FIST strategy and the FIST checklist as they gather information from a paragraph for their assignment.

Research Base

Allington & Cunningham (2002)

Cole (1995)

Dang, Dang, & Ruiter (2005)

Derwinger, Stigsdotter Neely, & Baeckman (2005)

Ellis & Lenz (1987)

Moore, Alvermann, & Hinchman (2000)

Odean (1987)

What to Watch for With ELL/CLD Students

i. Newcomers will need to have the FIST steps modeled and explained in their most proficient language before they can proceed independently.

ii. Students can be paired with partners who are slightly more bilingual than themselves to facilitate their learning this process.

READING STRATEGY—PARTNERS

Purpose of the Strategy

i. Adapt content to meet individual or unique student needs

ii. Build academic transfer skills

FIST Element	What am I to do at this step?	What did I do about it?	Notes
First sentence is read			
Indicate a question based on first sentence			
Search for the answer to the question			
Tie question and answer together through paraphrasing			

iii. Build awareness of learning process

iv. Build foundation for learning

v. Ensure that each student is familiar with specific academic and behavioral expectations

vi. Build upon students' existing language skills

vii. Develop basic interpersonal communication

viii. Develop, reinforce, and strengthen content knowledge foundation

ix. Develop extended time on task

x. Facilitate discussion about new learning

xi. Recognize importance of working together

xii. Reduce misperceptions

xiii. Facilitate students' comfort with learning environment

xiv. Develop constructive peer relationships

xv. Improve motivation

xvi. Minimize behavior problems

How to Do It

i. This strategy is a reading/listening technique that can be used in any content area. Students read aloud to one another from the textbook.

ii. The teacher matches a stronger reader with a student who needs more practice. The reading/listening pairs can be switched out as often as needed to give everyone a chance.

iii. With partners, each student participates either as an interested listener or as reader, while the teacher moves from pair to pair listening. Reading can be varied by changing partners. Children can reread parts of a story in pairs after the directed reading activity rather than have one student read while the others all listen. During this time, the students have a chance to help each other.

iv. With science and math lessons, different partners may be used by matching a successful learner with one just slightly less successful and so on down the line. Problem solution can be revisited by changing partners and redoing the problem and solution.

Research Base

Kamps (2007)

Koskinen & Blum (1984)

Wood & Algozzine (1994)

Wood & Harmon (2001)

Zutell & Rasinski (1991)

What to Watch for With ELL/CLD Students

i. Partners must be selected carefully with specific objectives in mind. If competence and understanding of the content is the goal, then similar language skills are necessary.

ii. If expansion and transition of learning is the goal, then paring a less proficient student with a more proficient bilingual partner will help.

iii. If challenging application is the goal, then paring very differently skilled parties may work.

READING STRATEGY—RIDER

Purpose of the Strategy

    i. Build transfer skills

    ii. Expand and elaborate on learning foundation

    iii. Build learners' confidence in their control of the learning process

    iv. Develop analytical skills

    v. Expand and elaborate on learning

    vi. Expand comprehension

    vii. Facilitate access of prior knowledge

    viii. Develop association skills

    ix. Build metacognition skills

    x. Develop thinking and planning skills

    xi. Improve access to prior knowledge

    xii. Improve retention of information

    xiii. Improve reading comprehension

    xiv. Strengthen language development

How to Do It

    i. This visualization strategy cues the learner to form a mental image of what was read and assists the student in making connections with previously learned materials.

    ii. The teacher prepares a poster or projects an overhead of the frame RIDER with each word highlighted. He or she explains each step in RIDER and explains what to do at each step.

    iii. Students may be given individual worksheets when first learning to use the strategy but usually only need reminders to follow the steps on the poster as they become more familiar with the process.

    iv. The following are the steps in RIDER:

        1. Read a sentence

        2. Image (form a mental picture)

        3. Describe how new information differs from previous

        4. Evaluate image to ensure it is comprehensive

        5. Repeat process with subsequent sentences

Research Base

Cole (1995)

Collier (2008)

What to Watch for With ELL/CLD Students

    i. Newcomers will need to have the RIDER steps modeled and explained in their most proficient language before they can proceed independently.

    ii. Students can be paired with partners who are slightly more bilingual than themselves to facilitate their learning this process.

RIDER Element	What am I to do at this step?	What did I do about it?	Notes
Read a sentence			
Image (form a mental picture)			
Describe how new information differs from previous			
Evaluate image to ensure it is comprehensive			
Repeat process with subsequent sentences			

READING AND WRITING STRATEGY—SSCD

Purpose of the Strategy

i. Access and use prior knowledge

ii. Build awareness of learning

iii. Build awareness of academic language

iv. Build transfer skills

v. Develop analytical skills

vi. Develop association skills

vii. Develop field sensitive skills

viii. Develop higher persistence

ix. Develop higher tolerance

x. Build metacognition skills

xi. Develop thinking and planning skills

xii. Improve access to prior knowledge

xiii. Reduce off-task behaviors

xiv. Strengthen language development

How to Do It

i. The teacher posts the letters and phrases for SSCD on the wall where students can refer to them as they work. He or she also gives them individual sheets to make notes for themselves.

ii. The teacher goes over each step in SSCD to show the students how to do this while reading text or when reviewing their own writing. He or she reminds them to use sound clues to read difficult or unfamiliar words as well as to use word structure clues. The teacher shows them how to use context clues and how to look words up in the dictionary, if possible.

iii. Bilingual dictionaries can also be used.

iv. SSCD encourages students to remember to use sound, structure, and context clues to address unfamiliar vocabulary. This is followed by dictionary usage if necessary.

v. The following are the steps in SSCD:

1. Sound clues used

2. Structure clues used

3. Context clues used

4. Dictionary used

Research Base

Opitz (1998)

What to Watch for With ELL/CLD Students

i. Newcomers will need to have the SSCD steps modeled and explained in their most proficient language before they can proceed independently.

ii. Students can be paired with partners who are slightly more bilingual than themselves to facilitate their learning this process.

READING STRATEGY—VISUALIZATION

Purpose of the Strategy

i. Access prior knowledge

ii. Adapt to meet individual or unique student needs

iii. Adapt the mode of response required of students

iv. Build academic transfer skills

v. Build foundation for learning

vi. Build metacognition skills

vii. Develop analytical skills

viii. Develop association skills

ix. Develop extended time on task

x. Enhance ability of students to focus on learning

xi. Enhance ability of students to learn new things

xii. Expand and elaborate on learning

xiii. Expand comprehension

xiv. Facilitate access of prior knowledge

xv. Improve access to prior knowledge

xvi. Improve comprehension

xvii. Strengthen language development

xviii. Strengthen learning to learn skills

xix. Strengthen retention and application abilities

xx. Develop higher tolerance

xxi. Develop thinking and planning skills

xxii. Improve mnemonic retrieval

xxiii. Improve retention

How to Do It

i. The teacher introduces the visualization strategy as a way to facilitate understanding and retaining what is being read. He or she has students learn the steps of visualization: stopping; asking who, what, where, when, why, and how; creating an image in the mind, and putting it all together.

ii. Students put small, red stop signs or other marks indicating stopping points at the end of sentences in an assigned reading. As they read the passage, they stop at each sign and answer questions about the passage. They then make a picture in their mind of what the passage means. This is repeated for each subsequent passage with the pictures forming a moving visualization or motion picture of what the passage means. (I usually remind students to think of TV shows.) This visualization strategy can also be used with other content activities, in science and social studies for example.

iii. The following are the steps for students to follow in implementing this strategy:

1. Where do I stop?

2. Who is doing what, where, when, how, and why?

3. What do I see in my mind?

4. How does this all go together?

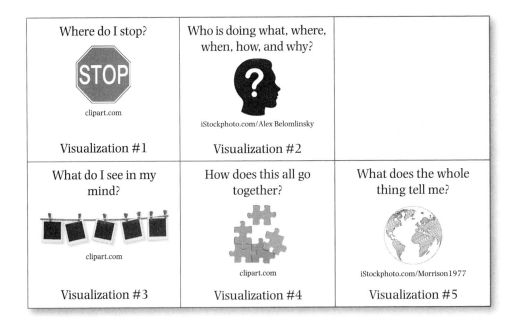

Where do I stop?	Who is doing what, where, when, how, and why?	
STOP clipart.com Visualization #1	? iStockphoto.com/Alex Belomlinsky Visualization #2	
What do I see in my mind?	How does this all go together?	What does the whole thing tell me?
clipart.com Visualization #3	clipart.com Visualization #4	iStockphoto.com/Morrison1977 Visualization #5

iv. When applying the visualization strategy, students work through problems or tasks using the above sequence of self-monitoring questions.

v. Suppose you are having your students read *The Story of Ferdinand* by Munro Leaf. You would have students work in pairs or in small mixed skill groups as they read this story together. They would help put small red "Post-It" circles at the end of each sentence or at the end of two sentences, depending upon their skill level (Step 1 of rehearsal, "Where should I stop to think?"). Suppose one group was reading this passage, for example:

1. All the other bulls who had grown up with him in the same pasture would fight each other all day. They would butt each other and stick each other with their horns. What they wanted most of all was to be picked to fight at the bull fights in Madrid. But not Ferdinand—he still liked to sit just quietly under the cork tree and smell the flowers.

vi. Students would take turns reading out loud to one another. The first reader would read up to the first red spot and stop. The students would then review the five "W" and one "H" questions about what had just been read (Step 2 of rehearsal, "Who is doing what, where, when, how, and why?"). Who = the other bulls, what = fight each other, where = in the pasture, when = all day. As this is the first sentence, the readers do not yet know the answers to all the questions (how and why = don't know yet). After answering the questions, the group will next take turns telling the others how they visualize this sentence (Step 3 of rehearsal, "What picture do I see in my mind regarding these?"). The picture in the book shows the bulls gazing up at a poster about the bull fights in Madrid, so they will have to use their imagination about what it might look like to see these young bulls play fighting. They will then go on to read the next sentence and repeat Steps 2 and 3, this time adding Step 4, Who = the bulls, what = fight each other, where = in the pasture, when = all day, how = butt each other and stick each other with their horns, why = still don't know. They can now expand their first imaginative picture of these bulls by adding some action to the movie they are making in their minds (Step 5 of rehearsal, "What do I see when I put the pictures from each stop together?"). The group goes on to the next sentence and repeats Steps 2, 3, 4, and 5. Who=the young bulls, what = fighting, where = in the pasture, how = butting heads, why = to be picked to fight in Madrid. They expand their visualization to showing the longing of the young bulls while they are fighting. They then read the final sentence and complete the movie in their minds. Who = the young bulls and Ferdinand, what = the young bulls fighting and Ferdinand sitting, where = fighting in the pasture while Ferdinand is under the cork tree, how = fighting by butting their heads while Ferdinand is smelling flowers, why = the young bulls want to be picked to fight in Madrid, but Ferdinand doesn't want to do anything but smell the flowers.

vii. The use of the visualization strategy will slow impulsive learners down, reinforce reflective habits, and guide students to more accurate understanding of what they are reading.

Research Base

Harwell (2001)

Klingner, Vaughn, & Boardman (2007)

Naughton (2008)

Tomlinson (1998)

Tovani (2000)

What to Watch for With ELL/CLD Students

   i. Students with limited school experience will not know what visualization means and will need to have direct instruction in the vocabulary and actions expected.

   ii. This can be introduced in the primary language and examples given from literature and art with which the students are more familiar.

REALITY-BASED LEARNING APPROACHES

Purpose of the Strategy

   i. Build awareness of learning

   ii. Build transfer skills

   iii. Develop academic language

   iv. Develop confidence in academic interactions

   v. Develop confidence in school culture interactions

   vi. Develop confidence in school language

   vii. Build upon existing language skills of students

   viii. Develop field independent skills

   ix. Develop independence in learning situations

   x. Develop self-esteem

   xi. Encourage questioning and exploration of new learning

   xii. Enhance ability of students to focus on learning

   xiii. Build upon existing language strengths of students

   xiv. Build vocabulary

   xv. Build awareness of adaptation process

   xvi. Reduce confusion in locus of control

   xvii. Reduce off-task behaviors

   xviii. Improve motivation

How to Do It

i. Teachers provide students with real purposes and real audiences for reading, writing, and speaking to real people.

ii. The teacher provides students with real audiences and real application situations for presenting mathematical and scientific hypotheses or calculations, like science fairs or poster presentations.

iii. When students write and speak to intended purposes and audiences, they are more likely to be motivated and to obtain valuable feedback on their efforts.

Research Base

Cole (1995)

What to Watch for With ELL/CLD Students

i. In some societies and cultures, children are actively discouraged from speculation and make believe and are encouraged to stay focused on real life and real objects and real interactions.

ii. It is not always apparent when your students come from homes where make believe and fantasy are not supported. Always introducing new content by giving real examples and real applications will assist students in accessing and comprehending the content of the lesson.

iii. The teacher can begin introducing make believe examples and applications as students become comfortable with the general learning process. Teachers should always make it clear when something is nonfiction and when something is fiction.

REDUCED STIMULI

Purpose of the Strategy

i. Adapt content to meet individual or unique student needs

ii. Build awareness of adaptation process

iii. Build first language to English transfer skills

iv. Build upon existing language skills of students

v. Build upon existing language strengths of students

vi. Build upon family language and culture

vii. Build upon the diverse language foundations of students and parents

viii. Develop personal control of situations

ix. Encourage questioning and exploration of new learning

    x. Enhance ability of students to focus on learning

    xi. Facilitate connections between known and new

    xii. Facilitate school adaptation process

    xiii. Facilitate students' comfort with learning environment

    xiv. Lower anxiety in classroom

    xv. Reduce culture shock

    xvi. Reduce response fatigue

    xvii. Reduce stress for new students

How to Do It

i. This strategy is done at the beginning of the school year and possibly at the beginning of each semester depending on the time of year new students enroll and may be done by pairing students within an integrated classroom.

ii. The teacher may start the year with very little on the walls or hanging from the ceiling of the room. The goal is fewer distractions and less visual auditory noise, that is, sights and sounds that may be meaningless to students who are unfamiliar with them.

iii. The teacher does not display or use visual/auditory materials until students have been introduced to the content or have produced the materials themselves.

iv. Visual, tactile, and auditory experiences are introduced gradually and with demonstration.

Research Base

Nelson, Kohnert, Sabur, & Shaw (2005)

Wortham (1996)

What to Watch for With ELL/CLD Students

i. Newcomers may become overly stimulated by lots of bright, new, unfamiliar, or strange objects, signs, sounds, and miscellany within their new classroom. They do not know what is important to attend to and what is not important. It is all new and exciting.

ii. This is also going to impact students with undiagnosed neurological conditions that they have not yet learned to accommodate.

iii. It is better to start out with less and add as students become comfortable and familiar with what is in the classroom.

RECIPROCAL QUESTIONING

Purpose of the Strategy

    i. Build academic transfer skills

    ii. Build appreciation that everyone has a contribution to make

    iii. Develop cognitive learning strategies

    iv. Develop confidence in academic interactions

    v. Develop confidence in school culture interactions

    vi. Develop confidence in school language

    vii. Facilitate connections between known and new

    viii. Facilitate discussion about new learning

    ix. Build upon existing language strengths of students

    x. Build awareness of appropriate cognitive academic language

    xi. Build awareness of appropriate communication behaviors for school language

    xii. Improve reading comprehension

    xiii. Improve use of discourse techniques

    xiv. Improve ability to organize and prioritize information

    xv. Recognize importance of working together

    xvi. Improve retention

    xvii. Strengthen knowledge of content

    xviii. Strengthen retention and application abilities

    xix. Develop thinking and planning skills

How to Do It

    i. The teacher engages individual students in reciprocal questioning to establish appropriate question-and-answer techniques and enhance comprehension of content.

    ii. Students or an assistant and student ask each other questions about a selection. Students model the teacher's questions and answers. The teacher provides feedback about the exchanges.

    iii. The focus allows learners to explore the meaning of the reading material.

Research Base

Cole (1995)

Moore, Alvermann, & Hinch (2000)

What to Watch for With ELL/CLD Students

i. Provide initial set up in the students' most proficient language.

ii. Students can practice reciprocal questioning with each other in their native language and then proceed with English proficient students.

RETENTION STRATEGY—CAN-DO

Purpose of the Strategy

i. Improve access to prior information

ii. Develop higher tolerance

iii. Build academic transfer skills

iv. Develop higher persistence

v. Build academic transfer skills

vi. Develop problem-solving skills

vii. Build awareness of learning process

viii. Build foundation for learning

ix. Develop analytic skills

x. Develop higher tolerance

xi. Develop thinking and planning skills

xii. Improve mnemonic retrieval

xiii. Improve retention

xiv. Use prior knowledge

How to Do It

i. This is in essence a mnemonic retrieval strategy for retaining information, particularly an itemized list. CAN-DO provides the learner with a structure for organizing items to be learned or remembered.

ii. These could be the steps in a process or elements in a unit or assignment. They could be vocabulary words in a selection of current reading or in a content area, such as math or science terms.

iii. CAN-DO may be done in mixed, integrated classrooms or as part of small group focused interventions within a tiered support program such as response to intervention (RTI).

iv. The teacher makes a poster or other visual aid illustrated the steps of CAN-DO and shows students how to organize the information or vocabulary list they are working on in the CAN-DO framework.

    v. The following are the steps in CAN-DO:

       1. Create list of items to learn

       2. Ask self if list is complete

       3. Note details and main ideas

       4. Describe components and their relationships

       5. Overlearn main items followed by learning details

Research Base

Derwinger, Stigsdotter Neely, & Baeckman (2005)

Eskritt & McLeod (2008)

Jutras (2008)

Lee (2005)

What to Watch for With ELL/CLD Students

    i. Newcomers will need to have the CAN-DO steps modeled and explained in their most proficient language before they can proceed independently.

    ii. Students can be paired with partners who are slightly more bilingual than themselves to facilitate their learning this process.

C Create list of items to learn	
A Ask self if list is complete	
N Note details and main ideas	
D Describe components and their relationships	
O Overlearn main items followed by learning details	

Source: Collier (2008).

RETENTION STRATEGY—PARS

Purpose of the Strategy

i. Build academic transfer skills

ii. Develop cognitive learning strategies

iii. Access prior knowledge

iv. Build awareness of school culture expectations

v. Develop thinking and planning skills

vi. Improve retention of content

vii. Increase students' time on task

viii. Increase the frequency of appropriate responses or behaviors

ix. Increase time on task

x. Strengthen knowledge of academic content

xi. Strengthen language development

xii. Strengthen learning to learn skills

xiii. Sustain engagement

xiv. Expand and elaborate on learning

xv. Facilitate reading process

xvi. Expand and improve comprehension

xvii. Build awareness of learning process

xviii. Develop academic language

xix. Improve mnemonic retrieval

xx. Reduce confusion in locus of control

xxi. Retention of content

xxii. Develop expanded time on task

How to Do It

i. The PARS retention strategy framework provides a structure for understanding what is being learned and retaining the information for later application.

ii. The teacher or assistant introduces students to PARS with charts and diagrams going through each step before giving students their own PARS chart or sheet with the PARS frame upon it.

iii. The teacher models each PARS element with a lesson with which the students are familiar, showing students what is meant by previewing the content, then asking questions about the content, going on and reading the materials completely, and finally summarizing what has been read in their own words.

iv. PARS is recommended for use with students who have limited experiences with study strategies. Students can create cue cards or use posters to remind themselves of the steps.

v. The following are the steps in PARS:

1. Preview
2. Ask questions
3. Read
4. Summarize

Research Base

Derwinger, Stigsdotter Neely, & Baeckman (2005)

Lee (2005)

Smith (2000)

What to Watch for With ELL/CLD Students

i. Newcomers will need to have the PARS steps modeled and explained in their most proficient language before they can proceed independently.

ii. Students can be paired with partners who are slightly more bilingual than themselves to facilitate their learning this process.

PARS Element	What am I to do at this step?	What did I do about it?	Notes
Preview			
Ask questions			
Read			

(Continued)

(Continued)

PARS Element	What am I to do at this step?	What did I do about it?	Notes
Summarize			

REST AND RELAXATION TECHNIQUES

Purpose of the Strategy

    i. Adapt to meet individual or unique student needs

    ii. Enhance ability of students to focus on learning

    iii. Facilitate nondirective guidance about student misbehavior

    iv. Facilitate school adaptation process

    v. Lower anxiety

    vi. Reduce response fatigue

    vii. Facilitate student regaining control over self

    viii. Enhance ability of students to learn new things

    ix. Develop self-monitoring skills

    x. Reduce anxiety and stress responses

    xi. Reduce culture shock

How to Do It

    i. There are many different ways to introduce different rest and relaxation techniques to students. These can include mindfulness exercises as well as just quiet times.

    ii. Relaxation techniques are shown in video or demonstration form with an explanation in the home and community language when possible. Students discuss when they might need to use these techniques.

Research Base

Allen & Klein (1997)

Page & Page (2003)

Thomas (2006)

What to Watch for With ELL/CLD Students

i. Heightened anxiety, distractibility, and response fatigue are all common side effects of the acculturation process and attributes of culture shock.

ii. English language learner (ELL) and culturally and linguistically diverse (CLD) students need more time to process classroom activities and tasks. Building in rest periods will provide thinking and processing breaks in their day.

RIDER—READING STRATEGY

Purpose of the Strategy

i. Build transfer skills

ii. Expand and elaborate on learning foundation

iii. Build learners' confidence in their control of the learning process

iv. Develop analytical skills

v. Expand comprehension

vi. Facilitate access of prior knowledge

vii. Develop association skills

viii. Build metacognition skills

ix. Develop thinking and planning skills

x. Improve access to prior knowledge

xi. Improve retention of information

xii. Improve reading comprehension

xiii. Strengthen language development

How to Do It

i. This visualization strategy cues the learner to form a mental image of what was read and assists the student in making connections with previously learned materials.

ii. The teacher prepares a poster or projects an overhead of the frame RIDER with each word highlighted. He or she explains each step in RIDER and explains what to do at each step.

iii. Students may be given individual worksheets when first learning to use the strategy but usually only need reminders to follow the steps on the poster as they become more familiar with the process.

iv. The following are the steps in RIDER:

1. Read a sentence

2. Image (form a mental picture)

3. Describe how new information differs from previous

4. Evaluate image to ensure it is comprehensive

5. Repeat process with subsequent sentences

Research Base

Cole (1995)

Collier (2008)

What to Watch for With ELL/CLD Students

i. Newcomers will need to have the RIDER steps modeled and explained in their most proficient language before they can proceed independently.

ii. Students can be paired with partners who are slightly more bilingual than themselves to facilitate their learning this process.

RIDER Element	What am I to do at this step?	What did I do about it?	Notes
Read a sentence			
Image (form a mental picture)			
Describe how new information differs from previous			

RIDER Element	What am I to do at this step?	What did I do about it?	Notes
Evaluate image to ensure it is comprehensive			
Repeat process with subsequent sentences			

ROLE-PLAYING

Purpose of the Strategy

i. Build awareness of appropriate cognitive academic language

ii. Build awareness of appropriate communication behaviors for school language and rules

iii. Build transfer skills

iv. Develop cognitive academic language

v. Develop confidence in school language

vi. Develop higher tolerance

vii. Facilitate language development

viii. Sustain engagement

ix. Develop personal control of situations

x. Develop thinking and planning skills

xi. Improve retention of content

xii. Reduce code switching

xiii. Reduce distractibility

xiv. Reduce response fatigue

xv. Use prior knowledge

How to Do It

i. Teachers and assistants model the appropriate and inappropriate ways to use cognitive academic language and cognitive learning strategies. Students take different roles in the interactions and practice them with each other and the teacher. Students practice the cognitive learning strategies in varied academic content areas with the teacher or assistant monitoring.

ii. Students identify a number of uncomfortable or uncertain social or formal interactions. The teacher and assistant model the appropriate and inappropriate ways to handle these interactions. Students take different roles in the interaction and practice with each other and the teacher. Students read dialogue prepared by the teacher or by other students.

iii. The teacher and assistant model the appropriate and inappropriate ways to use basic interpersonal communication and cognitive academic language in various school settings, both in and out of the classroom. Students take different roles in the interactions and practice them with each other and with the teacher. Students may suggest communication situations they want specific assistance with, and the teacher facilitates role-plays. Students create dialogues and interaction situations to enact.

iv. The teacher assigns students specific roles and creates situations where roles are acted out based upon how the students believe their characters would act. A specific problem, such as discrimination, is identified and described. Students role-play how they would confront the problem and discuss their roles or behaviors upon completion. Students learn how to confront the reactions of others and ways to deal with situations similar to the role-play.

v. Using role-playing in the classroom has many benefits:

1. Empathy: When students are participating in role-play activities, they are likely to be supportive of their classmates as they understand that putting yourself out there in these types of activities makes you vulnerable. This type of supportive and understanding atmosphere increases empathy among the students.

2. Authentic language experiences: Role-play activities give students practice communicating in authentic ways and situations. This will give them more confidence when presented with those scenarios when they are outside of class.

3. Memorable learning experience: The process students go through when they are doing a role-play activity (creating or learning the dialogue, practicing, presenting) will help solidify the new information they are learning. Dramatic activities provide "some of the richest and most memorable experiences (students) have in their struggle with the second language" (Celce-Murcia & Olshtain, 2000, p.71).

4. Adaptable for multiple levels: Role-play activities can be modified to fit upper- and lower-level students within the same activity.

Lower-level students can stick to the previously generated script, and upper-level students can modify the dialogue or improvise on their own. Students can take on as much or as little spontaneity as they feel comfortable.

5. Decreases inhibitions: Parrish (2004) states that "because learners are taking on a different persona to a degree, they sometimes are less inhibited than they might be with other fluency activities" (p.106).

6. Increases motivation and self-esteem: I have personally had students with attention issues become more fully engaged when we use role-play in our language lessons. It revives their interest and shows them they have a place and purpose in learning a new language. It frequently improves their ability to express themselves. We use real interaction situations that re-create school communicative situations.

7. Builds confidence: Raising students' self-esteem and showing them that they can be successful in communicative scenarios by using role-playing activities will help build their confidence when they need to communicate in real-life situations.

Research Base

Collier (2003a)

Johnson, Christie, & Yawkey (1999)

Kim & Kellogg (2007)

Livingstone (1983)

Magos & Politi (2008)

Rymes, Cahnmann-Taylor, & Souto-Manning (2008)

Webster-Stratton & Reid (2004)

What to Watch for With ELL/CLD Students

i. Many societies and cultures have specific beliefs and understandings about pretending to be something one is not in reality; there are cultural guidelines for make-believe, play, and assuming the role or character of someone or something.

ii. Be clear that in public schools and classrooms we sometimes are like actors in movies or television stories (although understanding that some people may think those are all real) for the purpose of illustrating or demonstrating something.

iii. Be clear that students will not become the character or thing and that it is a temporary action to illustrate or demonstrate a particular interaction you want them to learn.

iv. It may be easier with some students to start with puppets or drawings and then work up to individual people doing the actions.

ABCDEFGHIJKLMOPQR**S**TUVW

SCAFFOLDING

Purpose of the Strategy

   i. Access and use prior knowledge

   ii. Build academic transfer skills

   iii. Build awareness of learning process

   iv. Build foundation for learning

   v. Enhance ability of students to focus on learning

   vi. Enhance ability of students to learn new things

   vii. Facilitate student assuming responsibility for learning

   viii. Improve access to prior knowledge

   ix. Improve comprehension and retention

   x. Reinforce content

   xi. Strengthen retention and application abilities

   xii. Strengthen language development

How to Do It

   i. Teacher introduces scaffolding to students as a way to support, elaborate, and expand upon students' language as they learn to read (and write).

ii. Scaffolds are temporary frameworks that offer students immediate access to the meanings and pleasure of print.

iii. For example, one scaffolding strategy is paired reading. The teacher has students sit in pairs with one copy of the same book between them. All students are to read along during the activity, but only those students who the teacher taps or stands behind are to read aloud. The teacher may move around the room in a random manner, tapping or standing behind different pairs of students. When he or she taps the new pair, they start reading wherever the previous pair stopped reading. The voices may overlap slightly. The same story may then be read by groups of various sizes in the same manner.

iv. Another scaffolding technique is to have various students holding puppets or models representing characters or passages in the reading, and when the person or persons reading get to that passage, the puppets or pictures representative of that passage are held up for all to see. Sentence level scaffolds and discourse scaffolds (such as story mapping) are further examples of supporting language and reading.

Figure S.1 Example of Scaffolding

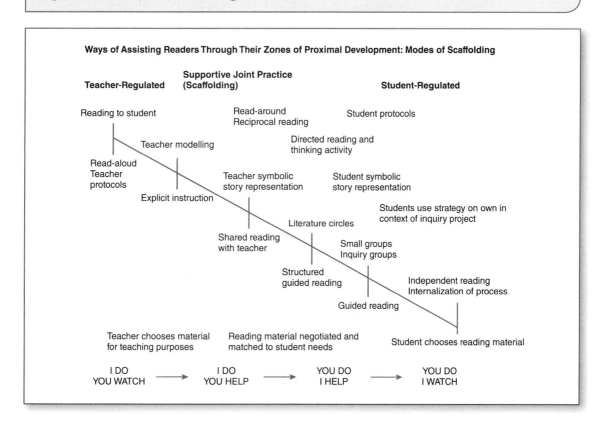

Research Base

Opitz (1998)

Vygotsky (1978)

What to Watch for With ELL/CLD Students

i. Teachers will need to lay a foundation for learning and continue to support new learners through the process until they are ready to do it on their own.

ii. It is important to remember not to continue extensive scaffolding beyond the point of skill acquisition. The learner must become empowered to proceed on his or her own. Vygotsky (1978) discusses this in the context of the zone of proximal development.

SCORER—TEST TAKING STRATEGY

Purpose of the Strategy

i. Access and use prior knowledge

ii. Improve test-taking skills

iii. Build awareness of learning process

iv. Develop cognitive learning strategies

v. Develop and extend time on task

vi. Develop field independent skills

vii. Develop higher persistence

viii. Develop problem-solving skills

ix. Reduce impulsivity

x. Sustain engagement

How to Do It

i. This test-taking strategy provides a structure for completing various tests by assisting the students to carefully and systematically complete test items.

ii. The teacher creates a poster or chart illustrating SCORER and explains each word and the actions to take at each step. He or she demonstrates how to do each step and reinforces these by stopping periodically during a trial test and asking what the students have done for each SCORER item.

iii. Students are given small cue cards with the SCORER frame on it to remind them of each step while taking a test or reading something requiring answers and responses.

iv. The following are the steps in SCORER:

1. Schedule time effectively

2. Clue words identified

3. Omit difficult items until the end

4. Read carefully

5. Estimate answers requiring calculations

6. Review work and responses

Research Base

Elliot & Thurlow (2005)

Ritter & Idol-Maestas (1986)

SCORER Test-Taking Element	What am I to do at this step?	What did I do about it?	Notes
Schedule time effectively			
Clue words identified			
Omit difficult items until the end			
Read carefully			
Estimate answers requiring calculations			
Review work and responses			

What to Watch for With ELL/CLD Students

    i. Newcomers will need to have the SCORER steps modeled and explained in their most proficient language before they can proceed independently.

    ii. Students can be paired with partners who are slightly more bilingual than themselves to facilitate their learning this process.

SELF-CONCEPT ACTIVITIES

Purpose of the Strategy

    i. Build awareness of adaptation process

    ii. Build transfer skills

    iii. Build appreciation that everyone has a contribution to make

    iv. Build awareness of appropriate academic behaviors

    v. Build confidence in independent work

    vi. Develop confidence in school interactions

    vii. Develop self-esteem

    viii. Encourage pride in students' personal history

    ix. Facilitate student regaining control over self

    x. Facilitate student self-concept as a successful person

    xi. Facilitate students' comfort with learning environment

    xii. Facilitate students' ownership in their education

    xiii. Develop self-monitoring skills

    xiv. Enhance awareness of school adaptation process

    xv. Reduce anxiety and stress

    xvi. Reduce confusion in locus of control

    xvii. Reduce culture shock

    xviii. Develop personal control of situations

    xix. Reduce resistance to change

    xx. Reduce response fatigue

    xxi. Reduce stress for new students

How to Do It

    i. The teacher sets aside one period each day, if possible, or at least twice a week for one or more of these activities.

    ii. The teacher or assistant demonstrates what is expected from the students during each exercise and keeps copies of acceptable responses posted on the wall.

iii. The following are examples of self-concept activities:

- Do well: Sitting in a circle, ask the children to share with the group something they like to do and that they do well.
- Pen pal: Ask the students to write a letter describing themselves to an imaginary pen pal. Encourage them to go beyond mere physical descriptions, adding things like hobbies, family composition, favorite subjects, and so on.
- My body: Ask the students to consider the following questions: What are the beautiful parts of your body? The ugliest? Where did you get your notions of beauty? How do TV commercials affect your notion of beauty? How does your body influence your self-image? What are bodies for anyway?
- My assets: Ask students to write a paragraph about themselves describing the assets they have, the negative traits they would like to eliminate, and the positive characteristics they would like to obtain or develop. In dealing with the negative aspects, it is important to distinguish between things that can be changed (a bad disposition) and things that cannot be changed (a weak chin).
- Puppets: Ask a group of elementary students to work alone or together to make up a story about themselves. Then have them make hand puppets representing the characters and to act out the story they have written. Encourage them to focus on the positive qualities of the participants.
- Self-worth: Have the students write a story about something they can do to make other people feel worthy.
- Drawing: Ask the students to draw a picture of the things they do that make other people feel worthy.
- Get well: When a student is sick for an extended period of time, initiate a class project to make or buy a gift for the sick child. One class we know of constructed a giant "We miss you!" card from individual paintings done by the children. The effort of caring and giving is as powerful on the class as is the effect of receiving and being cared for on the child who is ill.
- Class mural: Tape a long sheet of butcher paper to the wall, provide the class with lots of crayons, and ask the students to draw a "class mural" depicting the things they do in common and the things they do that are more uniquely their own.
- Bulletin boards: Create a large bulletin board in your room just for posting individual and group work and kids' pictures and drawings. The bulletin board should always be plastered with pictures and the work of the kids. Some themes teachers have used successfully are "What Would You Like to Be?" (pictures of occupational choice with stories written by children displayed by the picture that matches their choice) and "I am proud of" (stories and pictures drawn by students illustrating an achievement or an event they are proud of). Polaroid pictures of kids next to correct homework, poems, stories, and drawings they have created are also

very reinforcing. Names and pictures should change weekly in order to give everyone recognition for something every two or three weeks. Use your ingenuity to discover strengths in each student.

- Classroom or school newspaper: The creation of a classroom newspaper is a good way to provide children with the opportunity to see their names and their work in print. Articles can also be written about the children's achievements. Recognition, in print, of positive services, activities, and achievements does a lot to increase and improve self-concept. Students can select the name of the paper, choose editors and reporters, conduct interviews, and draw illustrations. On a school basis, each room could have a reporter, who might change from time to time, to collect and gather material for publication. The writing of the newspaper also helps strengthen written language skills. The newspaper could also be used in various classrooms for reading instruction.

- Write a story: Ask the students to write a story about themselves as "neat" people. Specifically instruct them to deal with personality and character—what they like about the way they are. In other words, discourage them from thinking of themselves as only their talents, skills, or achievements but rather their feelings, thoughts, and behaviors.

- The nicest things ever: Have the whole class write *the nicest thing ever* book. Let each child write and illustrate three contributions: "the nicest thing I ever did for anyone" (ask them to explain what it was, why they did it, and how it made them feel), "The nicest thing anyone ever did for me" (ask them to describe it, why they think someone did it, and how it made a difference in what might have happened), and "the nicest thing I ever did for myself."

- Teaching: Ask students to share with the class one area in which they feel confident enough to teach another person. This could be a hobby, a skill, a sport, a musical instrument, a special interest, or so on. Also ask them what they would like to learn if someone in the class had the skill to teach them.

- Breaking a record: Ask students what record they would break if they could break any record in the world. Why would they do it?

- It's neat to be me: Ask the students to consider the fact that they are one of a kind. Encourage them to write a short poem (or story) titled, "It's neat to be me!" This should be a free exercise, not forced writing assignment.

- I can: Ask the students to write a story about a boy or girl who faces a physical test of courage and resourcefulness and succeeds or a story about a teenager who suddenly finds himself or herself in trouble and gets out of it.

- Flower: Have students discuss or write their responses to the following questions: If you were a flower, what kind would you be? What color? Where would you be planted? If you were picked, who would pick you? To whom would you like to be given? Where would you be placed?

- Graffiti board: Get some butcher paper or newsprint, and designate an area where kids can write or draw anything they want. It's their place to let off steam in a nondestructive way. Periodically, place a new paper over the old so that new graffiti can be collected.

Research Base

Borba (2001)

Strickland, Ganske, & Monroe (2002)

Tomlinson (1999)

What to Watch for With ELL/CLD Students

i. All cultures have expectations about how to consider a person successful or whole or deserving of attention. This is related to differences in cultural practices regarding locus of control. Understand that in some cultures children are taught not to stand out and, in some cases, are teased if they put themselves forward as better than their peers.

ii. Students can learn this strategy and benefit from it, but the teacher has to directly teach each process and not assume students automatically know about the purpose.

iii. Use the students' most proficient language to explain the process and purpose of the strategy.

SELF-MONITORING TECHNIQUES

Purpose of the Strategy

i. Adapt to meet individual or unique student needs

ii. Alleviate power struggles between teacher and student

iii. Clarify responsibilities, assignments, and rewards

iv. Build awareness of relation between cause and effect

v. Build awareness of school culture expectations

vi. Build students' self-awareness of behavior

vii. Develop awareness of cause and effect

viii. Develop extended time on task

ix. Develop self-monitoring skills

x. Enhance ability of students to focus on learning

xi. Ensure that students are aware of and responsible for their own actions

xii. Facilitate students assuming responsibility for learning

xiii. Facilitate student regaining control over self

xiv. Facilitate students' ownership in their education

xv. Facilitate student self-evaluation skills

xvi. Minimize ambiguity in classroom

xvii. Minimize behavior problems

xviii. Improve motivation

xix. Reduce confrontations over minor misbehaving

xx. Reduce confusion in locus of control

xxi. Reduce frustration in students due to unclear expectations

xxii. Reduce impulsivity

xxiii. Reduce inappropriate behaviors

xxiv. Reduce low-persistence behaviors

xxv. Reduce misperceptions

xxvi. Reduce number of conflicts with other students

xxvii. Reduce off-task behaviors

xxviii. Build awareness of academic expectation

xxix. Build awareness of appropriate behaviors for school language and rules

xxx. Adapt the mode of response required of students

How to Do It

i. The teacher works with individual students to identify something they need to remember to do, either in terms of behavior in the classroom or on an academic goal or task. Together they create a checklist or other way to keep track of what they are to do and each time they complete the action correctly.

ii. This can also be done for specific academic benchmarks or goals to achieve. For example, we have used this with benchmarks in language acquisition for specific English language students as they accomplish specific levels of proficiency.

iii. This can also be done for specific classroom behaviors that an individual student finds challenging such as putting their work away, not bothering their neighbors, and so on.

iv. Individual students monitor their own learning behaviors using teacher or student made checklists. For example, students record a checkmark each time they catch themselves being distracted, each time they catch themselves tapping their pencils on their desks, or each time they complete a specified portion of an assignment.

Research Base

Collier (2010a)

Harwell (2001)

Strickland, Ganske, & Monroe (2002)

Tomlinson (1999)

What to Watch for With ELL/CLD Students

i. All cultures have expectations and rules about the degree to which a child is responsible for his or her actions. This is related to differences in cultural practices regarding locus of control.

ii. Students can learn this strategy and benefit from it, but the teacher has to directly teach this process and not assume students automatically know about the purpose.

iii. Use the students' most proficient language to explain the process and purpose of the strategy.

iv. The teacher must familiarize himself or herself with the self-control rules of the various cultures represented in the classroom before expecting to use self-monitoring strategically to promote learning.

v. Examples should be provided from the students' family or community experiences. Each desired outcome can be written in simple language and illustrated with a graphic prompt that shows exactly what is expected.

Self-Monitoring Chart

Name:

Date:

I want to be able to:

1. Work quietly during cooperative group activities.											
2. Listen to the teacher's directions and take notes of what I need to do.											
3. Put the materials away in their proper boxes when I am done using them.											

SELF-REINFORCEMENT

Purpose of the Strategy

i. Build awareness of learning

ii. Build awareness of school culture expectations

iii. Develop personal control of situations

iv. Develop self-monitoring skills

v. Build students' self-awareness of behavior

vi. Facilitate student regaining control over self

vii. Facilitate student self-concept as a successful person

viii. Facilitate students' comfort with learning environment

ix. Facilitate students' ownership in their education

x. Reduce confusion in locus of control

xi. Build transfer skills

xii. Build upon existing language skills of students

xiii. Develop thinking and planning skills

xiv. Facilitate access of prior knowledge

xv. Reduce impulsivity

xvi. Reduce inappropriate behaviors

xvii. Facilitate language development

xviii. Improve motivation and response

xix. Reduce off-task behaviors

How to Do It

i. The teacher assists students in developing checklists for task completion and appropriate classroom behavior.

ii. At first, the teacher stops the class occasionally and points out appropriate learning or behavior taking place, rewarding with points or praise.

iii. As students become familiar with what is desired, they can check off points on their own checklists.

iv. Individual students reward themselves for appropriate behavior and performance at specific check-in points during the lesson. Eventually, each student uses a self-developed checklist and gives rewards to self upon completion of tasks.

Research Base

Tomlinson (1999)

What to Watch for With ELL/CLD Students

  i. English language learner (ELL) students who are limited English proficient (LEP) may need the process explained in their most proficient language.

  ii. Points are not intrinsically reinforcing. What is rewarding to one person is not necessarily rewarding to another. This is another learned preference.

  iii. The points may be paired with some more directly rewarding action and then gradually just use points.

SHELTERED INSTRUCTION

Purpose of the Strategy

  i. Build appreciation that everyone belongs and is needed

  ii. Build appreciation that everyone has a contribution to make

  iii. Build awareness of academic expectations

  iv. Build awareness of adaptation process

  v. Build awareness of the appropriate content language in English culture/language

  vi. Build first language to English transfer skills

  vii. Build academic transfer skills

  viii. Build upon existing language skills of students

  ix. Build upon existing language strengths of student

  x. Build upon family language and culture

  xi. Build upon the diverse language foundations of students and parents

  xii. Develop cognitive academic language proficiency

  xiii. Develop confidence in school culture interactions

  xiv. Develop higher tolerance

  xv. Facilitate access of prior knowledge

  xvi. Facilitate language development

  xvii. Improve confidence in academic interactions

  xviii. Improve confidence in home and community culture/school culture interactions

  xix. Improve confidence in school interactions

  xx. Improve vocabulary

  xxi. Reduce anxiety and stress

xxii. Reduce anxiety and stress responses

xxiii. Reduce anxiety in social/academic interactions

xxiv. Reduce code switching

xxv. Reduce conflicts with other students

xxvi. Reduce culture shock

xxvii. Strengthen ability to discuss what is happening

xxviii. Strengthen language development

How to Do It

i. Sheltered instruction is an approach for teaching content to students in strategic ways that make the subject matter concepts comprehensible while promoting the students' language development. Sheltered instruction is something all teachers can use with all students. Teachers don't need to speak the students' native language. Sheltered instruction is not watered down instruction. Oftentimes "watered down" refers to simplified language. The purpose of sheltered instruction is to implement approaches that open the door to high level language for all students.

ii. Sheltered instruction is good teaching, but not all good teaching is sheltered instruction.

iii. The teacher always presents lessons with concrete, physical models and demonstrations of both content and expected performance. Language is simplified and content focused.

Expansion

i. Students are encouraged to discuss lessons in home and community language and work in small groups on content activities. The teacher develops a game or other casual group interaction activity. The teacher or specialist explains, in home and community language when possible, what is going to occur and whom the students are going to meet. The home and community culture students are introduced to the school culture students, and they engage in the game or activity together.

Research Base

Cloud, Genesee, & Hamayan (2000)

Echevarria (1995)

Echevarria & Graves (2006)

Echevarria, Vogt, & Short (2007)

Garber-Miller (2006)

Gibbons (2002)

Hansen-Thomas (2008)

Short & Echevarria (2004)

What to Watch for With ELL/CLD Students

i. It is important to have the example speakers be people with whom the students are familiar and comfortable.

ii. This can be paired with role-play of school interactions.

iii. The teacher presents lessons with concrete models and demonstrations of both content and expected performance. Language is simplified and content focused.

iv. Building familiarity is critical for the success of this strategy. Not all ELL/CLD students will know what the objects or models represent.

v. The teacher will need to introduce the models or objects in full scale representations or use the actual items to build a true understanding. Only after students have actually seen, felt, smelled, and possibly tasted an apple will they respond to a picture of an apple.

SHORTENING STUDENT ASSIGNMENTS

Purpose of the Strategy

i. Access prior knowledge

ii. Adapt the mode of response required of students

iii. Build confidence in independent work

iv. Build foundation for learning

v. Build learners' confidence in their control of the learning process

vi. Encourage questioning and exploration of new learning

vii. Enhance ability of students to focus on learning

viii. Enhance ability of students to learn new things

ix. Build awareness of learning

x. Develop personal control of situations

xi. Reduce off-task behaviors

xii. Facilitate school adaptation process

xiii. Facilitate students assuming responsibility for learning

xiv. Sustain engagement

xv. Develop thinking and planning skills

How to Do It

i. The teacher provides the students with shortened versions of specific assignments, or the complete assignment is presented in several short segments rather than all at one time. This helps make difficult or complex tasks become more manageable, less threatening, and less overwhelming to the students.

ii. For example, teacher assigns a student one section of a geography text. Then, the teacher structures a group to jigsaw information from the rest of the text to share with the student.

Research Base

Echevarria & Graves (2006)

Gibbons (2002

What to Watch for With ELL/CLD Students

i. Learning to survive and thrive in a new environment is challenging for anyone. This can be especially difficult for English language learners (ELL) and culturally and linguistically divers (CLD0 learners as they learn to interact in a new language and with new academic content and expectations.

ii. Breaking a task into specific short segments while retaining the core content objectives will facilitate learning for diverse learners.

SIGNALS

Purpose of the Strategy

i. Adapt to meet individual or unique student needs

ii. Build awareness of adaptation process

iii. Build awareness of appropriate academic behaviors

iv. Build awareness of appropriate behaviors for school language and rules

v. Build awareness of relation between cause and effect

vi. Build awareness of school culture expectations

vii. Build students' self-awareness of behavior

viii. Build transfer skills

ix. Develop personal control of situations

x. Develop self-monitoring skills

xi. Eliminate inappropriate behavior

xii. Reduce acting out behaviors

xiii. Facilitate nondirective guidance about student misbehavior

xiv. Prevent minor inappropriate behaviors from escalating

xv. Reduce specific attention to the students' misbehaving

How to Do It

i. The teacher selects and uses various nonverbal cues or signals to control inappropriate behavior or guide students to attend to specific aspects of the lessons or school routine.

ii. For example, teacher flicks the classroom lights on and off when the noise level in the class becomes too loud.

iii. I have done this with a sound cue, the opening bars of Beethoven's 5th, when it is time for students to stop and reflect on what they have just read in the textbook.

Research Base

Marable & Raimondi (1995)

Petrie, Lindauer, Bennett, & Gibson. (1998)

Rogers (2006)

What to Watch for With ELL/CLD Students

i. Always introduce signals to ELL and CLD students by explaining them in their most proficient language.

ii. ELL/CLD students who have had prior schooling might be asked what sort of signals they are familiar with, and that could become part of the classroom routine.

SORTING

Figure S.2   Example of the Sorting Strategy

Purpose of the Strategy

i. Access prior knowledge

ii. Build awareness of appropriate academic behaviors

iii. Build academic transfer skills

iv. Build appreciation that everyone belongs and is needed

v. Build appreciation that everyone has a contribution to make

vi. Build foundation for learning

vii. Build metacognition skills

viii. Develop cognitive academic language

ix. Develop cognitive learning strategies

x. Develop problem-solving skills

xi. Encourage questioning and exploration of new learning

xii. Enhance ability of students to focus on learning

xiii. Enhance ability of students to learn new things

xiv. Expand and elaborate on learning

xv. Expand comprehension

xvi. Facilitate access of prior knowledge

xvii. Facilitate discussion about new learning

xviii. Facilitate language development

xix. Improve students' ability to organize and prioritize information

xx. Reinforce content lessons

xxi. Retention of content

xxii. Strengthen ability to discuss what is happening

xxiii. Strengthen awareness of learning process

xxiv. Strengthen knowledge of academic content

xxv. Strengthen language development

xxvi. Strengthen learning to learn skills

xxvii. Strengthen retention and application abilities

xxviii. Sustain engagement

xxix. Use prior knowledge

xxx. Develop analytical skills

xxxi. Build awareness of learning process

xxxii. Develop association skills

xxxiii. Develop categorization skills

xxxiv. Develop field independent skills

xxxv. Improve mnemonic retrieval

How to Do It

i.   In essence, the teacher divides students into small groups and gives each group of students a bag of items related to some topic of discussion or recent unit of instruction. These can be models of objects or the actual items themselves such as colored balls, square blocks, toy animals, plastic fruit, coins, items from a place just visited, items related to a specific topic, and so on. The students are instructed to group or sort the items into groups or sets according to categories selected by the teacher or by the nature of the lesson.

ii. The following are the steps for students to follow in implementing this strategy:

1. What items go together, and why?

2. What attribute of these am I using to group them?

3. What do we call each set of items?

4. How are the groups similar to one another?

5. How are the groups different from one another?

6. How can we generalize this information?

iii. The teacher may assign students of similar language and ability to either heterogeneous or homogeneous groups depending upon the specific goals. Rather than preparing a bag of items, the teacher could also direct students to empty out their backpacks and work in small groups. Each small group goes through the steps, sorting all the items in their piles together. They make lists of their groups of items to share with the class.

iv. When applying the sorting strategy, students work through problems or tasks using the above sequence of self-monitoring questions. For example, you are going to have a new unit about rocks and minerals, that is, igneous, sedimentary, conglomerate, and so on. Many of the students are unfamiliar with these ways of grouping natural materials that they consider generically as rocks. One group of students comes from a culture where rocks are grouped by hard versus soft and another from a culture that groups rocks by whether they can be used to produce something in the home. You might introduce your class to the lesson by having actual examples of the rocks to handle or take the class on a field trip to the museum or a local mine or industrial area to observe them. You could also show pictures or videos of chemists interacting with the materials. Have the students look for patterns in appearance, use, environment, chemical reactions, and so on. They could chart the attributes and characteristics of the rocks and minerals on a graph or in Venn diagrams (Step 1 of sorting, "What items go together, and why?"). Now they should look for distinctive patterns of commonality between rocks and minerals that show whether or not they go together (Step 2 of sorting, "What attribute of these am I using to group them?"). Ask the students what they would name the group of rocks and minerals based upon the major attributes. Now introduce them to the common English name of the group (Step 3 of sorting, "What do we call each set of items?"). Discuss how the materials within each group share certain common characteristics, and then discuss the characteristics that all rocks and minerals share in common as rocks and minerals (Step 4 of sorting, "How are the groups similar to one another?"). Discuss how the rocks within each group might differ from each other, how each group of rocks and minerals differs from the other groups, and how rocks differ from nonrocks (Step 5 of sorting, "How are the groups different from one another?"). Finish the unit with a discussion of how to find patterns in anything you are studying (Step 6 of sorting, "How do we generalize this information?").

v. You might now step back from the lesson and discuss the enhanced cognitive learning that you have provided students, the learning to learn lesson that is represented by the strategy you had them use. At this point, you would discuss how everything in the world is composed of various elements that need to be identified in order to understand the whole thing being studied (field independence) and that when all the parts are put together the meaning of the whole thing results (field sensitive).

Research Base

Ferris & Hedgcock (2005)

Iachini, Borghi, & Senese (2008)

What to Watch for With ELL/CLD Students

i. The strategy preparation can be done in the native language or dialect of the students to assure their understanding of your expectations and their tasks prior to carrying the assignment out in English or other communication mode.

ii. Understand that all cultures have different ways of thinking of common attributes of a group of similar objects. What constitutes the criteria to pay attention to will vary based upon cultural values and learning practices. While it seems obvious to one group that the predominant surface color of a set of objects is what links them together as a set of objects, to another group it might be that surface texture or size is more important as an attribute for sorting out similarity and difference.

Participant	Weight	Where Object Found	Name of Thing	Color	Function or Use	Size	What Made Of	Shape
1								
2								
3								
4								
5								
Other sorting categories								

Participant	Taste or Smell	Color	Function or Use	Size	What Made Of	Shape	Texture	Weight
1								
2								
3								
4								
5								
Other sorting categories								

SQ3R—READING STRATEGY

Purpose of the Strategy

i. Develop cognitive academic language

ii. Develop extended time on task

iii. Develop higher persistence

iv. Develop problem-solving skills

v. Facilitate discussion of new learning

vi. Facilitate reading process

vii. Access and use prior knowledge

viii. Build transfer skills

ix. Improve and strengthen retention of content

x. Expand and elaborate on learning foundations

xi. Improve access to prior knowledge

xii. Improve comprehension

xiii. Strengthen and facilitate language development

How to Do It

i. The teacher puts the steps of SQ3R up on the board with the words survey, question, read, recite, and review. He or she explains what each term means and what a student should do while reading a passage. This strategy reminds students to go through any passage or lesson carefully and thoughtfully.

ii. The teacher models how to use each step of SQ3R while reading a passage or story, making notes to remind students what they should do at each point.

iii. Students can make cue cards to remember each step. The following are the steps in SQ3R:

1. Survey

2. Question

3. Read

4. Recite

5. Review

Research Base

Allington & Cunningham (2002)

Artis (2008)

Cole (1995)

Fisher & Frey (2004)

Irvin & Rose (1995)

Law & Eckes (2000)

Moore, Alvermann, & Hinchman (2000)

Robinson (1946)

Sakta (1999)

Tovani (2000)

What to Watch for With ELL/CLD Students

    i. Newcomers will need to have the SQ3R steps modeled and explained in their most proficient language before they can proceed independently.

    ii. Students can be paired with partners who are slightly more bilingual than themselves to facilitate their learning this process.

SQ3R Element	What am I to do at this step?	What did I do about it?	Notes
Survey			
Question			
Read			
Recite			
Review			

SQRQCQ—MATH STRATEGY

Purpose of the Strategy

    i. Build awareness of academic expectations

    ii. Build learners' confidence in their control of the learning process

    iii. Build awareness of appropriate academic behaviors

    iv. Build awareness of appropriate behaviors for school language and rules

v. Build awareness of appropriate cognitive academic language

vi. Develop cognitive academic language

vii. Develop cognitive learning strategies

viii. Develop field independent skills

ix. Develop higher persistence

x. Develop thinking and planning skills

xi. Expand and elaborate on learning

xii. Expand comprehension

xiii. Facilitate students assuming responsibility for learning

xiv. Improve comprehension

xv. Improve mnemonic retrieval

xvi. Increase students' probability of generating a correct response

xvii. Increase students' time on task

xviii. Increase the frequency of appropriate responses or behaviors

xix. Increase time on task

xx. Improve students' ability to organize and prioritize information

xxi. Retention of content

xxii. Strengthen ability to discuss what is happening

xxiii. Strengthen awareness of learning process

xxiv. Sustain engagement

xxv. Strengthen retention and application abilities

xxvi. Develop analytical skills

xxvii. Improve comprehension

xxviii. Develop problem-solving skills

xxix. Facilitate language development

xxx. Improve retention of information

xxxi. Improve problem solving of math word problems

xxxii. Strengthen language development

How to Do It

i. This strategy provides a systematic structure for identifying the question being asked in a math word problem, computing the response, and ensuring that the question in the problem was answered.

ii. The teacher projects the SQRQCQ frame upon a chart and goes through it step by step while students look at sheet copies of the pattern at their desks. The teacher presents a math word problem and shows how using the SQRQCQ frame helps understand the word problem and the steps to solve the word problem: (1) what am I to do at this step, (2) what did I do about it, and (3) any notes to themselves about what worked or didn't work to solve the problem.

iii. The following are the steps in SQRQCQ:

1. Survey word problems
2. Question asked is identified
3. Read more carefully
4. Question process required to solve problem
5. Compute the answer
6. Question self to ensure that the answer solves the problem

Research Base

Cole (1995)

Elliot & Thurlow (2005)

What to Watch for With ELL/CLD Students

i. Newcomers will need to have the SQRQCQ steps modeled and explained in their most proficient language before they can proceed independently.

ii. Students can be paired with partners who are slightly more bilingual than themselves to facilitate their learning this process.

SSCD—READING AND WRITING STRATEGY

Purpose of the Strategy

i. Access and use prior knowledge
ii. Build awareness of learning
iii. Build awareness of academic language
iv. Build transfer skills
v. Develop analytical skills
vi. Develop association skills
vii. Develop field sensitive skills
viii. Develop higher persistence
ix. Develop higher tolerance

SQRQCQ Element	What am I to do at this step?	What did I do about it?	Notes
Survey word problems			
Question asked is identified			
Read more carefully			
Question process required to solve problem			
Compute the answer			
Question self to ensure that the answer solves the problem			

    x.   Build mctacognition skills

   xi.   Develop thinking and planning skills

  xii.   Improve access to prior knowledge

 xiii.   Reduce off-task behaviors

 xiv.   Strengthen language development

How to Do It

i. The teacher posts the letters and phrases for SSCD on the wall where students can refer to them as they work. He or she also gives them individual sheets to make notes for themselves.

ii. The teacher goes over each step in SSCD to show how to do this while reading text or when reviewing their own writing. He reminds them to use sound clues to read difficult or unfamiliar words as well as how to use word structure clues. He or she shows them how to use context clues and how to look words up in the dictionary, if possible.

iii. Bilingual dictionaries can also be used.

iv. SSCD encourages students to remember to use sound, structure, and context clues to address unfamiliar vocabulary. This is followed by dictionary usage if necessary.

v. The following are the steps in SSCD:

1. Sound clues used

2. Structure clues used

3. Context clues used

4. Dictionary used

SSCD Elements	What am I to do at this step?	What did I do about it?	How many times did I do this?
Sound clues used			
Structure clues used			
Context clues used			
Dictionary used			

Research Base

Collier (2003b)

Opitz (1998)

What to Watch for With ELL/CLD Students

i. Newcomers will need to have the SSCD steps modeled and explained in their most proficient language before they can proceed independently.

ii. Students can be paired with partners who are slightly more bilingual than themselves to facilitate their learning this process.

STAR—CONTROL AND ATTENTION STRATEGY

Purpose of the Strategy

i. Build transfer skills

ii. Build awareness of appropriate academic behaviors

iii. Develop extended time on task

iv. Develop field independent skills

v. Develop thinking and planning skills

vi. Develop higher persistence

vii. Expand and elaborate on learning

viii. Expand comprehension

ix. Facilitate access of prior knowledge

x. Facilitate acquisition of content knowledge

xi. Build awareness of and foundation for learning

xii. Increase students' probability of generating a correct response

xiii. Increase students' time on task

xiv. Develop personal control of situations

xv. Improve access to prior knowledge

xvi. Reduce off-task behaviors

xvii. Strengthen language development

How to Do It

i. The teacher introduces students to the use of the STAR for assisting in regaining control over their actions, paying attention to what is going on, and as a way to take time during reading and writing or other lessons.

ii. The teacher can make a poster or chart showing STAR and what is to be done at each step. He or she can also model each action and tell students that whenever he or she stops in a lesson, and says "what does the STAR say," they are to stop and think about what is happening or what they are doing and then act appropriately. The teacher can have review points during the day as students become more familiar with this technique.

iii. This strategy can be used for all content areas and for behavior modification. Students can make cue cards for each step.

iv. The following are the steps in STAR:

1. Stop
2. Think
3. Act
4. Review

STAR Elements	What am I to do at this step?	What did I do about it?	How many times did I do this?
Stop			
Think			
Act			
Review			

Research Base

Agran, King-Sears, Wehmeyer, & Copeland (2003)

Carpenter (2001)

Lee et al. (2006)

What to Watch for With ELL/CLD Students

i. Newcomers will need to have the STAR steps modeled and explained in their most proficient language before they can proceed independently.

ii. Students can be paired with partners who are slightly more bilingual than themselves to facilitate their learning this process.

STORY STAR—READING COMPREHENSION STRATEGY

Purpose of the Strategy

i. Access and use prior knowledge

ii. Build vocabulary

iii. Develop content knowledge foundation

iv. Develop extended time on task

v. Develop problem-solving skills

vi. Develop thinking and planning skills

vii. Enhance ability of students to focus on learning

viii. Enhance ability of students to learn new things

ix. Build transfer skills

x. Expand and elaborate on learning

xi. Expand comprehension

xii. Facilitate access of prior knowledge

xiii. Facilitate acquisition of content knowledge

xiv. Increase students' probability of generating a correct response

xv. Increase students' time on task

xvi. Build awareness of learning

xvii. Reduce off-task behaviors

xviii. Reduce misperceptions

xix. Reinforce content

How to Do It

i. This strategy can be used to introduce a story. This gives the students the opportunity to predict where the story takes place, who the characters are, when the story takes place, what the problem is, and how it is solved.

ii. It organizes learning activity for preview, view, and review and provides structure for the learning process from beginning to end while providing structure for specific tasks through each step of the lesson:

1. (Step 1) The teacher or assistant uses a star (or other shape) with the *W* questions on it as a preview/view/review structure for all lesson content, outlining key issues, rehearsing vocabulary, and reviewing related prior knowledge.

2. (Step 2) The teacher shows the students the cover of the book or the pictures in the story and then asks them the five questions on each point of the star. Their guesses are recorded on the points.

3. (Step 3) The teacher leads the students through the star structure step by step: Where did this story take place? Who is this story about? When did this story happen? What do you think happens in this story? Why do the characters in the story do what they do? How do you think the characters get along?

4. (Step 4) Add other *W* questions. Use review or retention techniques to spiral back to and reinforce the use of KWL during lesson.

Research Base

Collier (2002)

Harwell (2001)

Heacox (2002)

Moore, Alvermann, & Hinchman (2000)

Opitz (1998)

What to Watch for With ELL/CLD Students

i. There are cultural differences in cognitive/learning style, and some ELL/CLD students may not respond to the brainstorming construct behind the story star.

ii. This is another activity that works best with preparation in the students' most proficient language and relevance to their culture before proceeding.

Figure S.3 Example of Story Star

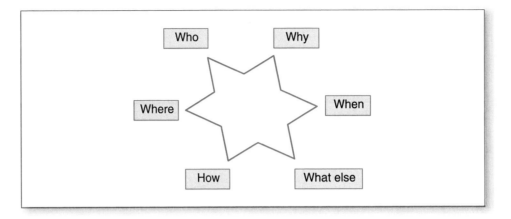

STUDENT INPUT

Purpose of the Strategy

   i. Build awareness of learning

   ii. Build upon existing language skills of students

   iii. Build upon existing language strengths of students

   iv. Develop personal control of situations

   v. Encourage questioning and exploration of new learning

   vi. Enhance ability of students to focus on learning

   vii. Facilitate students' ownership in their education

   viii. Access prior knowledge

   ix. Improve students' ability to organize and prioritize information

   x. Reduce distractibility

   xi. Retention of content

   xii. Strengthen ability to discuss what is happening

   xiii. Strengthen awareness of learning process

   xiv. Improve motivation

   xv. Increase time on task

   xvi. Expand and elaborate on learning

   xvii. Sustain engagement

   xviii. Build transfer skills

How to Do It

   i. Include students in the decision-making process as general curricular activities are developed. Allow students to select some specific topics to be covered in an upcoming unit of study. The learner is encouraged to provide ideas and suggestions for selected daily curricular activities, keeping within the general parameters of the required elements. This gives the students greater ownership and more motivation to complete challenging assignments.

Research Base

Beaudoin (2005)

Brophy (2004)

Curwin & Mendler (1999)

What to Watch for With ELL/CLD Students

i.   Some ELL and CLD students will have limited experience with schooling in settings where they are expected to speak out and volunteer information or ideas.

ii. These students will need to be directly taught how and when to provide input in an appropriate manner.

iii. Discussion about providing input may be done in any language to facilitate understanding.

SUCCESS

Purpose of the Strategy

i.   Adapt to meet individual or unique student needs

ii.   Adapt the mode of response required of students

iii. Build appreciation that everyone belongs and is needed

iv.   Build appreciation that everyone has a contribution to make

v.   Build awareness of learning process

vi.   Build foundation for learning

vii. Clarify responsibilities, assignments, and rewards

viii. Enhance ability of students to focus on learning

ix.   Reduce low-persistence behaviors

x.   Develop personal control of situations

xi.   Develop thinking and planning skills

xii. Facilitate student self-concept as a successful person

xiii. Improve confidence and self-esteem

xiv. Improve retention

xv.   Facilitate access and use of prior knowledge

How to Do It

i. The teacher ensures that each student successfully completes assigned tasks, by initially reducing the level of difficulty of materials and gradually increasing the level of difficulty as easier tasks are met with success. The teacher also reduces the complexity level of vocabulary or concepts in written material to help the students complete a reading task. Through this strategy, learners may read material similar to others in the class without requiring an excessive amount of individual attention from the teacher.

Example

i. The teacher places a transparency over a page of written material and, with a fine-point marker, crosses out the more difficult words and writes simpler equivalents of those words above or in the margin next to the crossed-out words. As the student reads, he or she substitutes the simpler words for those marked out.

Research Base

Gibbons (2003)

Krumenaker, Many, & Wang (2008)

Leki (1995)

Tomlinson (1999)

What to Watch for With ELL/CLD Students

i. The teacher needs information or professional development about all of the diverse learning styles, cultures, and languages in the classroom in order to design accessible learning activities for all students.

ii. There is as much diversity within the ELL and CLD population as there is between the non-ELL and ELL population as a whole.

SURVIVAL STRATEGIES FOR PARENTS/FAMILIES

Purpose of the Strategy

i. Build awareness of appropriate behaviors for school language and rules

ii. Build awareness of appropriate cognitive academic language

iii. Build awareness of appropriate communication behaviors for school language and rules

iv. Build awareness of school culture expectations

v. Build transfer skills

vi. Build upon the diverse language foundations of students and parents

vii. Improve confidence in home and community culture/school culture interactions

viii. Strengthen school/parent partnerships

ix. Develop confidence in school culture interactions

x. Develop personal control of situations

xi. Reduce culture shock

How to Do It

i. The liaison or specialist identifies basic rules of social and formal interaction that parents will need to know immediately. Parents may identify situations where they have made mistakes or which they would like assistance with. Facilitator and parents discuss situations and what is expected within these situations. Parents practice and discuss their responses and strategies in these situations, with opportunity for student input.

Research Base

Carrigan (2001)

Collier (2003)

What to Watch for With ELL/CLD Students

i. Particular social groups and cultures have different expectations of adults and children when it comes to being accountable for task completion. This is a learned difference between cultures. The teacher needs to be aware that the expectations in an American school may need to be taught directly to CLD students and not just assumed to be understood.

ii. One way to introduce the idea of behavior and strategies specific to your classroom is to ask students about how their parents have them behave at home or what they have learned playing games. This can then be expanded to the idea of acting appropriately in a classroom.

iii. Demonstrate all of the desired behaviors and strategies. Some role-play may be helpful. Examples of bad behaviors may be used with caution.

SURVIVAL STRATEGIES FOR STUDENTS

Purpose of the Strategy

i. Adapt to meet individual or unique student needs

ii. Adapt the mode of response required of students

iii. Build awareness of academic expectations

iv.   Build awareness of adaptation process

v.   Build awareness of appropriate academic behaviors

vi.   Build awareness of appropriate behaviors for school language and rules

vii. Build awareness of school culture expectations

viii. Build awareness of the appropriate content language in English culture/language

ix.   Develop confidence in academic interactions

x.   Develop confidence in school culture interactions

xi.   Develop confidence in school language

xii. Enhance awareness of school adaptation process

xiii. Enhance students' interaction with family during transition

xiv. Build awareness of appropriate behaviors for school language and rules

xv.   Build transfer skills

xvi. Develop confidence in school culture interactions

xvii. Facilitate students' comfort with learning environment

xviii. Reduce anxiety and stress

xix. Reduce anxiety and stress responses

xx.   Reduce anxiety in social/academic interactions

xxi. Develop personal control of situations

xxii. Reduce response fatigue

How to Do It

i.   The teacher identifies basic rules of social and formal interaction that students will need to know immediately. Students may identify situations where they made mistakes. The teacher, assistant, and peers discuss situations and what interactions are expected. Students may need to practice these interactions.

Research Base

Ashworth & Wakefield (2004)

Felix-Brasdefer (2008)

Jackson, Boostrom, & Hansen (1998)

Johnson, Juhasz, Marken, & Ruiz (1998)

What to Watch for With ELL/CLD Students

i. Particular social groups and cultures have different expectations of adults and children when it comes to following rules. This is a learned difference between cultures. The teacher needs to be aware that the expectations in an American school may need to be taught directly to CLD students and not just assumed to be understood.

ii. One way to introduce the idea of behavior and strategies specific to your classroom is to ask students about how their parents have them behave at home or what they have learned playing games. This can then be expanded to the idea of acting appropriately in a classroom.

iii. Demonstrate all of the desired behaviors and strategies. Some role-play may be helpful. Examples of bad behaviors may be used with caution.

ABCDEFGHIJKLMOPQRS**T**UVW

TEST-TAKING STRATEGY—PIRATES

Purpose of the Strategy

    i. Build academic transfer skills

    ii. Build awareness of learning process

    iii. Build awareness of school culture expectations

    iv. Clarify responsibilities, assignments, and rewards

    v. Develop confidence in academic interactions

    vi. Develop extended time on task

    vii. Develop thinking and planning skills

    viii. Improve confidence and self-esteem

    ix. Improve mnemonic retrieval

    x. Improve test-taking skills

    xi. Increase students' probability of generating a correct response

    xii. Increase students' time on task

    xiii. Reduce anxiety and stress

    xiv. Reduce distractibility

    xv. Sustain engagement

xvi. Develop problem-solving skills

xvii. Expand and elaborate on learning

xviii. Improve students' ability to organize and prioritize information

xix. Build awareness of learning process

xx. Improve test-taking skills for typical achievement tests

PIRATES Step	PIRATES Test-Taking Outcomes
P Prepare to succeed	
I Inspect instructions carefully	
R Read entire question, remember strategies, and reduce choices	
A Answer question or leave until later	
T Turn back to the abandoned items	
E Estimate unknown answers by avoiding absolutes and eliminating similar choices	
S Survey to ensure that all items have a response	

How to Do It

i. PIRATES may assist learners to complete tests more carefully and successfully. Students can create cue cards of the mnemonic and use them to work through each test and individual test item.

ii. The following are the steps in PIRATES:

1. Prepare to succeed

2. Inspect instructions carefully

3. Read entire question, remember strategies, and reduce choices

4. Answer question or leave until later

5. Turn back to the abandoned items

6. Estimate unknown answers by avoiding absolutes and eliminating similar choices

7. Survey to ensure that all items have a response

Research Base

DeVries Guth & Stephens Pettengill (2005)

Hughes, Deshler, Ruhl, & Schumaker (1993)

Lebzelter & Nowacek (1999)

What to Watch for With ELL/CLD Students

i. Newcomers will need to have the PIRATES steps modeled and explained in their most proficient language before they can proceed independently.

ii. Students can be paired with partners who are slightly more bilingual than themselves to facilitate learning this process.

TEST-TAKING STRATEGY—SCORER

Purpose of the Strategy

i. Build academic transfer skills

ii. Build awareness of learning process

iii. Build awareness of school culture expectations

iv. Clarify responsibilities, assignments, and rewards

v. Develop confidence in academic interactions

vi. Develop thinking and planning skills

vii. Improve confidence and self-esteem

viii. Improve mnemonic retrieval

ix. Improve test-taking skills

x. Increase students' probability of generating a correct response

xi. Reduce anxiety and stress

xii. Reduce distractibility

xiii. Sustain engagement

xiv. Increase students' time on task

xv. Develop problem-solving skills

xvi. Expand and elaborate on learning

xvii.   Improve students' ability to organize and prioritize information

xviii. Build awareness of learning process

xiv.   Improve test-taking skills for typical achievement tests

xx.   Develop and extend time on task

xxi.   Develop field independent skills

xxii.   Develop higher persistence

xxiii. Develop problem-solving skills

xxiv.   Reduce impulsivity

xxv.   Sustain engagement

How to Do It

i.   This test-taking strategy provides a structure for completing various tests by assisting the students to carefully and systematically complete test items.

ii. The teacher creates a poster or chart illustrating SCORER and explains each word and the actions to take at each step. He or she demonstrates how to do each step and reinforces these by stopping periodically during a trial test and asking what the students have done for each SCORER item.

iii. Students are given small cue cards with the SCORER frame on it to remind them of each step while taking a test or reading something requiring answers and responses.

iv. The following are steps in SCORER:

1. Schedule time effectively
2. Clue words identified
3. Omit difficult items until the end
4. Read carefully
5. Estimate answers requiring calculations
6. Review work and responses

Research Base

Elliot & Thurlow (2005)

Ritter & Idol-Maestas (1986)

What to Watch for With ELL/CLD Students

i. Newcomers will need to have the SCORER steps modeled and explained in their most proficient language before they can proceed independently.

ii. Students can be paired with partners who are slightly more bilingual than themselves to facilitate their learning this process.

SCORER Test-taking Element	What am I to do at this step?	What did I do about it?	Notes
Schedule time effectively			
Clue words identified			
Omit difficult items until the end			
Read carefully			
Estimate answers requiring calculations			
Review work and responses			

TIME-OUT

Purpose of the Strategy

    i. Adapt to meet individual or unique student needs

    ii. Adapt the mode of response required of students

    iii. Alleviate power struggles between teacher and students

iv. Build awareness of academic expectations

v. Build awareness of adaptation process

vi. Build awareness of appropriate academic behaviors

vii. Build awareness of relation between cause and effect

viii. Build awareness of school culture expectations

ix. Eliminate inappropriate behavior

x. Minimize behavior problems

xi. Reduce inappropriate behaviors

xii. Facilitate student regaining control over self

How to Do It

i. Time-outs can promote student thinking about own behavior and behavioral expectations of teacher.

ii. The teacher removes the student temporarily from the immediate environment to reduce external stimuli. This can be simply pulling the student's chair out of a circle or area and turning it around or can be a separate corner or place within the room.

iii. Be cautious about how long the student is removed—shorter is better, and be sure that it is absolutely clear why it is being done.

iv. For example, teacher removes a student to a quiet or time-out area for 3 to 5 minutes when student is unable to respond to a situation in a nonaggressive manner.

Research Base

Harwell (2001)

What to Watch for With ELL/CLD Students

i. Some English language learner (ELL) and culturally and linguistically diverse (CLD) students have limited experience with public schools and the rules expected in the classroom.

ii. Time-outs should be explained to the student in their most proficient language before using them or while taking them out of a situation.

TOTAL PHYSICAL RESPONSE—TPR

Purpose of the Strategy

i. Build transfer skills

ii. Access prior knowledge

iii. Adapt to meet individual or unique student needs

iv. Adapt the mode of response required of students

v. Build awareness of appropriate cognitive academic language

vi. Build awareness of appropriate social and academic language

vii. Build first language to English transfer skills

viii. Build foundation for learning

ix. Build home and community language to English transfer skills

x. Build learners' confidence in their control of the learning process

xi. Build transfer skills

xii. Build upon existing language skills of students

xiii. Build upon existing language strengths of student

xiv. Facilitate connections between known and new

xv. Facilitate discussion about new learning

xvi. Reduce anxiety and stress and responses

xvii. Reduce anxiety in social/academic interactions

xviii. Reduce code switching

xix. Improve comprehension

xx. Improve vocabulary

xxi. Build awareness of appropriate communication behaviors for school language and rules

xxii. Develop confidence in school language and rules for academic and social interactions

xxiii. Develop cognitive academic language

xxiv. Reduce stress for new students

How to Do It

i. Total physical response strategy was developed by James Asher and is a very simple strategy to enhance language learning in the context of movement and demonstration.

ii. Total physical response (TPR) is a popular and effective way of teaching language that actively involves the students and focuses on understanding the language rather than speaking it. The TPR method asks the students to demonstrate that they understand the new language by responding to a command with an action. At first, the teacher gives the commands and does the actions along with the student. As the student understands the vocabulary, the teacher stops doing the action and has the student do the action alone. Later, the student can give commands to other students or to the teacher.

iii. The teacher or assistant models words and phrases in action in various school settings, both in and out of the classroom. For example, he or she may teach the response to a question such as "what is this" or "what can you do with this" by saying and acting out the phrases "This is a pencil." "This pencil is used for writing on paper." Students take different roles in the interactions and practice them with each other and with the teacher.

Expansion

i. Students may suggest communication situations in which they would like specific assistance.

Research Base

Asher (1980)

Collier (2003a)

Law & Eckes (2000)

What to Watch for With ELL/CLD Students

i. Although this is a common beginner or newcomer strategy for use with ELL students, the teacher must still be cautious about making assumptions about CLD students' understanding of the actions required in the classroom.

ii. The teacher must clearly model and act out every action required before asking students to repeat the action.

TOUCH

Purpose of the Strategy

i. Adapt to meet individual or unique student needs

ii. Adapt the mode of response required of students

iii. Build awareness of adaptation process

iv. Build awareness of appropriate academic behaviors

v. Enhance ability of students to focus on learning

vi. Ensure that students are aware of and responsible for their own actions

vii. Facilitate nondirective guidance about student misbehavior

viii. Minimize behavior problems

ix. Reduce confrontations over minor misbehaving

x. Eliminate inappropriate behavior

xi. Develop self-monitoring skills

xii. Increase time on task

xiii. Build students' self-awareness of behavior

How to Do It

i. The teacher uses light taps or touches to minimize misbehaviors and convey messages to learners.

ii. For example, if a student is looking around the room during independent work time, the teacher can walk up to the student and gently tap on the student's shoulder as a signal to focus on the assignment.

Research Base

Koenig (2007)

Little & Akin-Little (2008)

Marable & Raimondi (1995)

What to Watch for With ELL/CLD Students

i. All cultures have guidelines about how a person can touch another person. These are mostly unspoken and learned through being raised in the culture and community where touching another person is seen and remarked upon by those around you.

ii. These touch relations are also affected by whether someone is related to the other person. These relative positions convey power and control relationships that vary from culture to culture.

iii. The teacher must familiarize himself or herself with the touch rules of the various cultures of the students in the classroom before expecting to use touch strategically to promote learning.

TOWER—WRITING STRATEGY

Purpose of the Strategy

i. Access and use prior knowledge

ii. Develop cognitive academic language

iii. Develop thinking and planning skills

iv. Build awareness of learning

v. Expand and elaborate on learning

vi. Develop personal control of situations

vii. Develop thinking and planning skills

viii. Facilitate students' writing

ix. Improve sequencing skills

x. Increase students' time on task

xi. Strengthen retention and application abilities

xii. Sustain engagement with reading and writing

xiii. Improve access to prior knowledge

xiv. Reduce off-task behaviors

xv. Strengthen language development

How to Do It

i. The TOWER writing strategy framework provides a structure for completing initial and final drafts of written reports.

ii. It may be used effectively with the COPS proofreading strategy structure.

iii. The teacher introduces TOWER by writing the steps on the board next to a passage from a hypothetical student written paragraph or sentence depending upon the grade level of the class. The teacher then has the class walk through the steps in TOWER explaining each point: thinking, ordering, writing, editing, rewriting.

iv. The teacher can provide a large TOWER frame as a poster or as a projection on the screen and walk through the steps with the students.

v. To help the students remember the steps in TOWER, the teacher can provide the students with a printed form with the letters T, O, W, E, and R down the left side and their meaning under each letter.

vi. The following are the steps students follow in TOWER:

1. Think

2. Order ideas

3. Write

4. Edit

5. Rewrite

Research Base

Cole (1995)

Ellis & Colvert (1996)

Ellis & Lenz (1987)

Goldsworthy (2003)

What to Watch for With ELL/CLD Students

i. Newcomers will need to have the TOWER steps modeled and explained in their most proficient language before they can proceed independently.

ii. Students can be paired with partners who are slightly more bilingual than themselves to facilitate their learning this process.

TOWER Elements	What am I to do at this step?	What did I do about it?	How many times did I do this?
Think			
Order ideas			
Write			
Edit			
Rewrite			

TPR—TOTAL PHYSICAL RESPONSE

Purpose of the Strategy

i. Build transfer skills

ii. Access prior knowledge

iii. Adapt to meet individual or unique student needs

iv. Adapt the mode of response required of students

v. Build awareness of appropriate cognitive academic language

vi. Build awareness of appropriate social and academic language

vii. Build first language to English transfer skills

viii. Build foundation for learning

ix. Build home and community language to English transfer skills

x. Build learners' confidence in their control of the learning process

xi. Build transfer skills

xii. Build upon existing language skills of students

xiii. Build upon existing language strengths of student

xiv. Facilitate connections between known and new

xv. Facilitate discussion about new learning

xvi. Reduce anxiety and stress and responses

xvii. Reduce anxiety in social/academic interactions

xviii. Reduce code switching

xix. Improve comprehension

xx. Improve vocabulary

xxi. Build awareness of appropriate communication behaviors for school language and rules

xxii. Develop confidence in school language and rules for academic and social interactions

xxiii. Develop cognitive academic language

xxiv. Reduce stress for new students

How to Do It

i. The total physical response strategy was developed by James Asher and is a very simple strategy to enhance language learning in the context of movement and demonstration.

ii. TPR is a popular and effective way of teaching language that actively involves the students and focuses on understanding the language rather than speaking it. TPR method asks the students to demonstrate that they understand the new language by responding to a command with an action. At first, the teacher gives the commands and does the actions along with the student. As the student understands the vocabulary, the teacher stops doing the action and has the student do the action alone. Later, the student can give commands to other students or to the teacher.

iii. The teacher or assistant models words and phrases in action in various school settings, both in and out of the classroom. For example, he or she may teach the response to a question such as "what is this" or "what can you do with this" by saying and acting out the phrases "This is a pencil." "This pencil is used for writing on paper." Students take different roles in the interactions and practice them with each other and with the teacher

Expansion

Students may suggest communication situations in which they would like specific assistance.

Research Base

Asher (1980)

Collier (2003a)

Law & Eckes (2000)

What to Watch for With ELL/CLD Students

i. Although this is a common beginner or newcomer strategy for use with ELL students, the teacher must still be cautious about making assumptions about CLD students' understanding of the actions required in the classroom.

ii. The teacher must clearly model and act out every action required before asking students to repeat the action.

TQLR—LISTENING STRATEGY

Purpose of the Strategy

i. Access and use prior knowledge

ii. Expand and elaborate on learning

iii. Expand comprehension

iv. Facilitate acquisition of content knowledge

v. Improve retention of content

vi. Improve mnemonic retrieval

vii. Improve comprehension

viii. Increase time on task

ix. Reduce distractibility

x. Reduce off-task behaviors

xi. Retention of content

xii. Sustain engagement

xiii. Build awareness of appropriate academic behaviors

xiv. Clarify responsibilities, assignments

xv. Build awareness of learning

xvi. Encourage questioning and exploration of new learning

xvii. Enhance ability of students to focus on learning

xiii. Develop personal control of situations

xix. Build awareness of academic expectations

xx. Build academic transfer skills

xxi. Improve access to prior knowledge

xxii. Strengthen language development

How to Do It

i. This strategy assists with listening comprehension. Students generate questions and listen for specific statements related to those questions.

ii. The teacher hands out sheets of paper or uses other individualized ways for students to follow and use the TQLR frame. He or she demonstrates how to use the TQLR frame to take notes while listening to an oral or video presentation. The teacher guides students through thinking about TQLR by asking them to consider what they are to do when (1) tuning in, (2) questioning, (3) listening, (4) reviewing. She then has the students consider what they did and how many times they did these active listening actions.

iii. The teacher creates posters or projections showing the TQLR steps and points them out step by step at the beginning of each new discussion and lesson until he or she is sure students know how to use this active listening strategy.

iv. After this detailed introduction, with demonstration and modeling if necessary, the teacher or assistant can then just refer to the poster to remind students to use the strategy while listening to someone present information.

v. The following are the steps in TQLR:

1. Tuning in

2. Questioning

3. Listening

4. Reviewing

Research Base

Artis (2008)

Fisher & Frey (2004)

Irvin & Rose (1995)

Law & Eckes (2000)

Popp (1997)

Sakta (1999)

What to Watch for With ELL/CLD Students

i. Newcomers will need to have the TQLR steps modeled and explained in their most proficient language before they can proceed independently.

ii. Students can be paired with partners who are slightly more bilingual than themselves to facilitate their learning this process.

Steps in the TQLR Process	What am I to do at this step?	What did I do about it?	How many times did I do this?
Tuning In			
Questioning			
Listening			
Reviewing			

ABCDEFGHIJKLMOPQRST U vw

USE OF FIRST LANGUAGE

Purpose of the Strategy

   i. Access prior knowledge

   ii. Build awareness of appropriate academic behavior

   iii. Build academic transfer skills

   iv. Build transfer skills

   v. Build upon existing language skills and strengths of student

   vi. Encourage pride in home language and culture

   vii. Encourage pride in students' personal history

   viii. Enhance awareness of school adaptation process

   ix. Enhance student interaction with family during transition

   x. Ensure that each student is familiar with specific academic and behavioral expectations

   xi. Improve access to prior knowledge

   xii. Improve comprehension

   xiii. Reduce stress for new students

   xiv. Strengthen ability to discuss what is happening

   xv. Strengthen awareness of learning process

   xvi. Strengthen home/school relationship

xvii. Reduce anxiety and stress

xviii. Reduce culture shock

xix. Develop basic interpersonal communication

xx. Develop cognitive academic language

xxi. Develop confidence in school language and rules for academic and social interactions

xxii. Develop content knowledge foundation

xxiii. Improve motivation

xxiv. Minimize behavior problems

xxv. Strengthen learning to learn skills

xxvi. Reduce code switching

xxvii. Strengthen knowledge of academic content

How to Do It

i. This strategy is done within the general education classroom with a bilingual student, assistant, or other volunteer working in coordination with the classroom teacher.

ii. The teacher directs an advanced-fluency student or volunteer to lead a guided activity in the home or community language.

iii. Students can retell parts of a story in pairs after the directed activity rather than have one student speak while the others all listen. Students then write their own summaries of what they have heard.

iv. Writing can be in either home or community language or English. During this time, the students have a chance to help each other. Advanced-fluency students can dramatize and create dialogue to illustrate the action.

Research Base

Carrigan (2001)

What to Watch for With ELL/CLD Students

i. The language helper can prepare the English language learner (ELL)/ limited English proficiency (LEP) students for an English lesson by reviewing key vocabulary words, explaining what will be occurring, and discussing what the teacher's expectations will be for the students' performance. This would then be followed by the teacher presenting the lesson in English. Students would be given the opportunity to ask for specific clarification in their first language.

ii. Students could work on their projects subsequent to the English lesson with the assistance of the bilingual helper, as needed. Content discussion and clarification should be in the students' most proficient language while they are preparing their task or project for presentation in English with the rest of the class.

ABCDEFGHIJKLMOPQRSTU**V**W

VARIED GROUPING

Purpose of the Strategy

    i. Facilitate discussion about new learning

    ii. Increase students' probability of generating a correct response

    iii. Increase students' time on task

    iv. Increase the frequency of appropriate responses or behaviors

    v. Reduce fears associated with assignments

    vi. Reduce frustration

    vii. Facilitate students' comfort with learning environment

    viii. Build academic transfer skills

    ix. Build appreciation that everyone belongs and is needed

    x. Build appreciation that everyone has a contribution to make

    xi. Build awareness of learning process

    xii. Build vocabulary

    xiii. Develop cognitive academic language

    xiv. Develop cognitive learning strategies

    xv. Develop confidence in academic interactions

    xvi. Develop confidence in school culture interactions

xvii. Encourage questioning and exploration of new learning

xviii. Enhance ability of student to focus on learning

xix. Enhance ability of students to learn new things

How to Do It

i. Teacher uses flexible grouping arrangements to facilitate learning among diverse groups of learners. For example, large group setting for introducing the general unit, small groups for research and jigsaw activities, pairs for sharing information and ideas about the topic, then returning to large group where individual teams can share their information with the whole class.

ii. The classroom instructional setting refers to the various groupings and independents at work situations often found in today's schools. These may include large group (entire class); small group; one-to-one instructional settings; work completed individually at tables, desks, or in centers located throughout the classroom; or some combination of the above limited only by the creativity of each individual teacher.

iii. The selection of the classroom instructional setting requires careful decision making and thought. Equally important is the understanding that much content can be taught in a variety of classroom instructional settings. In addition, many different instructional strategies can be successfully implemented in different instructional settings.

iv. Although influenced by content or instructional strategies, the decision to teach specific content or employ specific instructional strategies does not automatically lead to or require a specific type of classroom instructional setting. For example, use of a lecture-type technique may be employed in an individual, small group, or large group setting. Although this technique is typically used with larger groups of students, a teacher could use this method with an individual student.

v. When selecting the most appropriate classroom grouping for diverse learners, one must consider several factors. The classroom instructional setting must show the students that they are expected to learn as well as complete the required tasks. It is very important that students perceive the setting as a forum that minimizes their risk for failure while it simultaneously conveys the message that they are expected to complete and learn the task at hand.

vi. The teacher must also consider the students' prior educational successes and failures relative to grouping situations, the difficulty level of the material to be learned, the length of time required by the student to complete the task, the importance (for the specific task) of direct interaction between the teacher and student or student-student interaction, as well as the best classroom instructional setting necessary to implement the selected instructional strategy. By carefully weighing each of these factors as well as the other important areas discussed for the previous two elements, the best classroom instructional setting for each diverse learner can be determined.

Research Base

Collier (2010a)

Heacox (2002)

What to Watch for With ELL/CLD Students

i. Many cultures have guidelines about who children may associate with and how they are to interact with others. Familiarize yourself with these beliefs and values enough to prepare for specific difficulties that might arise, for example, boys not allowed to sit next to girls or two members of old political enemies next to each other (one may know that the other's parents slaughtered their grandmother).

ii. This is not to say you cannot mix and match groups in your classroom, but by preparing ahead, you can be sensible about what works most effectively for different activities.

iii. Build in numerous variations so students become familiar with your expectation that group work will occur in many different configurations and that their work partners will be quite varied.

iv. Start with easy, comfortable groupings, and work gradually to the more complex ones.

v. Grouping for English language learner (ELL) students can vary: Group ELL students with a range of bilingual peers when understanding the language of the activity is crucial to success. Group ELL students with heterogeneous language speakers when demonstration and nonverbal task completion are crucial to success. Group ELL students with homogeneous language speakers when concept mastery is crucial to success.

VIDEOS ABOUT INTERACTION PATTERNS

Purpose of the Strategy

i. Build awareness of appropriate communication behaviors for school language and rules

ii. Build transfer skills

iii. Build vocabulary

iv. Build awareness of school culture expectations

 v. Develop confidence in academic interactions

 vi. Develop confidence in school culture interactions

 vii. Facilitate family adaptation to new community

 viii. Improve confidence in home and community culture/school culture interactions

 ix. Strengthen school/parent partnerships

 x. Develop familiarity with school language and rules for academic and social interaction patterns

 xi. Reduce culture shock

How to Do It

 i. The teacher draws upon videos or films showing typical patterns of interaction and language use in your school and community. She points out key features of appropriate and inappropriate interactions and the meaning of any idiosyncratic gestures or phrases.

 ii. Groups of students or their families view videos developed locally or available from national organizations and others about public schools and about interacting with community service personnel. These are best shown in home and community language and with facilitator. Students are encouraged to discuss with their families what they see and experience in school.

 iii. The focus here is on videos about how to interact to be most effective in communicating.

Research Base

Carrigan (2001)

Kamps (2007)

Koskinen & Blum (1984)

Prasad (2005)

Wood & Algozzine (1994)

Wood & Harmon (2001)

Zutell & Rasinski (1991)

What to Watch for With ELL/CLD Students

 i. There are many versions of spoken English and differences of opinion about what is the proper dialect to use as the model for ELL/ culturally and linguistically diverse (CLD) students.

 ii. The teacher should be aware of the diversity of reaction to versions of spoken English in North America and be prepared to address expressions of prejudice or value judgments about certain speakers shown on the videos.

iii. The most practical way to deal with this is to prescreen the videos and select segments that most closely represent the dialects common in your local communities, plus a few as examples of the diversity that exist in our country.

iv. There are some excellent locally produced materials about school and service options within and for specific communities. The local school district may keep these in the media center. They may also be available through a local college or university.

v. The teacher should be aware of the diversity of reaction to depictions of official or government agencies and laws. These can raise the affective filter or emotional response of both students and parents to discussions about services.

vi. Always have interpreters available for in-depth discussion of the materials presented.

vii. Always introduce school expectations and rules to ELL and CLD students by explaining them in their most proficient language.

viii. ELL/CLD students who have had prior schooling might be asked what sort of rules and expectations they were familiar with, and that could become part of the classroom routine.

VISUALIZATION—READING STRATEGY

Purpose of the Strategy

i. Access prior knowledge

ii. Adapt to meet individual or unique student needs

iii. Adapt the mode of response required of students

iv. Build academic transfer skills

v. Build foundation for learning

vi. Build metacognition skills

vii. Develop analytical skills

viii. Develop association skills

ix. Develop extended time on task

x. Enhance ability of students to focus on learning

xi. Enhance ability of students to learn new things

xii. Expand and elaborate on learning

xiii. Expand comprehension

xiv. Facilitate access of prior knowledge

xv. Improve access to prior knowledge

xvi. Improve comprehension

xvii. Strengthen language development

xviii. Strengthen learning to learn skills

xix. Strengthen retention and application abilities

xx. Develop higher tolerance

xxi. Develop thinking and planning skills

xxii. Improve mnemonic retrieval

xxiii. Improve retention

How to Do It

i. The teacher introduces the visualization strategy as a way to facilitate understanding and retaining what is being read. She has students learn the steps of visualization: stopping; asking who, what, where, when, how, and why; creating an image in the mind; and putting it all together.

ii. Students put small, red stop signs or other marks indicating stopping points at the end of sentences in an assigned reading. As they read the passage, they stop at each sign and answer questions about the passage. They then make a picture in their mind of what the passage means. This is repeated for each subsequent passage with the pictures forming a moving visualization or motion picture of what the passage means. (I usually remind students to think of TV shows.) This visualization strategy can also be used with other content activities, in science and social studies for example.

iii. The following are the steps for students to follow in implementing this strategy:

1. Where do I stop?

2. Who is doing what, where, when, how, and why?

3. What do I see in my mind?

4. How does this all go together?

iv. When applying the visualization strategy, students work through problems or tasks using the above sequence of self-monitoring questions.

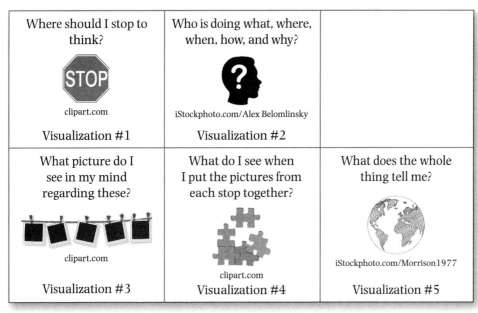

Where should I stop to think?	Who is doing what, where, when, how, and why?	
clipart.com	iStockphoto.com/Alex Belomlinsky	
Visualization #1	Visualization #2	
What picture do I see in my mind regarding these?	What do I see when I put the pictures from each stop together?	What does the whole thing tell me?
clipart.com	clipart.com	iStockphoto.com/Morrison1977
Visualization #3	Visualization #4	Visualization #5

Source: Collier (2008).

v. Suppose you are having your students read *The Story of Ferdinand* by Munro Leaf. You would have students work in pairs or in small mixed-skill groups as they read this story together. They would help put small red "Post-It" circles at the end of each sentence or at the end of two sentences, depending upon their skill level (Step 1 of rehearsal, "Where should I stop to think?"). Suppose one group was reading this passage, for example:

1. All the other bulls who had grown up with him in the same pasture would fight each other all day. They would butt each other and stick each other with their horns. What they wanted most of all was to be picked to fight at the bull fights in Madrid. But not Ferdinand—he still liked to sit just quietly under the cork tree and smell the flowers.

vi. Students would take turns reading out loud to one another. The first reader would read up to the first red spot and stop. The students would then review the five "W" and one "H" questions about what had just been read (Step 2 of rehearsal, "Who is doing what, where, when, how, and why?"). Who=the other bulls, what=fight each other, where=in the pasture, when=all day. As this is the first sentence, the readers do not yet know the answers to all the questions (how and why=don't know yet). After answering the questions, the group will take turns telling the others how they visualize this sentence (Step 3 of rehearsal, "What picture do I see in my mind regarding these?). The picture in the book shows the bulls gazing up at a poster about the bull fights in Madrid, so they will have to use their imagination about what it might look like to see these young bulls play fighting. They will then go on to read the next sentence and repeat Steps 2 and 3, this time adding Step 4, Who=the bulls, what=fight each other, where=in the pasture, when=all day, how=butt each other and stick each other with their horns, why=still don't know. They can now expand their first imaginative picture of these bulls by adding some action to the movie they are making in their minds (Step 5 of rehearsal, "What do I see when I put the pictures from each stop together?"). The group goes on to the next sentence and repeats Steps 2, 3, 4, and 5. Who=the young bulls, what=fighting, where=in the pasture, how=butting heads, why=to be picked to fight in Madrid. They expand their visualization to showing the longing of the young bulls while they are fighting. They then read the final sentence and complete the movie in their minds. Who=the young bulls and Ferdinand, what=the young bulls fighting and Ferdinand sitting, where=fighting in the pasture while Ferdinand is under the cork tree, how=fighting by butting their heads while Ferdinand is smelling flowers, why=the young bulls want to be picked to fight in Madrid. but Ferdinand doesn't want to do anything but smell the flowers.

vii. The use of the visualization strategy will slow impulsive learners down, reinforce reflective habits, and guide students to more accurate understanding of what they are reading.

Research Base

Harwell (2001)

Klingner, Vaughn, & Boardman (2007)

Naughton (2008)

Tomlinson (1998)

Tovani (2000)

What to Watch for With ELL/CLD Students

i. Students with limited school experience will not know what visualization means and will need to have direct instruction in the vocabulary and actions expected.

ii. This can be introduced in the primary language and examples given from literature and art with which the students are more familiar.

VISUALIZATION STRATEGY—RIDER

Purpose of the Strategy

i. Build transfer skills

ii. Expand and elaborate on learning foundation

   iii. Build learners' confidence in their control of the learning process

   iv. Develop analytical skills

   v. Expand and elaborate on learning

   vi. Expand comprehension

   vii. Facilitate access of prior knowledge

   viii. Develop association skills

   ix. Build metacognition skills

   x. Develop thinking and planning skills

   xi. Improve access to prior knowledge

   xii. Improve retention of information

   xiii. Improve reading comprehension

   xiv. Strengthen language development

How to Do It

   i. This visualization strategy cues the learner to form a mental image of what was read and assists the student in making connections with previously learned materials.

   ii. The teacher prepares a poster or projects an overhead of the frame RIDER with each word highlighted. She explains each step in RIDER and explains what to do at each step.

   iii. Students may be given individual worksheets when first learning to use the strategy but usually only need reminders to follow the steps on the poster as they become more familiar with the process.

   iv. The following are the steps in RIDER:

     1. Read a sentence

     2. Image (form a mental picture)

     3. Describe how new information differs from previous

     4. Evaluate image to ensure it is comprehensive

     5. Repeat process with subsequent sentences

Research Base

Cole (1995)

Collier (2008)

What to Watch for With ELL/CLD Students

   i. Newcomers will need to have the RIDER steps modeled and explained in their most proficient language before they can proceed independently.

ii. Students can be paired with partners who are slightly more bilingual than themselves to facilitate learning this process.

RIDER Element	What am I to do at this step?	What did I do about it?	Notes
Read a sentence			
Image (form a mental picture)			
Describe how new information differs from previous			
Evaluate image to ensure it is comprehensive			
Repeat the process with subsequent sentences			

Source: Collier (2008).

VOCABULARY PYRAMID

Purpose of the Strategy

i. Access and use prior knowledge

ii. Build confidence in independent work

iii. Develop academic language

> **Figure V.1** Vocabulary Pyramid Strategy

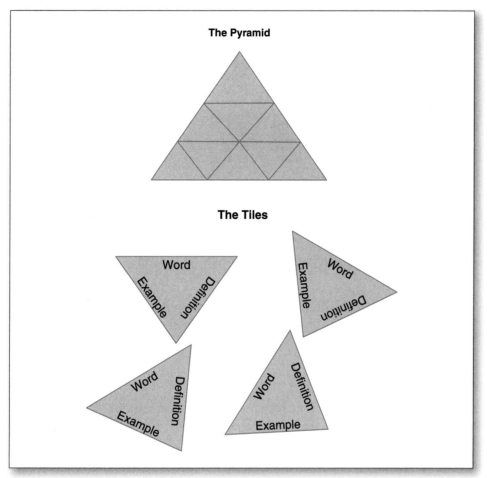

Source: © 2003 Dr. Catherine Collier.

    iv. Develop analytical skills

    v. Develop association skills

    vi. Build academic transfer skills

    vii. Expand and elaborate on learning foundation

    viii. Improve access to prior knowledge

    ix. Improve retention of information

    x. Improve reading comprehension

    xi. Strengthen language development

How to Do It

    i. The teacher uses this strategy to reinforce vocabulary and to build word association and definition skills.

Figure V.2   Vocabulary Pyramid Strategy

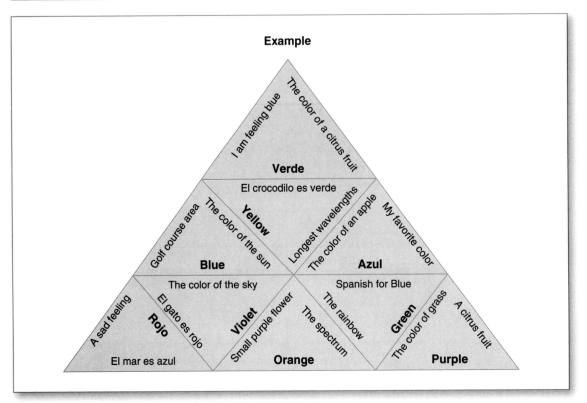

Source: © 2003 Dr. Catherine Collier.

Figure V.3   Example of Vocabulary Tile Pieces for the Vocabulary Pyramid Strategy

Source: © 2003 Dr. Catherine Collier.

ii. Have your students come up with a list of over 100 words, definitions, and examples of the word in use. You can also use mathematical formulas, chemical processes, story elements from fiction, historical events, or other content your students are learning and which you wish to reinforce and enhance.

iii. You can have these be in one, two, or three different languages depending upon what you are having your students learn.

iv. Make 100 or more vocabulary triangles with mixed-up words, definitions, and examples on each tile. They should not match on individual tiles! Your students can help you make all of these as part of their language arts lessons.

v. Make four or more pyramids with places for nine vocabulary triangles. Use the attached design, and copy it on to stiff index stock or shirt-board or other firm paper stock.

vi. Divide students into groups and give each group a pyramid and twenty or more triangles.

vii. Students work together to fill in their pyramid.

viii. The goal is to match a definition to a word or to an example, to match a word to a definition or an example, or to match an example to a word or a definition.

ABCDEFGHIJKLMOPQRSTUVW

WORDLESS PICTURE BOOKS

Purpose of the Strategy

    i. Access prior knowledge

    ii. Adapt to meet individual or unique student needs

    iii. Adapt the mode of response required of students

    iv. Build transfer skills

    v. Build upon existing language skills of students

    vi. Build upon existing language strengths of student

    vii. Encourage questioning and exploration of new learning

    viii. Enhance ability of students to focus on learning

    ix. Enhance ability of students to learn new things

    x. Improve sequencing skills

    xi. Facilitate reading process

    xii. Improve vocabulary

How to Do It

    i. Wordless picture books or books with strong graphic sequences and few printed words are very useful in dual language, bilingual, or English as an additional language instruction especially with non-English or limited English speakers or students with various learning challenges. These are great for language development in any language and a wide range of grade and ability levels.

ii. You can use them bilingually and in multilingual situations. They are also good for teaching sequencing, sorting, and cause and effect activities and lessons.

iii. Using wordless picture books with emerging readers of all ages is very effective. It builds upon the learner's oral language skills to develop the reading process. This allows for variations in phonology, syntax, vocabulary, intonation, and so on, to be accommodated in an integrated classroom, so that all students can participate in the activity regardless of reading level.

iv. The teacher selects a wordless picture book of high interest content to the students. Wordless picture books are available at all age/grade levels. The students can "read" the pictures in small groups or individually, telling the "story" as they see it. Students can also make their own wordless picture books.

v. Another variation on this strategy is to use modern "pop-up" books for telling the story. Some of these are quite sophisticated and may be used in math and science lessons as well.

Research Base

Collier (2010a)

Opitz (1998)

What to Watch for With ELL/CLD Students

i. Teachers may need to model how to go through a book to follow the sequence of the story through the pictures.

ii. Begin with pictures the students recognize from their own experiences. Introduce new and unusual illustrations after the students understand what the process of reading is like in a wordless picture book.

The following table includes some examples or wordless books to use in the classroom. The current or original publisher and date of publication are provided after the author and title. There are often more recent editions of these books, so check on Amazon or other online publishers.

WRITING STRATEGY—COPS

Purpose of the Strategy

i. Build awareness of learning

ii. Build awareness of adaptation process

iii. Facilitate and access prior knowledge

A	
Alexander, Martha, *Bobo's Dream*. Dial, 1970.	Alexander, Martha, *Out! Out! Out!* Dial, 1986.
Allsburg, Chris Van, *The Mysteries of Harris Burdick*. Houghton Mifflin, 1984.	Andreae, Giles and Guy Parker-Rees, *Giraffes Can't Dance*. Orchard Books, 2001.
Amoss, Berthe, *By the Sea*. Parents, 1969.	Anderson, Laurie, *The Package*. Bobbs, 1971.
Angel, Marie, *The Ark*. Harper and Row, 1973.	Anno, Mitsumasa, *Anno's Alphabet*. Crowell, 1974.
Anno, Mitsumasa, *Anno's Counting Book*. Crowell, 1975.	Anno, Mitsumasa, *Anno's Journey*. Collins-World, 1978.
Anno, Mitsumasa, *Dr. Anno's Magical Midnight Circus*. Weatherhill, 1972.	Anno, Mitsumasa, *Topsy-Turvies*. Weatherhill, 1970.
Anno, Mitsumasa, *Upside-Downers*. Weatherhill, 1971.	Ardizzone, Edward, *The Wrong Side of Bed*. Doubleday, 1970.
Aruego, Jose, *Look What I Can Do*. Simon & Schuster, 1971.	Asch, Frank, *In The Eye of the Teddy*. Harper & Row, 1973.
Asch, Frank, *The Blue Baloon*. McGraw-Hill, 1971.	

B	
Bang, Molly, *The Grey Lady and the Strawberry Snatcher*. Four Winds, 1980.	Barner, Bob, *The Elephant's Visit*. Little Brown, 1975.
Balint, Beata Noemi, *The Carrot Eating Monster*. Best Picture Books, 2014.	Banchek, Linda, *Snake in, Snake Out*. Crowell, 1978.
Barton, Byron, *Elephant*. Seabury, 1971.	Barton, Byron, *Harry Is a Scaredy Cat*. Macmillan, 1974.
Barnett, Mac and Jon Klassen, *Extra Yarn*. Balzer Bray, 2012.	Becker, Aaron, *Journey*. Candlewick, 2013.
Brinckloe, Julie, *The Spider Web*. Doubleday, 1974.	Baum, Willie, *Birds of a Feather*. Addison-Wesley, 1969.
Banyai, Istvan, *The Other Side*. Chronicle Books, 2005.	Banyai, Istvan, *Zoom*. Puffin, 1998.
Baum, Willie, *The Expedition*. Addison-Welsey, 1969.	Billout, Guy, *The Number 24*. Harlin Quiest, 1973.
Bolliger-Savelli, Antonella, *The Knitted Cat*. Macmillan, 1972.	Briggs, Raymond, *Father Christmas Goes On Holiday*. Coward, 1975.
Borden, Louise, *America Is. . . .* Margaret McElderry Books, 2005.	Bruna, Dick, *Another Story to Tell*. Methuen, 1974.
Briggs, Raymond, *The Snowman*. Random House, 1978.	Briggs, Raymond, *Father Christmas*. Coward, 1973.
Banyai, Istvan, *Re-Zoom*. Puffin, 1998.	Brown, Margaret Wise and Clement Hurd. *The Runaway Bunny*. HarperCollins, 2005.

C	
Cannon, Beth, *A Cat Had a Fish About a Dream.* Pantheon, 1976.	Carle, Eric, *A Very Long Tail.* Crowell, 1972.
Carle, Eric, *Do You Want to Be My Friend?* Crowell, 1971.	Carle, Eric, *I See a Song.* Crowell, 1973.
Carle, Eric, *My Very First Book of Colors.* Crowell, 1974.	Carle, Eric, *My Very First Book of Shapes.* Crowell, 1974.
Carle, Eric, *One, Two, Three, To The Zoo.* World, 1968.	Carle, Eric, *The Very Hungry Caterpillar.* World, 1970.
Carle, Eric, *The Very Long Train.* Crowell, 1972.	Carrick, Donald, *Drip, Drop.* Macmillan, 1973.
Carroll, Ruth and Latrobe Carroll, *The Christmas Kitten.* Walck, 1970.	Carroll, Ruth, *Rolling Downhill.* Walck, 1973.
Carroll, Ruth, *The Chimp and The Clown.* Walck, 1968.	Carroll, Ruth, *The Dolphin and The Mermaid.* Walck, 1974.
Carroll, Ruth, *The Witch Kitten.* Walck, 1973.	Carroll, Ruth, *What Whiskers Did.* Walck, 1965.
Charlip, Remy and Jerry Joyner, *Thirteen.* Simon & Schuster, 1994.	Charlot, Martin, *Sunnyside Up.* Weatherhill, 1972.
Crews, Donald, *Truck.* Greenwillow, 1980.	Cristini, Ermanno and Luigi Puricelli, *In My Garden.* Neugebauer Press, 1981.

D	
Dean, James, *Pete the Cat: I Love My White Shoes.* HarperCollins, 2010.	DeGroat, Diane, *Alligator's Toothache.* Crown, 1977.
dePaola, Tomie, *Pancakes for Breakfast.* Harcourt Brace, 1978.	dePaola, Tomie, *Pierot.* Harcourt Brace.
dePaola, Tomie, *The Cloud Book.* Holiday House, 1984.	dePaola, Tomie, *The Hunter and the Animals.* Holiday House, 1981.

E	
Elzbieta, *Chimp and the Clown.* Doubleday, 1974.	Elzbieta, *Little Mops at the Seashore.* Doubleday, 1974.
Elzbieta, *Little Mops and the Butterfly.* Doubleday, 1974.	Elzbieta, *Little Mops and the Moon.* Doubleday, 1974.
Emerley, Edward Randolph, *A Birthday Wish.* Little, 1974.	Espenschied, Gertrude, *Oh Ball.* Harper & Row, 1966.
Ets, Marie Hall, *I Can, Can't You?* Viking, 1968.	Ets, Marie Hall, *In the Forest.* Scholastic, 1989.
Ets, Marie Hall, *Play With Me.* Puffin, 1976.	

F	
Florian, Douglas, *The City.* Crowell, 1982.	Freeman, Don, *Corduroy.* Puffin, 1976.
Freeman, Don, *Forever Laughter.* Children's Press, 1970.	Fromental, Jean-Luc, *365 Penguins.* Abrams, 2006.
Fromm, Lilo, *Muffel and Plums.* Macmillan, 1973.	Fuchs, Erich, *Journey to the Moon.* Delacorte, 1969.

(Continued)

(Continued)

G	
Geisert, Arthur, *Hogwash*. HMH Books, 2008.	Geisert, Arthur, *Oops*. HMH Books, 2006.
Geisert, Arthur, *Thunderstorm*. Enchanted Lion Books, 2013.	Gerber, Preston, *Silliest Animals*.
Givoannetti, *Max*. Atheneum, 1977.	Giblert, Elliot, *A Cat*. Holt, Rinehart Winston, 1968.
Goodall, John S., *An Edwardian Holiday*. Atheneum, 1983.	Goodall, John S., *An Edwardian Christmas*. Atheneum, 1978.
Goodall, John S., *Naughty Nancy*. Atheneum, 1975.	Goodall, John S., *Creepy Castle*. Atheneum, 1975.
Goodall, John S., *Paddy's Evening Out*. Atheneum, 1973.	Goodall, John S., *Paddy Pork's Holiday*. Atheneum, 1967.
Goodall, John S., *The Adventures of Paddy Pork*. Harcourt, 1968.	Goodall, John S., *Shrewbettina's Birthday*. Harcourt, 1971.
Goodall, John S., *The Story of an English Village*. Atheneum, 1979.	Goodall, John S., *The Ballooning Adventures of Paddy Pork*. Harcourt, 1969.
Goodall, John S., *An Edwardian Summer*. Atheneum, 1976.	Goodall, John S., *The Surprise Picnic*. Atheneum, 1977.
Goodall, John S., *The Midnight Adventures of Kelly, Dot and Esmerelda*. Atheneum, 1973.	Goodwall, John S., *Jacko*. Harcourt, 1972.
H	
Hamberger, John, *The Lazy Dog*. Four Winds, 1971.	Hamberger, John, *A Sleepless Day*. Four Winds, 1973.
Hartelius, Margaret E., *The Chicken's Child*. Doubleday, 1975.	Hoban, Tana, *Big Ones, Little Ones*. Greenwillow, 1976.
Hoban, Tana, *Count and See*. Macmillan, 1972.	Hoban, Tana, *Circles, Triangles and Squares*. Macmillan, 1974.
Hoban, Tana, *Is It Red, Is It Yellow, Is It Blue?* Greenwillow, 1978.	Hoban, Tana, *Dig, Drill, Dump, Fill*. Greenwillow, 1975.
Hoban, Tana, *Over, Under and Through*. Macmillan, 1970.	Hoban, Tana, *Look Again!* Macmillan, 1971.
Hoban, Tana, *Shapes and Things*. Macmillan, 1970.	Hoban, Tana, *Push, Pull, Empty, Full*. Macmillan, 1973.
Hoban, Tana, *Take Another Look*. Greenwillow, 1978.	Hoest, William, *Taste of Carrot*. Atheneum, 1967.
Hogrogian, Nonny, *Apples*. Macmillan, 1972.	Hutchins, Pat, *Changes, Changes*. Macmillan, 1971.
J	
Jeffers, Oliver, *Stuck*. Philomet, 2011.	Johnson, Angela and E.B. Lewis, *All Different Now*. Simon & Schuster, 2014.
Jolivet, Joelle, *Zoo-ology*. Roaring Brook Press, 2003.	

K	
Keats, Ezra Jack, *Psst! Doggie.* Watts, 1973.	Keats, Ezra Jack, *Kitten for A Day.* Turtleback. 2002.
Keats, Ezra Jack, *Skates.* Watts, 1973.	Kent, Jack, *The Egg Book.* Macmillan, 1975.
Klassen, Jon, *This Is Not My Hat.* Candlewick Press, 2012.	Klassen, Jon, *I Want My Hat Back.* Candlewick Press, 2011.
Knobler, Susan, *The Tadpole and The Frog.* Harvey, 1974.	Kojima, Naomi, *Mr. And Mrs. Thief.* Crowell, 1981.
Kojima, Naomi, *The Flying Grandmother.* Crowell, 1981.	Krahn, Fernando, *A Flying Saucer Full of Spaghetti.* Dutton, 1970.
Krahn, Fernando, *April Fools.* Dutton, 1974.	Krahn, Fernando, *A Funny Friend From Heaven.* Lippincott, 1974.
Krahn, Fernando, *How Santa Clause Had a Long and Difficult Journey Delivering His Presents.* Delacorte, 1970.	Krahn, Fernando, *Catch the Cat.* Dutton, 1978.
Krahn, Fernando, *Little Love Story.* Lippincott, 1976.	Krahn, Fernando, *Journeys of Sebastian.* Delacorte, 1968.
Krahn, Fernando, *Sebastian and the Mushroom.* Delacorte, 1976.	Krahn, Fernando, *Robot-Bot-Bot.* Delacorte.
Krahn, Fernando, *The Great Ape.* Viking, 1978.	Krahn, Fernando, *The Biggest Christmas Tree on Earth.* Little, Brown, 1978.
Krahn, Fernando, *The Self-Made Snowman.* Lippincott, 1974.	Krahn, Fernando, *The Mystery of the Great Footprints.* Dutton, 1977.
Krahn, Fernando, *Who's Seen the Scissors?* Dutton, 1974.	Kranz, Linda, *Love You When . . .* Taylor Trade Publishing, 2012.
Kranz, Linda, *Only One You.* Cooper Square Publishing, 2006.	Kranz, Linda, *You Be You.* Taylor Trade Publishing, 2011.
L	
Lemke, Hurst, *Places and Places.*	Lewis, Stephen, *Zoo City.*
Lisker, Sonia, *The Attic Witch.* Four Winds, 1973.	Lisker, Sonia, *Lost.* Harcourt Brace, 1975.
Lobel, Anita and Arnold Lobel, *On Market Street.* Greenwillow, 1981.	Lustig, Loretta, *The Pop-up Book of Trucks.* Random, 1974.
M	
Mari, Iela and Enso Mari, *The Apple and the Moth.* Pantheon, 1970.	Mari, Iela and Enso Mari, *The Chicken and the Egg.* Pantheon, 1970.
Mari, Iela and Enso Mari, *The Red Balloon.* Pantheon, 1975.	Mari, Iela and Enso Mari, *The Magic Balloon.* Pantheon, 1970.
Mayer, Mercer and Marianna Mayer, *A Boy, A Dog, A Frog and A Friend.* Dial, 1971.	Mayer, Mercer and Marianna Mayer, *Mine.* Simon & Schuster, 1970.
Mayer, Mercer and Marianna Mayer, *One Frog Too Many.* Dial, 1969.	Mayer, Mercer, *A Boy, A Dog, and A Frog.* Dial, 1967.

(Continued)

(Continued)

Mayer, Mercer, *Ah-Choo*. Dial, 1970.	Mayer, Mercer, *Bubble, Bubble*. Parents, 1973.
Mayer, Mercer, *Frog Goes to Dinner*. Dial, 1974.	Mayer, Mercer, *Frog Where Are You?* Dial, 1969.
Mayer, Mercer, *Hiccup!* Dial, 1976.	Mayer, Mercer, *The Great Cat Chase*. Four Winds, 1974.
Mayer, Mercer, *Two More Moral Tales*. Four Winds, 1974.	Mayer, Mercer, *Two Moral Tales*. Four Winds, 1974.
McTrusty, Ron, *Dandelion Year*. Harvey, 1974.	Mendoza, George, *I Must Hurry for The Sea Is Coming In*. Prentice Hall, 1969.
Mendoza, George, *The Inspector*. Doubleday, 1970.	Meyer, Renate, *Hide and Seek*. Bradbury, 1972.
Meyer, Renate, *Vicki*. Atheneum, 1969.	Miller, Barry, *Alphabet World*. MacMillan, 1971.
Miyazaki, Hayan, *Howls Moving Castle*. VIZ Media, 2005.	Mordillo, Guillermo, *Crazy Cow Boy*. Quist, 1972.
Mordillo, Guillermo, *The Damp and Daffy Doings of a Daring Pirate Ship*. Quist, 1971.	Morris, Terry Nell, *Good Night, Dear Monster!* Alfred Knopf, 1980.
Morris, Terry Nell, *Lucky Puppy! Lucky Boy!* Alfred Knopf, 1980.	

O

Ogle, Lucille, *I Spy With My Little Eye*. McGraw-Hill, 1970.	Olschewski, Alfred, *Winterbird*. Houghton Mifflin, 1969.
Ommen, Sylvia Van, *The Surprise*. Lemniscaat USA, 2007.	Oughton, Jerrie and Lisa Desimini, *How the Stars Fell Into the Sky*. Paw Prints, 2009.

P

Panek, Dennis, *Catastrophe Cat at The Zoo*. Bradbury Press, 1979.	Pinkney, Jerry, *Noah's Ark*. Chronicle Books, 2002.
Pinkney, Jerry, *The Lion & the Mouse*. Little, Brown, 2009.	Pinkney, Jerry, *The Tortoise & the Hare*. Little, Brown, 2013.
Portis, Antoinette, *Not a Box*. Harper Festival, 2011.	Portis, Antoinette, *Not a Stick*. HarperCollins, 2007.

R

Raskin, Ellen, *Nothing Ever Happens On My Block*. Atheneum, 1974.	Reich, Hanns, *Laughing Camera for Children*.
Remington, Barbara, *Boat*. Doubleday, 1976.	Roberts, Thom, *The Barn*. McGraw-Hill, 1975.
Rojankovsky, Feodor Stepanovich, *Animals On the Farm*. Alfred Knopf, 1962.	Ross, Pat, *Hi Fly*. Crown, 1974.
Rubin, Adam and Daniel Salmieri, *Dragons Love Tacos*. Dial, 2012.	Rubin, Adam and Daniel Salmieri, *Secret Pizza Party*. Dial, 2013.
Rubin, Adam and Daniel Salmieri, *Those Darn Squirrels!* HMH Books, 2011.	

S	
Sara, *Across Town*. Orchard Books, 1991.	Saltzberg, Barney, *Beautiful Oops!* Workman Publishing, 2010.
Schick, Eleanor, *Making Friends*. MacMillan, 1969.	Seeger, Laura Vaccaro, *First the Egg*. Roaring Brook Press, 2007.
Sesame Street, *Can You Find What's Missing?* Random House, 1974.	Shimin, Symeon, *A Special Birthday*. McGraw-Hill, 1976.
Simmons, Ellie, *Cat*. McKay, 1968.	Simmons, Ellie, *Dog*. McKay, 1967.
Simmons, Ellie, *Family*. McKay, 1970.	Smith, Lane, *It's a Book*. Roaring Brook Press, 2010.
Smith, Lane, *It's a Little Book*. Roaring Brook Press, 2011.	Spier, Peter, *Noah's Ark*. Doubleday, 1977.
Spier, Peter, *Rain*. Doubleday.	Steiner, Charlotte, *I Am Andy*. Alfred Knopf, 1969.
Sugano, Yoshikatsu, *The Kitten's Adventure*. McGraw-Hill, 1971.	Sugita, Yutaka, *My Friend Little John and Me*. McGraw-Hill 1973.
T	
Taylor, Harriet Peck, *Coyote Places the Stars*. Simon & Schuster, 1993.	Thomson, Bill, *Chalk*. Two Lions, 2010.
Tillman, Nancy, *On the Night You Were Born*. Felwel & Friends, 2010.	Turkle, Brinton Cassady, *Deep in the Forest*. Dutton, 1976.
U	
Ueno, Noriko, *Elephant Buttons*. Harper & Row, 1973.	Ungerer, Tomi, *One, Two, Three, Where's My Shoe?* Harper & Row, 1964.
Ungerer, Tomi, *Snail, Where Are You?* Harper & Row, 1962.	
W – Y	
Ward, Lynd, *The Silver Pony*. Houghton Mifflin, 1973.	Wezel, Peter, *The Good Bird*. Harper & Row, 1966.
Wezel, Peter, *The Naughty Bird*. Follett, 1967.	Wiesner, David, *Flotsam*. Clarion Books, 2006.
Wiesner, David, *Free Fall*. HarperCollins, 1991.	Wiesner, David, *Mr Wuffles!* Clarion Books, 2013.
Wiesner, David, *Sector 7*. Clarion Books, 1999.	Wiesner, David, *Tuesday*. Clarion Books, 1991.
Willems, Mo, *Knuffle Bunny: A Cautionary Tale*. Hyperion, 2004.	Willems, Mo, *Don't Let the Pigeon Drive the Bus!* Hyperion, 2003.
Winter, Paula, *Sir Andrew Crown*. Houghton Mifflin, 1976.	Winter, Paula, *The Bear and The Fly*. Houghton Mifflin, 1973.
Wildsmith, Brian, *Circus*. Watts, 1970.	Wondriska, William, *A Long Piece of String*. Holt, Rinehart & Winston.
Wondriska, William, *A Long Piece of String*. Chronicle Books. 2010.	Yolen, Jane and John Schoenherr, *Owl Moon*. Philomet, 1987.

   iv. Build transfer skills

   v. Build vocabulary

   vi. Develop academic language

   vii. Develop analytical skills

   viii. Develop cognitive academic language

   ix. Develop cognitive learning strategies

   x. Develop extended time on task

   xi. Develop field independent skills

   xii. Facilitate student writing

   xiii. Facilitate student self-evaluation skills

   xiv. Improve access to prior knowledge

   xv. Facilitate language development

   xvi. Sustain engagement with reading and writing

   xvii. Use prior knowledge

   xviii. Strengthen learning to learn skills

   xix. Strengthen retention and application abilities

   xx. Improve mnemonic retrieval

   xxi. Improve test taking

   xxii. Reduce impulsivity

   xxiii. Improve writing strategies

How to Do It

   i. This strategy provides a structure for proofreading written work prior to submitting it to the teacher.

   ii. The teacher introduces COPS by writing the steps on the board next to a passage from a hypothetical student written paragraph or sentence depending upon the grade level of the class. The teacher then has the class walk through the steps in COPS, pointing out and correcting elements in the writing sample.

   iii. The teacher can provide a large COPS frame as a poster or as a projection on the screen and walk through the steps with the class.

   iv. The poster can remain up on the wall as a reminder of the COPS process during any writing activity, and students should be reminded to check it periodically as they work on writing assignments.

   v. Student can also be given worksheets with the COPS format to accompany desk work.

   vi. The following are the steps in COPS:

      1. Capitalization correct

      2. Overall appearance

3. Punctuation correct

4. Spelling correct

Research Base

Cole (1995)

What to Watch for With ELL/CLD Students

i. Newcomers will need to have the COPS steps modeled and explained in their most proficient language before they can proceed independently.

ii. Students can be paired with partners who are slightly more bilingual than themselves to facilitate their learning this process.

COPS Elements to Check	Correct?	Corrections Made
Capitalization		
Overall appearance		
Punctuation		
Spelling		

WRITING STRATEGY—DEFENDS

Purpose of the Strategy

    i. Assist learners to defend a particular position in a written assignment

    ii. Build academic transfer skills

    iii. Build awareness of learning

    iv. Develop academic language

    v. Develop thinking and planning skills

    vi. Expand comprehension

How to Do It

    i. The DEFENDS writing strategy framework provides a structure for completing initial and final drafts of written reports and may be used with any group of students including mixed language groups.

    ii. The teacher reads an example of a passage that defends a particular position on a topic or area of interest to the students. The teacher or assistant introduces the students to the vocabulary words decide, examine, form, expose, note, drive, and search. He or she explains how the example passage "defends" a position and points out how points are made supporting the position or idea. The teacher shows how the position is "driven" home.

    iii. Students are asked to read the passage and note each reason and its associated points, creating a list of points. The teacher then has students try writing their own version of the passage using DEFENDS.

    iv. The vocabulary of decide, examine, form, expose, note, drive, and search may be put on posters of each word with space for posting examples or on the chalkboard. As the teacher explains each term, he or she asks for examples from the example passage or a familiar previous reading.

    v. The teacher writes these examples under the word on the poster or chalkboard. Then students can combine them into a composition as an example.

    vi. When used within multitiered support systems, including response to intervention (RTI), this strategy may be done with small groups or one on one for focused intensive periods of time. It is also useful with whole classrooms where students are working on their writing assignments at varied levels.

    vii. DEFENDS can be combined effectively with the COPS proofreading strategy structure.

    viii. To help the students remember the steps in DEFENDS, the teacher can provide the students with a printed form with the letters D, E, F, E, N, D, and S down the left side with the meaning under each letter.

ix. The following are the steps in DEFENDS:

1. Decide on a specific position
2. Examine own reasons for this position
3. Form list of points explaining each reason
4. Expose position in first sentence of written task
5. Note each reason and associated points
6. Drive home position in last sentence
7. Search for and correct any errors

Research Base

Ellis & Colvert (1996)

Ellis & Lenz (1987)

Goldsworthy (2003)

What to Watch for With ELL/CLD Students

i. Newcomers will need to have the DEFENDS steps modeled and explained in their most proficient language before they can proceed independently.

ii. Students can be paired with partners who are slightly more bilingual than themselves to facilitate their learning this process.

DEFENDS Step	DEFENDS Outcome
D Decide on a specific position	
E Examine own reasons for this position	
F Form list of points explaining each reason	
E Expose position in first sentence of written task	
N Note each reason and associated points	

(Continued)

(Continued)

DEFENDS Step	DEFENDS Outcome
D Drive home position in last sentence	
S Search for and correct any errors	

WRITING STRATEGY—INVERTED PYRAMID

Purpose of the Strategy

   i. Build vocabulary

   ii. Assist learners to defend a particular position in a written assignment

   iii. Assist students to learn information through paraphrasing

   iv. Build academic transfer skills

   v. Develop cognitive academic language

   vi. Develop extended time on task

   vii. Develop thinking and planning skills

   viii. Expand and elaborate on learning

   ix. Expand comprehension

   x. Facilitate access of prior knowledge

   xi. Facilitate acquisition of content knowledge

   xii. Facilitate writing process

   xiii. Facilitate language development

   xiv. Improve retention of content

   xv. Improve sequencing skills

   xvi. Strengthen knowledge of academic content

   xvii. Strengthen language development

   xviii. Strengthen learning to learn skills

   xix. Strengthen retention and application abilities

   xx. Build transfer skills

   xxi. Develop content area skills

   xxii. Establish and elaborate on learning

   xxiii. Improve comprehension

How to Do It

i. The teacher introduces the inverted pyramid guide to writing by saying that one of the skills of a good writer is being able to tell a story clearly, concisely, and in a way that grabs the reader's attention right from the start.

ii. The teacher might give the example that is especially true of those working in journalism; a quick flick through any newspaper will reveal many examples of how to tell a story in as few words as possible.

iii. The teacher gives examples from selections showing reports that are attention grabbing and succinct and that have all the important information clearly summarized right at the beginning. He or she shows how to take the elements of writing, such as introductions, descriptions, conclusions, and explanations, and put them into order according to their importance.

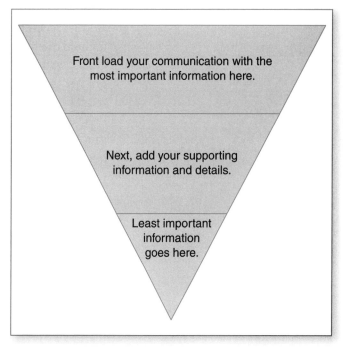

Figure W.1   Example of Writing Strategy Guidelines in the Inverted Pyramid

Front load your communication with the most important information here.

Next, add your supporting information and details.

Least important information goes here.

iv. The inverted pyramid is a simple, effective model for producing eye-catching, quickly digestible content. It takes the elements of writing, such as introductions, descriptions, conclusions, and explanations, and puts them into order according to their importance.

v. In the inverted pyramid model (see Figure W.1), the most important information goes first. This is called front loading. This opening section should summarize your entire message in a few sentences. Subsequent paragraphs then present less critical information, in order of diminishing importance.

vi. The following are four simple steps for using the inverted pyramid:

1. Choose the most important information: Pinpoint the most important part of your message, and work out the least amount of information you need to give people to get it across. Decide which details are less and least important, and plan a running order for your piece.

2. Front load your communication with a short, strong summary: Set a maximum of thirty words for your crucial opening section or as many as will fit on a screen before you have to scroll down. Limit it to a few short paragraphs or sentences that summarize the key details, and lead with your most important point. Covering the five Ws and one H of a story (what, who, where,

when, why, and how) here can be too much. Make your priority the what and the who. The where and when can follow next and then the why and how. Remember to keep things simple; use everyday language, and avoid jargon.

3. Add your supporting information and detail: This is where you include the bulk of your information, expand on your argument, describe the issues, or supply contextual material. Illustrations, quotes, and statistics can also go here. Such details will help the reader but aren't essential for understanding your message. Keep this section clear and concise. Your communication might have more room to breathe here than in your introduction, but you don't want to lose your readers by overwhelming them with detail. Split your points into separate paragraphs, and front load them by making your point and then elaborating on it.

4. Close your piece with background or bonus information: You can end your communication with information that may not be directly related to its main subject but which might help someone to understand it. This could include background or historical detail.

Avoiding potential pitfalls:

1. The inverted pyramid is a multipurpose writing tool, but it isn't a universal one. It doesn't group similar information together or present it in chronological order. So, if you don't shuffle your information with great care, you risk confusing your reader.

2. You also risk losing your readers after your summary. They will have the key points, but if that's all they read, they will miss out on the supporting information and other important but not necessarily attention-grabbing detail.

3. It's not appropriate for every writing situation, either. You often need to hook people with a good opening, but you may not always want to say everything straight away. For example, sometimes, you'll want to build a compelling step-by-step argument or follow a prescribed template for a report. Or, you may be writing for people with lots of time on their hands or who are looking for a more predictable storytelling approach, with a beginning, a middle, and an end.

Research Base

Peregoy & Boyle (2005)

What to Watch for With ELL/CLD Students

i. This strategy is for intermediate to fluent speakers, who are literate in their own or the target language. It will not be effective for newcomers, beginning level, or less proficient speakers or those who are not literate.

ii. However, it can be used in simplified form as students become more comfortable with reading and writing and could be introduced by showing existing examples of the inverted pyramid in reading for comprehension.

WRITING STRATEGY—PENS

Purpose of the Strategy

i. Facilitate access of prior knowledge

ii. Build academic transfer skills

iii. Build foundation for learning

iv. Build awareness of appropriate social and academic language

v. Build awareness of learning process

vi. Develop thinking and planning skills

vii. Facilitate language development

viii. Facilitate writing process

ix. Improve vocabulary

x. Improve writing strategies

xi. Increase focus on reading

xii. Reduce distractibility

xiii. Reduce impulsivity

xiv. Reinforce content lessons

xv. Strengthen language development

xvi. Strengthen learning to learn skills

xvii. Sustain engagement with reading and writing

xviii. Improve vocabulary

xix. Develop academic language

xx. Develop analytical skills

xxi. Develop basic sentence structure

xxii. Increase time on task

xxiii. Develop problem-solving skills

xxiv. Improve comprehension

xxv. Improve reading and writing strategies

How to Do It

i. PENS is a strategy for writing and composition skills to expand language arts capabilities and developing basic sentence structure.

ii. The teacher introduces PENS with charts and individual worksheets that students can use while working on a writing assignment. He or she gives the students several formulas for sentence construction using cloze techniques or other graphic frames and models. The teacher also provides word subject action object lists to choose from in completing the sentences.

iii. PENS assists students to write different types of sentences following formulas for sentence construction. The following are the steps in PENS:

1. Pick a formula
2. Explore different words that fit the formula
3. Note the words selected
4. Subject and verb selections follow

Research Base

Derwinger, Stigsdotter Neely, & Baeckman (2005).

Eskritt & McLeod (2008)

PENS Process Steps	What am I to do at this step?	What did I do about it?	Example of What I Used
Pick a formula			
Explore different words that fit the formula			
Note the words selected			
Subject and verb selections follow			

What to Watch for With ELL/CLD Students

i. Newcomers will need to have the PENS steps modeled and explained in their most proficient language before they can proceed independently.

ii. Students can be paired with partners who are slightly more bilingual than themselves to facilitate their learning this process.

WRITING STRATEGY—TOWER

Purpose of the Strategy

i. Access and use prior knowledge

ii. Develop cognitive academic language

iii. Develop thinking and planning skills

iv. Build awareness of learning

v. Expand and elaborate on learning

vi. Develop personal control of situations

vii. Develop thinking and planning skills

viii. Facilitate students' writing

ix. Improve sequencing skills

x. Improve time on task

xi. Strengthen retention and application abilities

xii. Sustain engagement with reading and writing

xiii. Improve access to prior knowledge

xiv. Reduce off-task behaviors

xv. Strengthen language development

How to Do It

i. The TOWER writing strategy framework provides a structure for completing initial and final drafts of written reports.

ii. It may be used effectively with the COPS proofreading strategy structure.

iii. The teacher introduces TOWER by writing the steps on the board next to a passage from a hypothetical student written paragraph or sentence depending upon the grade level of the class. The teacher then has the class walk through the steps in TOWER explaining each point: thinking, ordering, writing, editing, and rewriting.

iv. The teacher can provide a large TOWER frame as a poster or as a projection on the screen and walk through the steps with the students.

v. To help the students remember the steps in TOWER, the teacher can provide the students with a printed form with the letters T, O, W, E, and R down the left side and with the meaning under each letter.

vi. The following are the steps students follow in TOWER:

1. Think
2. Order ideas
3. Write
4. Edit
5. Rewrite

Research Base

Cole (1995)

Ellis & Colvert (1996)

Ellis & Lenz (1987)

Goldsworthy (2003)

TOWER Elements	What am I to do at this step?	What did I do about it?	How many times did I do this?
Think			
Order ideas			
Write			
Edit			
Rewrite			

What to Watch for With ELL/CLD Students

i. Newcomers will need to have the TOWER steps modeled and explained in their most proficient language before they can proceed independently.

ii. Students can be paired with partners who are slightly more bilingual than themselves to facilitate their learning this process.

W-STAR—READING COMPREHENSION STRATEGY

Purpose of the Strategy

i. Access and use prior knowledge

ii. Build vocabulary

iii. Develop content knowledge foundation

iv. Develop extended time on task

v. Develop problem-solving skills

vi. Develop thinking and planning skills

vii. Enhance ability of students to focus on learning

viii. Enhance ability of students to learn new things

ix. Build transfer skills

x. Expand and elaborate on learning

xi. Expand comprehension

xii. Facilitate access of prior knowledge

xiii. Facilitate acquisition of content knowledge

xiv. Increase students' probability of generating a correct response

xv. Increase students' time on task

xvi. Build awareness of learning

xvii. Reduce off-task behaviors

xviii. Reduce misperceptions

xix. Reinforce content

How to Do It

i. This cognitive strategy is conducted in the general classroom with all students. The teacher or assistant previews lesson content in the students' first language when possible, outlining key issues, rehearsing vocabulary, and reviewing related prior knowledge.

ii. The teacher has the target student preview the lesson for less-advanced students, outlining key issues, rehearsing vocabulary, and reviewing related prior knowledge. An advanced fluency student helps less-advanced students understand how to organize their reading and writing materials.

iii. This strategy is done in individualized, focused intensive periods of time. The teacher has the target student preview lesson for less-advanced students, outlining key issues, rehearsing vocabulary, and reviewing related prior knowledge. Advanced fluency student helps less-advanced students understand how to organize their reading and writing materials.

iv. This strategy is done in specially designed individual programs and may be included in the IEP. The teacher has the target student preview lesson for less-advanced students, outlining key issues, rehearsing vocabulary, and reviewing related prior knowledge. An advanced fluency student helps less-advanced students understand how to organize their reading and writing materials.

v. W-star is done by asking the students to brainstorm before beginning a reading: Who do you think this story/event is about? Where do you think the story/event is located? When do you think the story/event occurs? How do you think the story/event turns out? The answers are written onto the points of a star diagram, each point of which represents one of the "w" questions.

vi. When applying the w-star strategy, students work through problems or tasks using a sequence of ordering, sequencing, and connecting techniques. Suppose you want your students to write a short personal reflection about the story, *Everyone Cooks Rice* by Norah Dooley, that the class has just finished reading together. You would start by having your students work in small groups of similar ability level. You would show a copy of a graphic organizer form outline on the overhead projector or drawn on the whiteboard. Each group would be assigned two or three of the boxes in the graphic organizer. For example, you might assign the most challenged group to fill in the boxes about title, author, location, and country. Another group would be responsible for the main and supporting characters. Another group would be responsible for identifying the sequence of events in the story and a summary statement about these. Another group could be assigned to identify the main problem faced by the main character. After reading the story through the first time, the groups complete their tasks, and you or they write down their answers on the large or projected graphic organizer. Now as a group, you ask about how this main problem was resolved, the barriers to resolution, and things in the story that helped solve the problem. The students can now discuss the final resolution and what the moral of the story might be from their perspectives. You can expand this activity by comparing and contrasting the story with others like it or with happenings in the students' lives.

vii. You might now step back from the lesson and discuss the metacognitive learning that you have provided students, the learning to learn lesson that is represented by the strategy you had them use.

viii. The following are the steps for teaching w-stars:

1. *Inform* the students what w-stars is, how it operates, when to use it, and why it is useful. Begin by saying that w-stars is a way to help them (the students) plan and remember. They work by previewing or putting information concerning the lesson or assignment they are working on into graphic form. Once they learn how to use w-stars, they can use it anytime and with any content or lesson you give them to do.

2. *Use cues,* metaphors, analogies, or other means of elaborating on a description of w-stars combined with visual cues. One way to do this is to have the group look at a blueprint of a house or other building they are familiar with. Have them see how the architect had to plan for everything ahead of time and create a preview or graphic image of what everyone was going to have to do to complete the construction. Explain that almost anyone could help construct the house or building by reading the blueprint, and the ability to read and understand these is a special and critical skill that will be useful to them later in life.

3. *Lead group discussions* about the use of w-stars. Have students start with talking about a lesson they have just successfully completed. They can go back through the lesson or book using different w-star tools to see how they work and what is required. Encourage them to ask you anything about the learning process they want clarified.

4. *Provide guided practice* in applying w-stars to particular tasks. Work directly with student groups demonstrating and modeling how to identify elements. Have more skilled students demonstrate for the class.

5. *Provide feedback* on monitoring use and success of w-stars. While students use w-stars in small groups, you should move around the room listening and supplying encouragement for consistent use of the tools. As students get more comfortable using these tools, you can have them monitor one another in the use of the strategy.

Research Base

Collier (2002)

Harwell (2001)

Heacox (2002)

Moore, Alvermann, & Hinchman (2000)

Opitz (1998)

What to Watch for With ELL/CLD Students

i. There are cultural differences in cognitive/learning style, and some English language learner (ELL)/culturally and linguistically diverse (CLD) students may not respond to the brainstorming construct behind most advanced organizers.

ii. By keeping the graphic design of the w-star as close as possible to the illustrations in the text or some aspect of the lesson, the teacher can more tightly connect the concepts being studied with the what/who/where questioning that precedes the lesson.

iii. This is another activity that works best with preparation in the students' most proficient language and relevance to their culture before proceeding.

Figure W.2 Example of W-Star

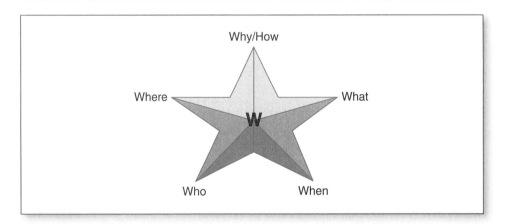

References

Agran, M., King-Sears, M., Wehmeyer, M., & Copeland, S. (2003). *Teachers' guides to inclusive practices: Student-directed learning.* Baltimore, MD: Paul H. Brookes.

Ainley, M. (2006). Connecting with learning: Motivation, affect and cognition in interest processes. *Educational Psychological Review, 18,* 391–405.

Ajibade, Y., & Ndububa, K. (2008). Effects of world games, culturally relevant songs, and stories on students' motivation in a Nigerian English language class. *TESL Canada Journal, 25*(2), 27–48.

Allen, J. S., & Klein, R. J. (1997). *Ready, set, relax: A research-based program of relaxation, learning and self-esteem for children.* Watertown, WI: Inner Coaching.

Allington, R. L., & Cunningham, P. M. (2002). *Schools that work: Where all children read and write.* Boston, MA: Allyn & Bacon.

Anderson, J. R. (2000). *Learning and memory: An integrated approach* (2nd ed.). New York, NY: Wiley.

Aram, D., & Shlak, M. (2008). The safe kindergarten: Promotion of communication and social skills among kindergartners. *Early Education and Development, 19*(6), 865–884.

Arkoudis, S. (2005). Fusing pedagogic horizons: Language and content teaching in the mainstream. *Linguistics and Education: An International Research Journal, 16*(2), 173–187.

Artis, A. (2008). Improving marketing students' reading comprehension with the SQ3R method. *Journal of Marketing Education, 30*(2), 130–137.

Asher, J. (1980). *Learning another language through actions: The complete teacher's guidebook.* Los Gatos, CA: Sky Oaks.

Ashworth, M., & Wakefield, P. (2004). *Teaching the world's children: ESL for ages three to seven* (2nd ed.). Toronto, Canada: Pippin.

Banchi, H., & Bell, R. (2008). The many levels of inquiry. *Science and Children, 46*(2), 26–29.

Beaudoin, N. (2005). *Elevating student voice: How to enhance participation, citizenship, and leadership.* Larchmont, NY: Eye on Education.

Becker, H., & Hamayan, E. V. (2008). *Teaching ESL K–12: Views from the classroom.* Boston, MA: Heinle & Heinle.

Beckett, G. H. (2002). Teacher and student evaluations of project-based instruction. *TESL Canada Journal, 19*(2), 52–66.

Beckett, G. H., & Miller, P. C. (Ed.). (2006). *Project-based second and foreign language education: Past, present, and future.* Charlotte, NC: Information Age.

Beckett, G. H., & Slater, T. (2005). The project framework: A tool for language, content, and skills integration. *ELT Journal, 59*(2), 108–116.

Benjamin, S. (2003). What counts as 'success'? Hierarchical discourses in a girls' comprehensive school. *Discourse, 24*(1), 105–118.

Bondi, W. (1988). *Designing interdisciplinary units.* Tampa, FL: Wiles Bondi.

Borba, M. (2001). *Building moral intelligence: The seven essential virtues that teach kids to do the right thing.* San Francisco, CA: Jossey-Bass.

Brechtel, M. (2001). *Bringing it all together: Language and literacy in the multilingual classroom.* Parsippany, NJ: Dominie Press (Pearson).

Brinton, D. M., Wesche, M., & Snow, M. A. (2003). *Content-based second-language instruction: Michigan classics edition.* Ann Arbor: University of Michigan Press.

Brophy, J. (2004). *Motivating students to learn.* Mahwah, NJ: Lawrence Erlbaum.

Brown, A. L., & Palincsar, A. S. (1987). Reciprocal teaching of comprehension strategies: A natural history of one program for enhancing learning. In J. Day & J. Borkowski (Eds.), *Intelligence and exceptionality: New directions in theory, assessment and instructional practices* (pp. 81–132). Norwood, NJ: Ablex.

Brownlie, F., & King, J. (2000). *Learning in safe schools: Creating classrooms where all students belong.* Markham, Ontario: Pembroke.

Bruner, J. S. (1961). The act of discovery. *Harvard Educational Review, 31,* 21–32.

Burnham, L., Mantero, M., & Hooper, L. (2009). Experiential training: Connecting school counselors-in-training, English as a second language (ESL) teachers, and ESL students. *Journal of Multicultural Counseling and Development, 37*(1), 2–14.

Carpenter, L. B. (2001). Utilizing travel cards to increase productive student behavior, teacher collaboration, and parent-school communication. *Education and Training in Mental Retardation and Developmental Disabilities, 36,* 318–322.

Carrigan, T. (2001). *Canada: Who are we and where are we going? Immigration, multiculturalism, and the Canadian identity.* Vancouver, British Columbia: Hawthorn Educational Group.

Carver, R. P. (1970). Effects of a "chunked" typography on reading rate and comprehension. *Journal of Applied Psychology, 54*(3), 288–290.

Casteel, C. A. (1988). Effects of chunked reading among learning disabled students: An experimental comparison of computer and traditional chunked passages. *Journal of Educational Technology Systems, 17*(2), 115–121.

Celce-Murcia, M., & Olshtain, E. (2000). *Discourse and context in language teaching.* New York, NY: Cambridge University Press.

Cloud, N., Genesee, F., & Hamayan, E. (2000). *Dual language instruction: A handbook for enriched education.* Boston, MA: Heinle & Heinle.

Coelho, E., & Rivers, D. (2003). *Adding English: A guide to teaching in multilingual classrooms.* Toronto, Canada: Pippin.

Cole, R. W. (Ed.). (1995). *Educating everybody's children: Diverse teaching strategies for diverse learners.* Alexandria, VA: Association for Supervision and Curriculum Development.

Collier, C. (2002). *Cognitive learning strategies for diverse learners.* Ferndale, WA: CrossCultural Developmental Education Services.

Collier, C. (2003a). *Separating difference from disability.* Ferndale, WA: CrossCultural Developmental Education Services.

Collier, C. (2003b). Curriculum materials for the bilingual exceptional child. In L. Baca & H. Cervantes (Eds.), *The bilingual special education interface* (4th ed.). New York, NY: Prentice Hall.

Collier, C. (2008). *Cognitive learning styles and strategies for diverse learners.* Ferndale, WA: CrossCultural Developmental Education Services.

Collier, C. (2010a). *RTI for diverse learners.* Thousand Oaks, CA: Corwin.

Collier, C. (2010b). *Seven steps to separating difference from disability.* Thousand Oaks, CA: Corwin.

Collier, C. (2012a). *Cognitive learning strategies for diverse learners* (2nd ed.). Ferndale, WA: CrossCultural Developmental Education Services.

Collier, C. (2012b). *Pearls of wisdom: Strategies for learning support and intervention of diverse learners.* Ferndale, WA: CrossCultural Developmental Education Services.

Collins Block, C., & Mangieri, J. N. (2003). *Exemplary literacy teachers: Promoting success for all children in grades K–5.* New York. NY: Guilford Press.

Cordova, D. I., & Lepper, M. R. (1996). Intrinsic motivation and the process of learning: Beneficial effects of contextualization, personalization and choice. *Journal of Educational Psychology, 88,* 715–730.

Croom, L., & Davis, B. H. (2006). It's not polite to interrupt, and other rules of classroom etiquette. *Kappa Delta Pi Record, 42*(3), 109–113.

Cummins, J. (1984). *Bilingualism and special education: Issues in assessment and pedagogy.* San Diego, CA: College Hill Press.

Cummins, J., Baker, C., & Hornberger, N. H. (2001). *An introductory reader to the writings of Jim Cummins.* Clevedon, UK: Multilingual Matters.

Curwin, R., & Mendler, A. (1999). *Discipline with dignity* (2nd ed.). Alexandria, VA: Association for Supervision and Curriculum Development.

Dang, T., Dang, P., & Ruiter, R. (2005). *Highway to E.S.L.: A user-friendly guide to teaching English as a second language.* Bloomington, IN: iUniverse.

Davey, B. (1983). Thinking aloud: Modeling the cognitive process of reading comprehension. *Journal of Reading, 27,* 44–47.

Davis, B. M. (2005). *How to teach students who don't look like you: Culturally relevant teaching strategies.* Thousand Oaks, CA: Corwin.

Derwinger, A., Stigsdotter Neely, A., & Baeckman, L. (2005). Design your own memory strategies! Self-generated strategy training versus mnemonic training in old age: An 8-month follow-up. *Neuropsychological Rehabilitation, 15*(1), 37–54.

DeVries Guth, N., & Stephens Pettengill, S. (2005). *Leading a successful reading program: Administrators and reading specialists working together to make it happen.* Newark, DE: International Reading Association

Donaldson, M. (1978). *Children's minds.* Glasgow, UK: Collins.

Echevarria, J. (1995). Sheltered instruction for students with learning disabilities who have limited English proficiency. *Intervention in School & Clinic, 30*(5), 302–305.

Echevarria, J., & Graves, A. (2006). *Sheltered content instruction: Teaching English language learners with diverse abilities* (3rd ed.). Old Tappan, NJ: Pearson.

Echevarria, J., Vogt, M. E., & Short, D. (2007). *Making content comprehensible for English learners: The SIOP model* (3rd ed.). Old Tappan, NJ: Pearson.

Elliot, J. L., & Thurlow, M. L. (2005). *Improving test performance of students with disabilities: On district and state assessments* (2nd ed.). Thousand Oaks, CA: Corwin.

Ellis, E. S., & Colvert, G. (1996). Writing strategy instruction. In D. D. Deshler, E. S. Ellis, & B. K. Lenz (Eds.), *Teaching adolescents with learning disabilities: Strategies and methods* (2nd ed.), (pp. 127–170). Denver, CO: Love.

Ellis, E. S., & Lenz, B. K. (1987). A component analysis of effective learning strategies for LD students. *Learning Disabilities Focus, 2*(2), 94–107.

Eskritt, M., & McLeod, K. (2008). Children's note taking as a mnemonic tool. *Journal of Experimental Child Psychology, 101*(1), 52–74.

Etscheidt, S. (1984). The effectiveness of teacher proximity as an initial technique of helping pupils control their behavior. *Pointer, 28*(4), 33–35.

Evertson, C. M., & Neal, K. W. (2006). *Looking into learning-centered classrooms implications for classroom management.* Washington DC: National Education Association.

Evertson, C. M., & Weinstein, C. S. (2006). *Handbook of classroom management: Research, practice, and contemporary issues.* New York, NY: Routledge.

Felix-Brasdefer, J. C. (2008). *Politeness in Mexico and the United States: A contrastive study of the realization and perception of refusals.* Amsterdam, Netherlands: John Benjamins.

Ferris, D., & Hedgcock, J. (2005). *Teaching ESL composition: Purpose, process, and practice* (2nd ed.). New York, NY: Routledge.

Feuerstein, R. (1986). The foster home group experiment. In Y. Kashti & M. Arieli (Eds.), *Residential settings and the community.* Tel Aviv, Israel: Freund.

Feuerstein, R., & Hoffman, M. (1982). Intergenerational conflict of rights: Cultural imposition and self-realization. *Viewpoints in Teaching and Learning, 58*(1), 44–63.

Fisher, D., & Frey, N. (2004). *Improving adolescent literacy: Strategies at work.* Upper Saddle River, NJ: Pearson Prentice Hall.

Fitzell, S. G. (1997). *Free the children! Conflict education for strong and peaceful minds. Conflict resolution skills for pre-K through grade 12.* Gabriola Island, British Columbia, Canada: New Society.

Flowerday, T., & Schraw, G. (2003). Effect of choice on cognitive and affective engagement. *The Journal of Educational Research, 96,* 207–215.

Flowerday, T., Schraw, G., & Stevens, J. (2004). The role of choice and interest in reader engagement. *Journal of Experimental Education, 72*(2), 93–114.

Flowerdew, J., & Peacock, M. (2001). *Research perspectives on English for academic purposes.* Cambridge, UK: Cambridge University Press.

Fuchs, D., Compton, D. L., Fuchs, L. S., & Bryant, J. (2008). Making "secondary intervention" work in a three-tier responsiveness-to-intervention model: Findings from the first-grade longitudinal reading study at the National Research Center on Learning Disabilities. *Reading and Writing: An Interdisciplinary Journal, 21,* 413–436.

Fuchs, D., & Fuchs, L. S. (2006). Introduction to responsiveness-to-intervention: What, why, and how valid is it? *Reading Research Quarterly, 4,* 93–99.

Fuchs, L. S., & Stecker, P. M. (2003). *Scientifically based progress monitoring.* Washington, DC: National Center on Student Progress Monitoring.

Garber-Miller, K. (2006). Playful textbook previews: Letting go of familiar mustache monologues. *Journal of Adolescent & Adult Literacy, 50*(4), 284–288.

Garcia, D. C., Hasson, D. J., Hoffman, E., Paneque, O. M., & Pelaez, G. (1996). *Family centered learning. A program guide for linguistically and culturally diverse populations.* Miami: Florida International University.

Garcia, E. E. (2005). *Teaching and learning in two languages: Bilingualism & schooling in the United States* (Multicultural Education). New York, NY: Teachers College Press.

Gardner, H. (1993a). *Multiple intelligences: The theory in practice.* New York, NY: Basic Books.

Gardner, H. (1993b). *Frames of mind: The theory of multiple intelligences* (10th ed.). New York, NY: Basic Books.

Gibbons, P. (2002). *Scaffolding language, scaffolding learning: Teaching second language learners in the mainstream classroom.* Portsmouth, NH: Heinemann.

Gibbons, P. (2003). Mediating language learning: Teacher interactions with ESL students in a content-based classroom. *TESOL Quarterly, 37*(2), 247–273.

Gibbons, P. (2006). *Bridging discourses in the ESL classroom: Students, teachers and researchers.* New York, NY: Continuum International.

Goldsworthy, C. L. (2003). *Developmental reading disabilities: A language-based treatment approach* (2nd ed.). Florence, KY: Cengage Learning.

Grossman, H. (2003). *Classroom behavior management for diverse and inclusive schools* (3rd ed.). Lanham, MD: Rowman & Littlefield.

Gunter, P. L., & Shores, R. E. (1995). On the move: Using teacher/student proximity to improve student's behavior. *Teaching Exceptional Children, 28*(1), 12–14.

Hafernik, J. J., Messerschmitt, D. S., & Vandrick, S. (2002). *Ethical issues for ESL faculty: Social justice in practice.* Philadelphia, PA: Lawrence Erlbaum.

Hall, R. V., & Hall, M. C. (1998). *How to use planned ignoring (extinction)* (2nd ed.). Austin, TX: Pro-Ed.

Hamachek, D. E. (1994). *Psychology in teaching, learning, and growth: Learning and growth* (5th ed.). Old Tappan, NJ: Allyn & Bacon.

Haneda, M. (2008). Contexts for learning: English language learners in a U.S. middle school. *International Journal of Bilingual Education and Bilingualism, 11*(1), 57–74.

Harwell, J. M. (2001). *Complete learning disabilities handbook: Ready-to-use strategies & activities for teaching students with learning disabilities.* Paramus, NJ: Center for Applied Research in Education.

Hamilton, L. S., Stecher, B. M., & Klein, S. P. (2002). *Making sense of test-based accountability in education.* Santa Monica, CA: Rand.

Haneda, M. (2008). Contexts for learning: English language learners in a U.S. middle school. *International Journal of Bilingual Education and Bilingualism, 11*(1), 57–74.

Hansen-Thomas, H. (2008). Sheltered instruction: Best practices for ELL/CLD in the mainstream, *Kappa Delta Pi Record, 44*(4), 165–169.

Heacox, D. (2002). *Differentiating instruction in the regular classroom: How to reach and teach all learners, grades 3–12.* Minneapolis, MN: Free Spirit.

Herrera, S. (2010). *Biography-driven culturally responsive teaching.* New York, NY: Teachers College Press.

Herrera, S. G., & Murry, K. G. (2004). Mastering ESL and bilingual methods. Boston, MA: Allyn and Bacon.

Hoover, & Collier. (1987). *Cognitive learning strategies for minority handicapped learners.* Lindale, TX: Hamilton.

Houghton, S., & Bain, A. (1993). Peer tutoring with ESL and below-average readers. *Journal of Behavioral Education, 3*(2), 125–142.

Hu, R., & Commeyras, M. (2008). A case study: Emergent biliteracy in English and Chinese of a 5-year-old Chinese child with wordless picture books. *Reading Psychology, 29*(1), 1–30.

Hughes, C. A., Deshler, D. D., Ruhl, K. L., & Schumaker, J. B. (1993). Test-taking strategy instruction for adolescents with emotional and behavioral disorders. *Journal of Emotional and Behavioral Disorders, 1*(3), 189–198.

Iachini, T., Borghi, A. M., & Senese, V. P. (2008). Categorization and sensorimotor interaction with objects. *Brain and Cognition, 67*(1), 31–43.

Irvin, J. L., & Rose, E. O. (1995). *Starting early with study skills: A week-by-week guide for elementary students.* Old Tappan, NJ: Pearson.

Jackson, P. W., Boostrom, R. E., & Hansen, D. T. (1998). *The moral life of schools.* San Francisco, CA: Jossey-Bass.

Jeffries, L., & Mikulecky, B. S. (2009). *Reading power 2* (4th ed.). White Plains, NY: Pearson Education.

Johnson, J. E., Christie, J. F., & Yawkey, T. D. (1999). *Play and early childhood development* (2nd ed.). New York, NY: Addison Wesley Longman.

Johnson, B., Juhasz, A., Marken, J., & Ruiz, B. R. (1998). The ESL teacher as moral agent. *Research in the Teaching of English, 32*(2), 161–81.

Johnson, R. (1995). ESL teacher education and intercultural communication: Discomfort as a learning tool. *TESL Canada Journal, 12*(2), 59–66.

Jutras, P. (2008). How do you teach students to practice memorization? *Keyboard Companion, 19*(1), 50.

Kamps, D. (2007). Use of evidence-based, small-group reading instruction for English language learners in elementary grades: Secondary-tier intervention (table). *Learning Disability Quarterly, 30*(3), 153–69.

Kaufman, D. (2001). Organizing and managing the language arts workshop: A matter of motion. *Language Arts, 79*(2), 114–123.

Kelly, B. W., & Holmes, J. (1979). The guided lecture procedure. *Journal of Reading, 22*(7), 602–604.

Kim, Y., & Kellogg, D. (2007). Rules out of roles: Differences in play language and their developmental significance. *Applied Linguistics, 28*(1), 25–45.

Kirschner, P. A., Sweller, J., & Clark, R. E. (2006). Why minimal guidance during instruction does not work: An analysis of the failure of constructivist, discovery, problem-based, experiential, and inquiry based teaching. *Educational Psychologist, 41*(2), 75–86.

Klingner, J. K., Vaughn, S., & Boardman, A. (2007). *Teaching reading comprehension to students with learning difficulties.* New York, NY: Guilford Press.

Koenig, L. J. (2007). *Smart discipline for the classroom: Respect and cooperation restored* (4th ed.). Thousand Oaks, CA: Corwin.

Koskinen, P. A., & Blum, I. H. (1984). Paired repeated reading: A classroom strategy for developing fluent reading. *The Reading Teacher, 40,* 70–75

Kovelman, I., Baker, S., & Petitto, L. A. (2008). Age of bilingual language exposure as a new window into bilingual reading development. *Bilingualism: Language and Cognition, 11*(2), 203–223.

Kragler, S., & Nolley, C. (1996). Student choices: Book selection strategies of fourth graders. *Reading Horizons, 36*(4), 354–365.

Krashen, S. (2003). *Explorations in language acquisition and use: The Taipei lectures.* Portsmouth, NH: Heinemann.

Krumenaker, L., Many, J., & Wang, Y. (2008). Understanding the experiences and needs of mainstream teachers of ESL students: Reflections from a secondary studies teacher. *TESL Canada Journal, 25*(2), 66–84.

Landis, D., Bennett, J. M., & Bennett, M. J. (Eds.). (2004). *Handbook of intercultural training.* Thousand Oaks, CA: Sage.

Lapp, D., Flood, J., Brock, C. H., & Fisher, D. (2007). *Teaching reading to every child.* New York, NY: Routledge.

Law, B., & Eckes, M. (2000). *The more-than-just-surviving handbook: ESL for every classroom teacher.* Winnipeg, Manitoba: Portage & Main Press.

Lebzelter, S., & Nowacek, E. J. (1999). Reading strategies for secondary students with mild disabilities. *Intervention in School and Clinic, 34*(4), 212–219.

Lee, S. W. (Ed.). (2005). *Encyclopedia of school psychology.* Thousand Oaks, CA: Sage.

Lee, S., Amos, B. A., Gragoudas, S., Lee, Y., Shogren, K. A., Theoharis, R., & Wehmeyer, M. L. (2006). Curriculum augmentation and adaptation strategies to promote access to the general curriculum for students with intellectual and developmental disabilities. *Education and Training in Developmental Disabilities, 41*(3), 199–212.

Leki, I. (1995). Coping strategies of ESL students in writing tasks across the curriculum. *TESOL Quarterly, 29*(2), 235–260.

Little, S. G., & Akin-Little, A. (2008). Psychology's contributions to classroom management. *Psychology in the Schools, 45*(3), 227–234.

Livingstone, C. (1983). *Role play in language learning.* New York, NY: Longman.

Ma, J. (2008). Reading the word and the world: How mind and culture are mediated through the use of dual-language storybooks. *Education 3–13, 36*(3), 237–251.

Magos, K., & Politi, F. (2008). The creative second-language lesson: The contribution of the role-play technique to the teaching of a second language in immigrant classes. *RELC Journal, 39*(1), 96–112.

Marable, M. A., & Raimondi, S. L. (1995). Managing surface behaviors. *LD Forum, 20*(2), 45–47.

Mathes, P. G., Pollard-Durodola, S. D., Cárdenas-Hagan, E., Linan-Thompson, S., & Vaughn, S. (2007). Teaching struggling readers who are native Spanish speakers: What do we know? *Language, Speech, and Hearing Services in Schools, 38,* 260–271.

McAllister, C., & Irvine, J. J. (2000). Cross cultural competency and multicultural teacher education. *Review of Educational Research, 70,* 3–24.

McCain, T. D. (2005). *Teaching for tomorrow: Teaching content and problem-solving skills.* Thousand Oaks, CA: Corwin.

McIntyre, E., Kyle, D., Chen, C., Kraemer, J., & Parr, J. (2009). *Six principles for teaching English language learners in all classrooms.* Thousand Oaks, CA: Corwin.

Moore, D. W., Alvermann, D. E., & Hinchman, K. A. (Ed.). (2000). *Struggling adolescent readers: A collection of teaching strategies.* Newark, DE: International Reading Association.

Movitz, A. P., & Holmes, K. P. (2007). Finding center: How learning centers evolved in a secondary student-centered classroom. *English Journal, 96*(3), 68–73.

Murrey, D. (2008). Differentiating instruction in mathematics for the English language learner. *Mathematics Teaching in the Middle School, 14*(3).

Naughton, V. M. (2008). Picture it! *Reading Teacher, 62*(1), 65–68.

Nelson, P., Kohnert, K., Sabur, S., & Shaw, D. (2005). Classroom noise and children learning through a second language: Double jeopardy? *Language, Speech, and Hearing Services in Schools, 36,* 219–229.

Nelson, J. R., Martella, R., & Galand, B. (1998). The effects of teaching school expectations and establishing a consistent consequence on formal office disciplinary actions. *Journal of Emotional and Behavioral Disorders, 6*(3), 153–161.

Nessel, D. D., & Nixon, C. N. (2008). *Using the language experience approach with English language learners: Strategies for engaging students and developing literacy.* Thousand Oaks, CA: Corwin.

Nishizawa, H., Yoshioka, T., & Fukada, M. (2010). The impact of a 4-year extensive reading program. In A. M. Stoke (Ed.), *JALT2009 conference proceedings.* Tokyo: JALT.

Odean, P. M. (1987). Teaching paraphrasing to ESL students. *MinneTESOL Journal, 6,* 15–27.

Olson S., & Loucks-Horsley, S. (Ed.). (2000). *The National Academies Press Inquiry and the National Science Education Standards: A guide for teaching and learning.* Washington, DC: National Academy Press.

Opitz, M. F. (Ed.). (1998). *Literacy instruction for culturally and linguistically diverse students.* Newark, DE: International Reading Association.

Padak, N., & Rasinski, T. (2008). The games children play. *Reading Teacher, 62*(4), 363–364.

Page, R. M., & Page, T. S. (2003). *Fostering emotional well-being in the classroom* (3rd ed.). Sudbury, MA: Jones & Bartlett.

Parrish, B. (2004). *Teaching adult ESL: A practical introduction.* New York, NY: McGraw-Hill.

Pelow, R. A., & Colvin, H. M. (1983, spring). PQ4R as it affects comprehension of social studies reading material. *Social Studies Journal, 12,* 14–22.

Peregoy, S. F., & Boyle, O. F. (2005). *Reading, writing, and learning in ESL: A resource book for K–12 teachers* (4th ed.). White Plains, NY: Pearson Education.

Petrie, G., Lindauer, P., Bennett, B., & Gibson, S. (1998). Nonverbal cues: The key to classroom management. *Principal, 77*(3), 34–36.

Popp, M. S. (1997). *Learning journals in the K–8 classroom: Exploring ideas and information in the content areas.* Mahwah, NJ: Lawrence Erlbaum.

Prasad, J. (2005). *Audio-visual education: Teaching innovative techniques.* Delhi, India: Kanishka

Pressley, M., Borkowski, J. G., & O'Sullivan, J. T. (1984). Memory strategy instruction is made of this: Metamemory and durable strategy use. *Educational Psychology, 19*, 94–107.

Rafferty, L. A. (2007). "They just won't listen to me": A teacher's guide to positive behavioral interventions. *Childhood Education, 84*(2), 102–104.

Reid, M. J., Webster-Stratton, C., & Hammond, M. (2007). Enhancing a classroom social competence and problem-solving curriculum by offering parent training to families of moderate- to high-risk elementary school children. *Journal of Clinical Child & Adolescent Psychology, 36*(4), 605–620.

Reggy-Mamo, M. (2008). An experiential approach to intercultural education. *Christian Higher Education, 7*(2), 110–122.

Ritter, S., & Idol-Maestas, L. (1986). Teaching middle school students to use a test-taking strategy. *Journal of Educational Research, 79*(6), 350–357.

Robertson, K. (2009). Math instruction for English language learners. Reading Rockets Website. Retrieved from http://www.readingrockets.org/article/math-instruction-english-language-learners

Robinson, F. P. (1946). *Effective study.* New York, NY: Harper & Row.

Roessingh, H., Kover, P., & Watt, D. (2005). Developing cognitive academic language proficiency: The journey. *TESL Canada Journal, 23*(1), 1–27.

Rogers, B. (2006). *Classroom behaviour: A practical guide to effective teaching, behaviour management and colleague support.* London, UK: Paul Chapman.

Rubenstein, I. Z. (2006). Educational expectations: How they differ around the world: Implications for teaching ESL college students. *Community College Journal of Research & Practice, 30*(5–6), 433–441.

Rymes, B., Cahnmann-Taylor, M., & Souto-Manning, M. (2008). Bilingual teachers' performances of power and conflict. *Teaching Education, 19*(2), 93–107.

Sakta, C. G. (1999). SQRC: A strategy for guiding reading and higher level thinking. *Journal of Adolescent & Adult Literacy, 42*, 265–269.

Sanacore, J. (1982). Transferring the PQ4R study procedure: Administrative concerns. *Clearing House, 55*(5), 234–236.

Sanacore, J. (1999). Encouraging children to make choices about their literacy learning. *Intervention in School and Clinic, 35*(1), 38–42.

Seuss. (1954). *Horton hears a who.* New York, NY: Random House.

Shores, C., & Chester, K. (2009). *Using RTI for school improvement.* Thousand Oaks, CA: Corwin.

Short, D., & Echevarria, J. (2004). Teacher skills to support English language learners. *Educational Leadership, 62*(4), 8–13.

Sink, D. W., Jr., Parkhill, M. A., Marshall, R., Norwood, S., & Parkhill, M. (2005). Learning together: A family-centered literacy program. *Community College Journal of Research & Practice, 29*(8), 583–590.

Smith, C. B. (2000). Reading to learn: How to study as you read. Bloomington, IN: ERIC Clearinghouse on Reading English and Communication.

Sousa, D. A., & Tomlinson, C. A. (2010). *Differentiation and the brain: How neuroscience supports the learner-friendly classroom.* Bloomington, IN: Solution Tree Press.

Sperling, D. (2016). *Flip for Krypto.* Retrieved from http://www.eslcafe.com

Strickland, D. S., Ganske, K., & Monroe, J. K. (2002). *Supporting struggling readers and writers: Strategies for classroom intervention 3–6.* Newark, DE: International Reading Association.

Thomas, P. (2006). *Stress in early childhood: Helping children and their careers.* Watson, ACT, Australia: Early Childhood Australia.

Tomlinson, B. (Ed.). (1998). *Materials development in language teaching.* Cambridge, UK: Cambridge University Press.

Tomlinson, C. A. (1999). *The differentiated classroom: Responding to the needs of all learners.* Alexandria, VA: Association for Supervision and Curriculum Development.

Toole, R. (2000). An additional step in the guided lecture procedure. *Journal of Adolescent & Adult Literacy, 44*(2), 166–168.

Tovani, C. (2000). *I read it, but I don't get it: Comprehension strategies for adolescent readers.* Portland, ME: Stenhouse.

Trudeau, K., & Harle, A. Z. (2006). Using reflection to increase children's learning in kindergarten. *Young Children, 61*(4), 101–104.

Vaughn, S., & Linan-Thompson, S. (2007). *Research-based methods of reading instruction for English language learners: Grades K–4.* Alexandria, VA: Association for Supervision and Curriculum Development.

Vygotsky, L. S. (1978). *Mind in society: The development of higher psychological processes.* Cambridge, MA: Harvard University Press.

Walker, D., Carta, J. J., Greenwood, C. R., & Buzhardt, J. F. (2008). The use of individual growth and developmental indicators for progress monitoring and intervention decision making in early education. *Exceptionality, 16*(1), 33–47.

Walter, C. (2004). Transfer of reading comprehension skills to L2 is linked to mental representations of text and to L2 working memory. *Applied Linguistics, 25*(3), 315–339.

Walters, J., & Frei, S. (2007). *Managing classroom behavior and discipline.* Huntington Beach, CA: Shell Education.

Wasik, B. H. (2004). *Handbook of family literacy.* Florence, KY: Routledge.

Webster-Stratton, C., & Reid, M. J. (2004). Strengthening social and emotional competence in young children—The foundation for early school readiness and success: Incredible year's classroom social skills and problem-solving curriculum. *Infants & Young Children, 17*(2), 96–113.

Weisman, E., & Hansen, L. (2007). Strategies for teaching social studies to elementary level ELL/CLD. *Education Digest, 73*(4), 61–65.

Williams, K. C. (2008). *Elementary classroom management: A student-centered approach to leading and learning.* Thousand Oaks, CA: Sage.

Wolpow, R., Johnson, M. M., Hertel, R., & Kincaid, S. O. (2009). *Learning and teaching: Compassion, resiliency, and academic success.* Olympia, WA: Office of the Superintendent of Public Instruction.

Wood, K. D., & Algozzine, B. (1994). Using collaborative learning to meet the needs of high-risk learners. In K. D. Wood & B. Algozzine (Eds.), *Teaching reading to high-risk learners. An integrated approach* (pp. 315–333). Boston, MA: Allyn & Bacon.

Wood, K. D., & Harmon, J. M. (2001). *Strategies for integrating reading and writing in middle and high school classrooms.* Westerville, OH: National Middle School Association.

Wortham, S. C. (1996). *The integrated classroom: The assessment-curriculum link in early childhood education.* Upper Saddle River, NJ: Prentice Hall Business.

Wright, A., Betteridge, D., & Buckby, M. (2006). *Games for language learning.* Cambridge, UK: Cambridge University Press.

Youb, K. (2008). The effects of integrated language-based instruction in elementary ESL learning. *Modern Language Journal, 92*(3), 431–451.

Zutell, J., & Rasinski, T. V. (1991). Training teachers to attend to their students' oral reading fluency. *Theory into Practice, 30*, 211–217.

Zweirs, J. (2008). *Building academic language: Essential practices for content classrooms.* New York, NY: John Wiley & Sons.

Zweirs, J. (2014). *Building academic language: Meeting common core standards across disciplines.* New York, NY: John Wiley & Sons.

Index

A SAGE Publishing Company

CORWIN HAS ONE MISSION: to enhance education through intentional professional learning.

We build long-term relationships with our authors, educators, clients, and associations who partner with us to develop and continuously improve the best evidence-based practices that establish and support lifelong learning.

Solutions you want. Experts you trust. Results you need.

Author Consulting

On-site professional learning with sustainable results! Let us help you design a professional learning plan to meet the unique needs of your school or district. www.corwin.com/pd

Institutes

Corwin Institutes provide collaborative learning experiences that equip your team with tools and action plans ready for immediate implementation. www.corwin.com/institutes

eCourses

Practical, flexible online professional learning designed to let you go at your own pace. www.corwin.com/ecourses

Read2Earn

Did you know you can earn graduate credit for reading this book? Find out how: www.corwin.com/read2earn

Contact an account manager at (800) 831-6640 or visit **www.corwin.com** for more information.